GEISHA

Liza Dalby is an anthropologist specialising in Japanese culture, and the only Westerner to have become a geisha. She is the author of *Tale of Murasaki* (2000), and is a consultant on Steven Spielberg's film of *Memoirs of a Geisha*. She lives in California with her husband and three children.

Liza Dalby

GEISHA

VINTAGE

Published by Vintage 2000

6 8 10 9 7

Copyright © Liza Dalby 1983
'Twenty-four Years Later' © Liza Dalby 1998

The right of Liza Dalby to be identified as the author of this
work has been asserted by her in accordance with the Copyright, Designs and Patents Act, 1988

First published in 1983 by
University of California Press

Vintage
Random House, 20 Vauxhall Bridge Road,
London SW1V 2SA

Random House Australia (Pty) Limited
20 Alfred Street, Milsons Point, Sydney,
New South Wales 2061, Australia

Random House New Zealand Limited
18 Poland Road, Glenfield,
Auckland 10, New Zealand

Random House (Pty) Limited
Endulini, 5A Jubilee Road, Parktown 2193,
South Africa

The Random House Group Limited Reg. No. 954009
www.randomhouse.co.uk

A CIP catalogue record for this book
is available from the British Library

ISBN 0 09 928638 6

Papers used by Random House are natural, recyclable
products made from wood grown in sustainable forests.
The manufacturing processes conform to the environ-
mental regulations of the country of origin

Printed and bound in Great Britain by
Cox & Wyman Limited, Reading, Berkshire

TO MICHAEL AND MARIE

CONTENTS

CONTENTS

PART TWO:
VARIATIONS

CONTENTS

CONTENTS

The secret of understanding the living essence of culture is to grasp it as it is, in all its real concreteness.

Kuki Shūzō, Iki no Kōzō (1930)

GEISHA AND ANTHROPOLOGY

THIS BOOK IS, first and last, about geisha. It is intended to speak to anyone whose curiosity has ever been piqued by the geisha's evocative image. It is secondarily a book about Japanese culture. What geisha do and what they represent are intelligible only within their cultural context. Thus it has been necessary to discuss Japanese customs, history, law, social interaction, psychology, business practice, male-female relations, religious beliefs, dress, food, music, aesthetics, and consciousness of cultural identity, among other things, in order to say anything revealing about geisha. But I have not used the geisha as a device for constructing general statements or theories about the Japanese. The geisha can offer insight into Japan, but this study makes no claims beyond that.

I do not view geisha as constituting a microcosm, a symbol, or a typification of the larger entity: Japanese society. But neither are they a marginal subculture. Geisha are embedded in Japanese culture – Japanese regard them as "more Japanese" than almost any other definable group – but only in showing how they differ from other Japanese does their multifaceted identity become clear.

Most important, geisha are different from wives. They are categorically different, in fact, and the categories are mutually exclusive. If a geisha marries, she ceases being a geisha. From the vantage point of the Japanese man, the role of wife and that of geisha are complementary. Although wives frequently work outside the home, socially they are still confined to it.[1] In contrast to Americans, Japanese married couples do very little entertaining as a couple. Further, romance is not necessarily a concomitant of marriage, even as an ideal. Geisha are supposed to be sexy where wives are sober, artistic where wives are humdrum, and witty where wives are serious – keeping in mind that any of these contrasts is culturally constituted, and that "sexy" for a Japanese does not necessarily mean what it might to an American.

Foreign women are frequently outraged by the idea of the geisha. "Playthings for men!" they say, decrying the very existence of such a profession. Certainly from an outside perspective, which by almost any lights shows Japan as an egregiously male-dominated society, this split nature of femininity seems unfair to women. Why can't wives go out with their husbands? Why can't geisha marry and work too? Why are there geisha at all? But Japanese wives and geisha themselves often have a different view of these institutions, one that we cannot simply dismiss as distorted or false consciousness.

I have concentrated on presenting the geishas' viewpoint in this book. Naturally, this is shaped by their perceptions of wives, wives' perceptions of them, and geishas' perceptions of wives' perceptions of geisha. Although geisha can hardly be labeled feminists, ironically they are among the few Japanese women who have managed to attain economic self-sufficiency and positions of authority and influence on their own merits. Geisha have a great deal of freedom not permitted to wives, and they are dedicated to a career they can pursue without fear of being jettisoned from the payroll when they reach age thirty-five.[2] I cannot join in the categorical Western feminist scorn for geisha as chattel, and I do not take the position that theirs is a degrading profession that must be rooted out before Japanese women can attain equality with men.[3] The reader may take his or her own stand on this question. I have tried, instead, to present a culturally sensitive perspective on how geisha see themselves in the context of their own society.

As an anthropologist, I conducted the research for this book as fieldwork; I went to Japan and lived with geisha. My knowledge of the *karyūkai*, the "flower and willow world," as geisha society is called in Japanese, is culled from a variety of sources. I interviewed geisha, ex-geisha, the owners of geisha houses, and registry office officials in fourteen geisha communities in different areas of Japan.[4] Some of these were single meetings, others required repeated visits over the course of the fourteen months devoted to fieldwork. Geisha may present a single image to foreigners, but within Japan as many differences exist among them as there are varieties of roses. In order to arrive at some quantifiable sense of these differences, I also distributed a questionnaire in the fourteen communities, to which one hundred geisha sent back responses.[5]

Interviews and questionnaires are standard tools of research. The notion of participant observation is also common in anthropological studies, and my joining the geisha ranks in the community of Pontochō in Kyoto has been called that. I myself dislike the term, as it implies a degree of emotional distance that only creates a false sense of objectivity. I was allowed to participate in the lives of these women, for which I am very grateful, and I tried to be a perceptive observer of all that went on; yet I soon found that I had plunged my whole heart into the endeavor and could not maintain the conventional researcher's separation from the object of study. I was totally absorbed in learning to be a geisha. The objectivity, the sorting of my experiences, and the analysis came much later.

Yet this remains a personal book, and I have included large parts of unabashedly subjective material. In particular, I have written as much about my own experience as the geisha Ichigiku as I have about the more orthodox geisha whom I went to study. I cannot pretend that I was the invisible observer, seeing but not seen, simply reporting what appeared before my eyes, and it would be disingenuous of me to say that my presence had no influence on the interactions I sought to record. On the contrary: during my brief career as a geisha, Ichigiku became rather famous in Japan, and I was interviewed almost as often as I conducted interviews.

There are several reasons why I have written so much about Ichigiku. One has to do with the question of how geisha become geisha. All new geisha go through a period of *minarai*, or learning by observation, a Japanese category that I was able to slip into easily.[6] The other geisha thought it perfectly reasonable that

I should undertake minarai; in fact, once they recognized that I was serious about understanding their world, they suggested it themselves. The transformation from Liza Crihfield, graduate student, to Ichigiku of Pontochō occurred bit by bit, and I have tried to reconstruct this gradual development in the chapters concerning Ichigiku. The question of how geisha become geisha I can, therefore, answer largely from firsthand experience. Ichigiku was by no means typical but, then, there is no such thing as a typical geisha.

The difficulties I experienced because I am an American often suggested deep cultural differences that I have taken some pains to elucidate. But initial hesitation in the face of the strange and unaccustomed will always give way to the familiar comfort of routine. So, too, with learning to be a geisha – for me, eventually, the Japanese perspective came to feel like the only natural one. I have combined two viewpoints in writing this book: that of the outsider seizing upon those things that appear most in need of explanation, and that of the insider, dwelling on things that may not even occur to the outsider to question but that in fact are of central importance in the geishas' view of their world.

This book could be called an ethnography, a descriptive study of the customs of a particular people. My goal, however, has not been to compile a catalog of customs of geisha in the various regions of Japan. Description always needs a reference point, and I have tried to make mine explicit. I think of this study as an interpretive ethnography; my goal is to explain the cultural meaning of persons, objects, and situations in the geisha world. Sometimes this has led to digressions on subjects (Japanese humor, for example) that initially might appear quite unrelated to geisha as such. The problem, as I see it, is that no culturally relevant topic – a person like Sakurako the geisha, an object such as a teabowl, or a situation like the sexual initiation of an apprentice geisha – can be plucked out and matter-of-factly described, as if it were not part of a "web of significance" that makes all the difference to the persons who actually live in the flower and willow world.

Of course, one has to make deliberate choices about how far to follow particular strands of this web. Because the choices are to some extent arbitrary, the figure of the writer should be of more than subsidiary interest. This is another reason why I have written much of this book in the first person. Unlike many ethnographies, where the presence of the writer is hardly acknowledged and things are recorded as if they were simply there to be observed, the reader here will not be permitted to forget that his understanding is being shaped by Ichigiku. This is more evident in some chapters than others (a friend who looked at an early draft of the chapter entitled "Country Geisha" said that it plainly reflected a Kyoto geisha's view of the cultural hinterlands); but I consider it a matter of intellectual honesty, if that is not too grandiose a term, to make no secret of my own biases, all the more because my own understanding of the geisha was formed in such an intense and peculiar way.

I have often been asked what sorts of women in other societies are comparable to geisha. As a student of anthropology, the discipline of cross-cultural studies, I have been under some pressure to consider this question, yet I have not done so here. The reasons are, first, that I am suspicious of the idea of functional equivalents and, second, I have proposed no theory of the geishas' function in Japan that would lend itself to cross-cultural comparison. The comparison of cultural traits necessitates a drastic simplification, a hacking away of cultural matrices in order to come up with some unit that can be compared. This study has gone in the opposite direction and attempts to elaborate upon what is culturally unique to geisha. Geisha undoubtedly have something in common with the hetaerae of classical Greece, the *kisaeng* of Korea, the *femmes savantes* of seventeenth-century France, and the *xiaoshu* of imperial China. But an analysis of these similarities is beyond the scope, and in any case is not the intention, of this book.

Some may wonder that I have not touched on one other aspect of geisha: their image or stereotype in the West. The idea of the exotic geisha, seductress skilled in the *Kama Sutra* arts of pleasing men, was part of the European-American cultural stereotype of the Orient even before Perry's ships. Pierre Loti's Madame Chrysanthème and Townsend Harris' Okichi (neither of whom was in fact a geisha) are stock examples of the women of allegedly easy virtue who are assumed by foreigners to typify the geisha. This may be a fascinating topic, but it remains one that says more about Western obsessions than it does about geisha themselves.

What does it mean to be a geisha? There are undoubtedly many possible answers. I have given my own, and I have tried to make clear the elements of culture that necessarily shape such a question.

TWENTY-FOUR YEARS LATER

What I described in the mid-1970s as a picture of geisha and their place in modern Japanese society has turned into a snapshot of a particular era. Geisha remain standard-bearers of tradition, but the fact of living in a changing world continues to affect the profession. How could it be otherwise? The geisha "mothers" who managed their communities in 1974–75 when I briefly joined their ranks were women who came of age before the Second World War. Their experiences and expectations were formed in a stricter and more circumscribed environment than that of the young geisha they in turn brought up or mentored in the postwar years. The mothers I wrote about in this book have retired or passed away. The young women who were my peers are now the figures of experience and authority.

Twenty-four years have passed since I appeared as the geisha Ichigiku in Pontochō. During this time, my geisha mother had her old-fashioned riverbank establishment, the Mitsuba, torn down and replaced with a modern five-story building housing a stylish restaurant, bar, and offices, with living quarters for herself on the top floor. I was shocked when she told me what she had done. She was not sentimental. Always interested in novel ventures, she was deeply involved in the community of Pontochō until she died in 1992 from a heart attack.

Tendencies that were evident a quarter century ago as signs that geisha life was modernizing are even stronger now. In 1989, Prime Minister Uno Sosuke was forced to resign because his geisha mistress publicly accused him of stinginess and arrogance. For the first time in Japanese political life, the Uno affair demonstrated that a married politician's association with a geisha (a liaison long taken for granted) could be criticized as womanizing. Japanese wives are not as complaisant as they once were in such matters.

In 1995 a disgruntled Kyoto apprentice brought civil suit against the geisha house where she was trained, charging the mother of the house with exploitation. When the case was settled out of court, she went on to open her own entertainment venture – a freelance dial-a-maiko. Being able to open such a business is a sign of how things have changed.

Yet the stage for this litigious "maiko from hell" (as Japanese journalists dubbed the outspoken apprentice) had already been set during my own geisha days. Even then the maiko of Kyoto were a tourist attraction, and many girls were pulled into the ranks simply in order to fill the demand for these doll-like symbols of the city. Most of them played at being maiko for a few years without any intention of undergoing the discipline and commitment required of full-fledged geisha. My own geisha friends regarded Prime Minister Uno's mistress as declassé and the impudent maiko as an ill-bred aberration. Yet the fact remains that their actions would have been unthinkable not so long ago. These public scandals have opened cracks in the walls surrounding the private world of the geisha.

Throughout its history, the "flower and willow world" has expanded or contracted according to the state of the country's finances. When customers are flush, geisha are busy and their numbers swell; when the economic tide ebbs, parties are canceled and geisha retire. With the deflation of Japan's bubble economy during the 1990s, the population of geisha has dwindled. Still, I think it unlikely that the twenty-first century will dawn on a Japan devoid of geisha. Their chosen function of upholding Japanese tradition – the defining mode of the profession – has not changed. As long as Japanese feel strongly about their cultural value, geisha are likely to withstand the scandals of modern life for some time to come. That their numbers will shrink further, however, is probably inevitable.

Liza Dalby
Berkeley, California
February 1998

PART ONE

RELATIONS

ONE

SISTERS

Ume no mi mo	Even the plums blush ripely
Irozuku koro ya	Around the time
Satsuki ame	Of the late spring rains.

Beginning phrase of a kouta

DEATH OF A GEISHA

APRIL IN KYOTO is a glorious season. Cherry trees blossom along the river banks and envelop the wooded mountainsides in a thin pink mist. In Maruyama Park, Japanese come at night to drink beer and sake under the blossom-dripping boughs of an ancient weeping cherry. This huge tree stands spotlighted in pale unearthly splendor amid the noisy carousers.

April is also one of the busiest months in the Kyoto geisha quarters. Every afternoon the Pontochō theater fills with spectators who have come to see the geisha perform the spring Kamo River Dance. In the evenings the "teahouses" and restaurants where geisha entertain are crowded with guests from Tokyo and other cities who have journeyed to Kyoto for the cherry blossoms and the geisha dance festival.

At night, students and young couples walk along the wide stone flanks of the Kamo River, where the only light is that reflected from the Pontochō teahouses on the embankment above. The river is always alluring, and the scent of a spring night makes it irresistible. The geisha and their well-to-do patrons look

3

down at the crowd of young romantics drifting alongside the slow-moving river. Much of the charm of Pontochō is due to its location, but whereas the customers of the geisha pay dearly for their privileged river views and charming companions, the students and young lovers below them stroll for free.

Some teahouses keep a spyglass in the banquet room overlooking the river, and a geisha will tease an elderly customer to look for illicit couplings under the dark shadows of the bridges. A young geisha may gaze out past the gray heads of her guests and, inhaling the spring night air, wish that she too were walking with a young man along the river below.

On one of those balmy late-April nights in 1978, a tendril of smoke drifted from the west bank of the Kamo River. Nobody noticed it issuing lazily from one of the closely spaced wooden buildings in the area where the geisha of Pontochō live and work. By four in the morning, a raging blaze had destroyed several houses. Distraught geisha clutched their cotton sleeping kimonos against the river breeze and splashed their roofs with buckets of river water in an effort to halt the spread of Japan's most feared natural catastrophe, fire. At daybreak, a dozen houses lay in smoldering ruins and one young geisha was dead.

Her mother and two sister geisha had managed to escape the house before the acrid smoke became poisonously thick, and in the smoky confusion of the narrow alley no one realized that the young woman was still inside. When the story was recounted to me three months later, one elderly geisha said she still had nightmares about a pitiful voice faintly crying *"okāsan"* – mother – though she couldn't be sure whether she had heard or imagined it.

THE GEISHA FAMILY

Geisha call the women who manage the teahouses okāsan. They call any geisha who has seniority by virtue of an earlier debut into the geisha world *onēsan*, older sister. Both are used as general terms of respect. When a geisha speaks of one particular older sister, however, she is referring to a senior geisha with whom she once "tied the knot" in a ceremony uniting them as sister geisha.

During the time I spent studying the flower and willow world by living within it, a geisha named Ichiume took the role of my older sister. Ichiume was twenty-two at the time and I was twenty-five. The fact that she was three years younger than I posed no problem in the kinship of the geisha world because actual age is not as important as experience. When we met, Ichiume had been a *maiko*, or apprentice, for four years and a full-fledged geisha for a year and a half.

As Ichiume's "younger sister," I went by the name Ichigiku. Ichiume had not had a younger sister before, but she did her best to help me learn the intricate etiquette of geisha society – to the extent, that is, that she had mastered it herself. "Blind leading the blind," sighed one of the mothers after having scolded us both for being late to an engagement. It was probably because Ichiume was something of a jokester that she was charged with sistering the American geisha in the first place. But eventually things worked out better than the mothers had dared hope. When it was time for me to leave Japan, they even told me that I had been a good influence on Ichiume. Having a younger sister, even an odd one like me, was, for Ichiume, a step toward greater responsibility as a member of the geisha community.

After a year in Pontochō as Ichigiku, I returned to the United States to write my thesis on geisha. I missed my geisha family and wrote or telephoned them often. I would occasionally get letters from my okāsan with a quick scribble appended by Ichiume. I was very sorry to miss the ceremony, about six months later, in which Ichiume celebrated the bond of sisterhood with a new, more legitimate, younger sister. At that time, the geisha of Pontochō threw themselves an elaborate party to welcome the new apprentice to their ranks. Okāsan sent me pictures of the affair, which included a coolly elegant new face – a face I remembered as that of the unsophisticated Midori, a junior high school girl who had been studying classical dance in preparation for her debut as a maiko.

To be a maiko, with the trailing embroidered kimono and high clogs with bells, had been a romantic dream for Midori. Many people think of the life of a maiko as old-fashioned, constricting, and boring – even some of the other maiko privately feel that way. Midori, however, was enthusiastic at the prospect. The mothers of the Pontochō teahouses were very proud of her and had high hopes for her future as a geisha. I had talked to them often about Midori.

The number of maiko has dwindled alarmingly in recent years. A couple of years before I had arrived, in fact, maiko had disappeared altogether from Pontochō, but when I was there in 1975 there were four. Midori, under her professional name of Ichitomi, would make five. Even in Kyoto a woman does not have to be a maiko before becoming a fully qualified geisha, but those who follow this traditional path of entrance into the profession enjoy higher prestige later as the true geisha of Kyoto.

Midori's natural mother was a retired geisha in the nearby area of Miyagawa-chō, one of the six recognized geisha communities (hanamachi) in Kyoto. Why didn't Midori become a geisha there? I wondered. This was the sort of thing one could not inquire about directly but about which my okāsan, ex-geisha, mistress of an elegant inn, and pillar of the Pontochō community, could enlighten me as we had tea in the afternoon or snacks late at night after a party at her establishment, the Mitsuba.

"You're making a study of this, Kikuko," she said, using my ordinary and familiar Japanese name, "so you should know about Miyagawa-chō. There's a word called 'double registration' – that's what many of the geisha in areas like that are. You can call them geisha if you like, but they do a bit more than dance for the customers."[1]

"Is that why Midori didn't want to work there?" I asked.

"This was her mother's idea, actually," replied my okāsan. "And it was a smart decision, in my opinion. When I was a girl, you had to be born in Pontochō to become a geisha here, but these days one can hardly insist on that. The customers love to have young maiko attend the banquets. This is Kyoto, after all. Having a maiko pour sake for you really makes you feel you're in Kyoto. Tokyo customers especially insist on it. There just aren't enough maiko to keep up with the demand. So when someone like Midori wants to work in Kyoto, why should she stay in

Miyagawa when she can make her debut in Pontochō? She'll get better training here, and she'll meet a better class of customer."

So in her last year of junior high school, Midori left her mother's house in Miyagawa-chō to live in the house called Hatsuyuki in Pontochō. At sixteen, she became the pampered pet of the other two geisha who lived there. Ichiume was closest to her in age; the other geisha, Ichihiro, was their senior by almost twenty years.

Midori called the mistress of the Hatsuyuki, a fifty-five-year-old woman who had once been a geisha herself, okāsan. Like most of the mothers of teahouses in Pontochō, this woman's knowledge of etiquette, speech, feminine deportment, classical dance, and music – that is, her knowledge of those things necessary for a geisha to know – is firsthand. As a geisha in her early twenties, she had found a patron; as is usual in such affairs, he was a much older man. She became his mistress, retiring from geisha life to live in relative ease. But when he died, she was left with a young son and barely enough money to purchase a small teahouse in Pontochō. That is where she had worked as a geisha, and she still knew important community figures. She began this second phase of her life in the geisha world by managing the Hatsuyuki, slowly building up a clientele and eventually bringing in geisha to train. I liked to visit this house, where I was always made to feel welcome by the bustling and energetic family of women. The son of the house, the one blood relation of its mistress, was never much in evidence. I had been introduced to him once, only after I inquired about the young man walking upstairs as if he belonged there.

SONS AND LOVERS

In the geisha world, men may claim the night, but women dominate the day. The son of the proprietress of the Hatsuyuki was one of a very few men who actually live in this quarter, and he spent as much time as possible with his cronies, away from what he found to be the suffocatingly female atmosphere of daytime Pontochō.

*Nighttime Pontochō. At the time of the
Kamogawa Dances, the eaves of the teahouses
are hung with red lanterns.*

The hours between 6:00 P.M. and early morning are the business hours here. The long, "narrow-as-an-eel's bed" block of Pontochō is illuminated by the rosy neon displays of bars interspersed with the more discreet monochrome signs of teahouses. Customers' voices drift down to the street, mingled with the plangent sounds of *shamisen* music. The cramped street is full of men, who in the small hours of the morning are often supported by a geisha or a hostess in their unsteady progress from bar to taxi. The customers (or anyone else who glimpses this scene during business hours) think that Pontochō is an entire world created for the delectation of men. That is the point, of course: to make them feel that way.

Few of these evening guests ever see the daytime side of this world, the geisha quarters when the customers have gone home. Even those who patronize geisha usually have only the vaguest idea of the realities of this professional community, whose members are linked one to another by the idiom of kinship. The

Paper lantern with Pontochō's special mark, the plover.

"mothers" of the teahouses, where geisha are employed, are the real businesswomen and entrepreneurs. The geisha are the "daughters" of these women, living their private and their professional lives as older and younger sisters to each other. There are a few positions for men whose services are necessary to the professional life of Pontochō, such as the lone wig stylist, the kimono dressers, and perhaps the hired accountants at the registry office. But the position of men, when they are not customers, is basically precarious in the ongoing everyday life of the geisha quarters.

Japanese men are accustomed to having women wait on them. This is not the only mode of male/female interaction in Japan,

Ichiume.

but Japanese men feel that there is nothing unusual about it. The cultural style of masculinity in Japan tends to demand female subservience (at least pro forma), and many things contribute to an ideology in which men are the sources of authority. As a consequence, life is notoriously hard on the egos of men who live within the geisha world. The refined nuances of exquisite service in which geisha are trained are not meant for them.

The pampering of the male ego, which geisha think of as one of their most important skills, does not extend to family. For men of geisha families, it is their mothers, sisters, daughters, or wives who are the principals of this world in terms of actual work and socially recognized authority.[2] The stigma, if there is one, of being the child of a geisha (and thus illegitimate) is felt far more keenly by male than by female children. In almost every case I am familiar with, males manifest their resentment by becoming wayward and profligate. Whereas a girl will fit easily into such a community of capable and self-supporting women, a boy will have endless trouble. This is perhaps the only place in Japanese society where the birth of a baby girl is always more welcome than that of a boy.

The okāsan of the Hatsuyuki, however, doted on her lackadaisical son. It was her fond hope that he would marry someone sensible and capable, a girl at home in the "flower and willow world" who would be able to take over as mistress of the Hatsuyuki when she retired. A geisha, for example, who would be willing to entertain customers in her altered role of proprietress, would be ideal. If her son's bride were not the sort who could handle teahouse business, that would probably end his chances of managing the establishment. As a man, he could not run it himself even if he were so inclined. At the time, I thought the okāsan of the Hatsuyuki was pinning false hopes on this sleepy-eyed son of hers. Better to depend on one of the daughters – even the mischievous Ichiume, it seemed to me.

Ichiume was popular with guests because of her transparent and naive manner. She could melt the ice of stiff propriety at the beginning of a party with her unselfconscious laughter and involved stories. Childlike as she was, her seemingly boundless credulity would entice guests to lead her further and further, until finally the realization of being fooled would break like a wave over her face. Then she would pout while everyone else laughed. When she thought something was not right, however, she could

11

be ingenuously stubborn, ignoring her mother or older sister tugging her sleeve from behind. She was not calculating. There were those who said she was not very clever.

Several months after I had left Japan, my okāsan told me over the phone that Ichiume had settled down quite a bit since becoming an older sister to Midori. The responsibility of being a model to someone, she said, had had a good effect. Okāsan also hinted that Ichiume had finally become involved with a man. I remember one of the older geisha saying once that the problem with Ichiume was that she was still a virgin, that her flightiness, spells of silliness, and sometimes uncomfortable intensity would be muted after she had an outlet for her sexuality. Ichiume and Midori had blushed at such remarks, but the older geisha merely repeated them matter-of-factly. Whatever the cause, time had passed, and my okāsan reported that Ichiume was blossoming and coming into her own.

Most geisha have a specialty among the arts required as part of their training. Ichiume's was classical Japanese dance. She would be dancing a solo, a section of the famous *Dōjōji* legend, in the spring geisha dances of Pontochō. My okāsan sent me a picture of the dress rehearsals, with Ichiume posed holding the strings of wide-brimmed red and gold hats that denote *Dōjōji*. This was to be the first public exhibition of her coming of age as a dancer, so all the older geisha and mothers had their eyes closely trained on her. Their preliminary comments were favorable. My older sister Ichiume clearly seemed one of the young geisha destined to become a mother and leader of the community in her time.

THE DANCE

May is a month of ebullient activity in Pontochō. So is October. Twice a yeal for a three-week period marked by pink cherry blossoms and a later three-week period of red maple leaves, the geisha of Pontochō give public performances at the Pontochō Recital Hall. These are the Kamogawa Odori, the Kamo River Dances, which since 1872 have been performed semiannually with but one break during the Second World War. There is an

*Poster advertising the Kamogawa Dances in 1976. Pontochō's four
maiko hold up their hems in a classic pose.*

坂東玉三郎　《名月八幡祭》の芸者美代吉

Male as female, female as male. Kabuki actor Bando Tamasaburō in a stage role as a geisha.

A geisha in a stage role as a samurai.

edge of excitement in the air during these months. Nearly every woman in Pontochō is drawn into the dances. Geisha who specialize in singing or shamisen provide the musical accompaniment for geisha dancers. The young maiko always do a simple dance number, essentially playing themselves rather than the more theatrical dance roles reserved for experienced geisha. But because of their distinctive and extravagant outfits, the maiko are usually the ones to pose for the poster advertising the dances to the public.

As ex-geisha, the mothers of the teahouses are the sharpest critics of the quality of these performances. They gather at the recital hall daily to coach their daughters and converse with one another. Even the retired mothers, the fragile, tiny ladies who dress in sober blues and grays and live quietly in the back rooms of teahouses now turned over to daughters, are tempted out for the dances. They shuffle between the front row and backstage during rehearsals, leaving only at the last possible minute in late afternoon to go back to their household chores, such as polishing the front stoop before the first customers arrive at the teahouses. There are children backstage too – little girls watching the rows of makeup tables where their mothers are transformed into gorgeous princesses, swaggering samurai, priests, and demons.

The program always includes one Kabukiesque dramatic piece, which may in fact be drawn from the Kabuki repertoire.

15

When geisha perform such works, all the male roles are of course played by women. This makes an interesting inversion for an audience accustomed to seeing the same plays done on the Kabuki stage, where male actors take the feminine roles.

Every geisha I have ever met is an enthusiastic Kabuki fan, and they know all the actors. The close tie between geisha and Kabuki players goes back several hundred years, to the origins of both professions, which have much in common. To begin with, they are both part of the business of entertainment. And, curiously, both have changed their appeal in similar ways over the centuries. Kabuki actors were once common, faintly disreputable sorts of entertainers; and in the nineteenth century even poor students could visit the geisha quarters. Gradually, the appeal of these arts has become a much more refined pursuit, requiring at least some money and a slight taste for the recherché. The popular entertainments of a century ago, Kabuki and geisha have become enshrined as symbols of Japanese tradition.

The fact that they have much in common may account for the remarkably high incidence of marriage between geisha and Kabuki actors. Until recently, love affairs between them were the prime stuff of scandal magazines and popular gossip, although now movie stars and pop singers have largely usurped their place. Shop talk for these people is dance. They have the same dance teachers, draw on the same repertoire, cultivate the same sensibilities. Kabuki actors hardly ever go to teahouses for enjoyment, however. As veteran Onoue Kuroemon says, "It's boring; all we do is talk about work. I certainly wouldn't visit geisha to relax."

Pontochō is usually one of the quietest streets in Kyoto before eleven in the morning. Because of their evening hours, most geisha like to sleep late. But during the months of the dances, rehearsals and lessons fill the days, while business goes on without a break in the evenings. So in April and September, the weary geisha faithfully drag themselves down to the recital hall at the unheard-of hour of 10:00 A.M. for rehearsal. A few will curtail their nighttime hours to conserve their strength, but most consider it a matter of pride not to admit to fatigue during these intense weeks of artistic activity and revelry.

It appears that Ichiume was out celebrating with friends on the evening of April 27. As I later heard the story, her friends said that they made her go home early for her own good. She was getting too drunk, the performances were starting soon, she needed her rest. When the fire broke out around 3:00 A.M. she was sleeping heavily. She must have been roused groggily by the cries of "Fire!" or else the heat, because they found what was left of her body slumped near the staircase. The newspaper said she had died of smoke inhalation.

TWO

KYOTO

Miyako hanarete	My lonely departure
Tabi no sō hitori sabishiku	From Kyoto.
Kisha no mado	Hiding tears
Namida kakushite	At the train window,
Ocha ocha ocha	Oh please, please,
Hitotsu chōdai na	Someone give me
	A cup of tea.

Kouta by novelist Izumi Kyōka (c. 1920)

GERALD FORD AND THE MAIKO

ICHIUME'S FUNERAL WAS held a week after the fire, a memorial service another week after that. Besides the numerous black-and-white ribboned floral tributes, there was also a telegram from former President of the United States Gerald Ford, addressed to Ichiume's mother in care of the Pontochō geisha office.

In November 1974, Gerald Ford had been the first American president to visit Japan, and the Japanese made this into a full state occasion, including an audience with the emperor, dinners with the prime minister, and the mobilization of thousands of flag-waving school children at every scenic spot he visited. Ford's side trip to Kyoto, renowned repository of traditional Japanese culture, would have been incomplete without a banquet with geisha in attendance.

The Ford entourage accordingly was bundled into a fleet of black limousines and driven past the Kyoto Zoo and the Heian Shrine to a restaurant called Tsuruya, in the eastern hills of the city. Queen Elizabeth had been entertained at Tsuruya on her trip to Japan a few years earlier. The menus of these dinners, proudly saved by the restaurant, show that both the president and the queen were served a raw dish, a vinegared dish, a boiled dish, a roasted dish, and so on in the Japanese sequence of formal banquet courses, but with Kobe beef and tempura (thought to be more palatable to foreigners) interspersed.

The geisha who attended President Ford's banquet came from three of the six Kyoto geisha communities: Gion, Pontochō, and Kamishichiken. These three, though sometimes ranked in descending order thus, are all considered first-class. On occasions when the city of Kyoto, or traditional Japan in general, must be officially represented, the geisha are diplomatically chosen from all three places. The geisha from these higher-ranked areas all know one another and their respective mothers, but they are considerably more vague about the women in the three "lower" communities.

Despite their status as first-class geisha, however, all of them were frisked by Secret Service men before entering the Tsuruya on the evening of the Ford banquet. Newsmen with television cameras traipsed across the tatami mats, vying with one another to shoot pictures of the president's attempts to eat with chopsticks, or the president being served sake by an apprentice geisha.

At that time I was in California, finishing the proposal for my dissertation research on geisha as a Japanese social institution. I was particularly intrigued, therefore, by the pictures of our president in *Time* and on the evening news, gamely enjoying his foreign sojourn in the company of two prim-faced maiko. Almost exactly one year later, sitting with my okāsan in one of the private rooms of her inn, I asked if she remembered Ford's trip to Japan.

"Before I came to Japan," I said, "I saw President Ford in the news with some maiko from Kyoto. Do you know where they held that banquet, Okāsan?"

19

President Gerald Ford visits Japan in 1974.
The maiko on the right is Ichiume.

"Of course. You've been there – it was the Tsuruya. One of those maiko was your older sister, Ichiume."

"Really? That means I saw Ichiume before I even heard of Pontochō. Her face was in the news all over America."

I went to my room to fetch a magazine clipping from the collection of miscellany about geisha that I had brought with me. There was no doubt about it, the plump-cheeked one looking slightly bewildered was Ichiume. The next time we met, I asked her what she thought of that banquet, and of President Ford. She replied that all she had done was pour sake into his cup once; then she was moved down to give another maiko a chance. "It was very hot with all those lights," she said.

Maiko are generally rather quiet at large formal banquets. As geisha-in-training they are still learning the skills, and most of them have not built up the reservoir of experience necessary to feel at ease in front of high government officials or foreigners or both. But a maiko doesn't have to be witty; it is quite enough if she sits demurely, looking like a beautiful painted doll. If she happens to be clever as well as pretty, that is to her advantage, but she is not expected to be a conversationalist. That can be left to an older geisha – who may have to dye her hair to achieve the desired glossy blackness but who, through years of experience, knows the best way to draw someone out with small talk.

Banquets are usually planned so that a mixture of younger and older geisha are present; the idea is that the young ones, especially the maiko in their distinctive dress, will provide atmosphere, whereas the older geisha are usually more entertaining. Customers have their own preferences, though, so at less formal engagements the ratio of maiko to geisha varies greatly. Some men hardly notice the individual maiko ("they all look the same with that white face paint") and instead call the geisha they have come to know and whose company they prefer. But other customers savor the nostalgia of a romanticized past and love to be surrounded by these figures out of woodblock prints. Even in such cases, though, at least a few older geisha come along; a party of all maiko is inconceivable. Besides the fact that they are always chaperoned, the conversation of a group of seventeen-year-olds is probably interesting only to other seventeen-year-olds.

However carefully banquets are planned, any arrangement is likely not to work when foreigners are involved. A hybrid "geisha party" creates a collision between two sets of expectations, one determined by a foreigner's Visit To Japan, the other arising because geisha are thought of as the epitome of Japanese Tradition. The very nature of the latter makes it likely that it will be included as a sine qua non of the former, although Westerners are usually more puzzled than entertained by geisha parties. It is nearly inevitable that the cues for etiquette and enjoyment will clash head-on.

For example, American curiosity is piqued by the maiko's painted face and gorgeous robes – and also by those of the geisha, when the geisha also happen to arrive in formal painted and bewigged attire. But this initial fascination with the "unnatural" soon gives way to distaste. The most common American comment I have heard about geisha is that "they wear too much makeup for my taste." Foreigners think geisha dances are grace-

*Pontochō maiko Ichiwaka wearing a summer hair ornament.
Photograph by Yuten Konishi.*

ful and exotic, but hardly erotic, and they think of their music as merely exotic. The fact that a middle-aged geisha is charming and highly sought after by Japanese is lost on an American who doesn't know the Japanese language. If she attempts to entertain him at a level where his lack of language is not crucial, a foreign guest will play along with her rock-paper-scissors finger games, then afterward chuckle about how childish the Japanese are.

Perhaps it is a sign of the strength of the geisha's position as a symbol of Japanese culture that, although foreigners seldom enjoy an evening with geisha as anything other than a curiosity, they nevertheless usually feel that a geisha party makes a visit to Japan complete. Lavish though the Ford banquet was, it was based on exactly this notion.

Seat of Honor

The person sitting at the place of honor in a Japanese banquet room is framed in the others' eyes by a floor-to-ceiling alcove called the tokonoma at his back. A seasonally appropriate hanging scroll and a vase of carefully arranged flowers placed in the *tokonoma* focus the aesthetic interest of the entire room. The guest of honor is not able to contemplate this display from his exalted seat directly in front of it, but he has the satisfaction of knowing that he is at the center of the tableau.

At any banquet with geisha in attendance, whoever occupies the place of honor will be the subject of the most attention by the most geisha at any one time. The guests are already seated when the geisha enter the room, in smooth phalanxes of five or six at a large banquet. The first group will go directly to the guests in the places of higher prestige. After all the geisha have entered and distributed themselves around the room at the elbows of guests, the first toast is made and the party officially begins. The geisha then circulate among the guests for the rest of the evening, but the pattern of distribution is never even. Each geisha must at some point spend time at the prestigious end of the table, so whenever space is vacated there, another geisha quickly moves to fill it. The older ones are very skillful at judging when to move. At first, the maiko have little sense about this subtlety, so they wait to be directed by their older sisters.

Ichiume was but one standing in the line of maiko waiting to pour a cup of sake for President Ford, who of course had been placed in front of the tokonoma. She happened to be with him when most of the pictures were snapped. Actually, none of the geisha were aware of the news releases in the United States, so when I showed them the picture, some of them teased Ichiume by calling her "Ford-san's girlfriend." This slender connection between Ichiume and Gerald Ford, created only by the chance coincidence of a photograph, is what prompted me to write President Ford, requesting that he send a telegram in time for the funeral.

BONCHI

My okāsan, mistress of the Mitsuba Inn, met me at the Osaka airport with her son Tsunehiko when I returned to Japan after completing my study of the geisha. I had been away a year. The first question she asked, as we stood outside waiting for Tsune-hiko to get the car, was whether I had had anything to do with the telegram from Ford. Ichiume's mother, she said, thought I had probably told him – who else did she know in America, after all. She was still in the hospital. The severe shock of losing her daughter, her house, and her livelihood had quite broken her health and her heart. When I saw her, said my okāsan, I would be taken aback at how old she had suddenly become.

The warm, moist air of Japanese summer made me gasp as we stepped out of the air-conditioned airport. During the summer months in Kyoto, the phrase "Mushiatsui ne?" (Hot and humid, isn't it?) is the most frequently heard salutation, as men wipe the backs of their necks and women dab their foreheads with loosely woven cotton handkerchiefs. We were grateful for a faint breeze rippling in from Osaka Bay by the time Tsunehiko drove up.

It was already dark. I couldn't see until the last minute that Tsunehiko was driving a brand-new Toyota Crown, the top of the Toyota line, with all the extras I knew came with such cars and some I wasn't aware of. Tsunehiko crushed a barely puffed cigarette under his heel and hefted my bags into the trunk. "Welcome back to Kyoto, mushiatsui ne?" he panted, turning the air conditioner on high after getting in behind the wheel.

It is a fifty-minute drive from the Osaka airport to Kyoto – at least, the way Tsunehiko drives. One of the extras on the dashboard was a beeper that sounded whenever the car exceeded the national speed limit of eighty kilometers (fifty miles) per hour. We attempted to talk over the beeper a good part of the way home.

During the year I had been away, most of the changes my okāsan had to report were deaths. Besides Ichiume, there was Kikugorō's patron; Kikugorō was a middle-aged geisha in Atami with whom I had stayed when I was investigating the somewhat honky-tonk but thriving geisha business in that resort town. Kikugorō, who had taken as her geisha name the stage name of a famous Kabuki actor, was an old friend of my okāsan. This late patron of hers, a Tokyo businessman, had long been a welcome visitor to the Mitsuba Inn. He was the link through which my okāsan, mistress of the Mitsuba, and Kikugorō had become acquainted. I remembered him as a genial, generous man and was sorry to hear of his death.

Also gone, the victim of a heart attack at age forty-three, was Kurochan (Blackie), from the *kouta* singing group (kouta are short lyrical songs). My okāsan and I had both taken kouta lessons from the same teacher, along with about fifty other students, including geisha, businessmen, and housewives. Some had lessons on the same day as I, so I came to know them fairly well, whereas others I would see only at the semiannual recital. I had trouble remembering which Kurochan was being referred to because there were several dark-complected customers to whom the geisha gave this nickname. Still, "What a shame," I said, "and at such an early age."

Approaching Kyoto, I noticed some familiar landmarks: the pagoda of the Nishi Honganji temple behind the looming space needle of the Kyoto Tower Hotel. Faint lights near the summit of Mount Hiei glittered in the distance. I have always loved Kyoto for its straightforward layout, its boundedness. Every guidebook to the city describes how it was built from raw countryside in the year 794, with a regular pattern of straight broad streets intersecting at right angles (so different from the convoluted maze of most later Japanese cities), and how its planners used as their model the Tang dynasty Chinese capital of Changan. At the time the city was built, the Japanese were carrying on a century-long infatuation with the brilliant contemporary culture of Tang

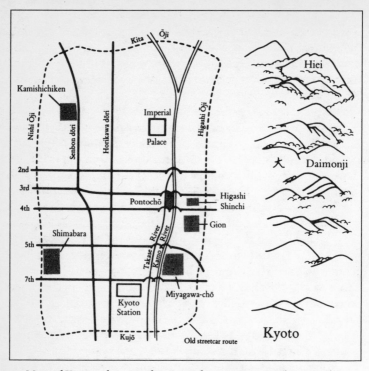

Map of Kyoto, showing the six geisha communities (hanamachi).

China. Kammu, conventionally counted as the fiftieth emperor of Japan, chose to move his entire court from the city of Nara (smaller, but also modeled after Changan) some thirty-five miles north to the wide Kyoto basin, ringed by rounded mountains. The imperial palace was built just west of the Kamo River. The grid of streets began from its north central position, just as in the Chinese model.

Because Kyoto lies in a flat plain closely surrounded by mountains, the general Japanese postwar tendency toward urban sprawl has been greatly curtailed. Kyoto has no heavy industry, furthermore (most is in Osaka or other nearby cities), so there has been no great influx of people looking for housing, either. Kyoto's main industry is Kyoto.

A city ordinance forbids the construction of new buildings over ten stories high. The idea is to protect the famous view of temple pagodas – for over a thousand years the highest manmade structures around. The ugly Kyoto Tower Hotel predates the ordinance, but perhaps it was this aggressively modern example of how such a structure could mar the landscape that provided impetus for the rule in the first place.

"Because Kyoto is a flat plain surrounded by mountains" is a favorite Kyoto way of explaining virtually anything. "Bonchi ya sakai ni . . ." people say. "Because it is a *bonchi*," a basin or valley, Kyoto has always been more contained than Tokyo. ("We are such-and-such, as opposed to Tokyo people, who are something else" is another favorite Kyoto maxim and is probably the notion underlying both ideas.) Because Kyoto is a bonchi, the humid summer air settles right into it, clinging to the ground like a fog of heat. And also because Kyoto is a bonchi, the chill of winter is especially damp and penetrating.

The fact that the city has had no place to expand, that it has folded back in on its cherished rich tradition, makes it, more than any other city I have ever lived in, feel like a bounded unit. Kyoto is a fine silk handkerchief with neatly hand-rolled edges, not a ragged scarf, raveling off inconclusively, like Tokyo.

From the southern end of the old city (for most purposes, Kyoto Station) to the Botanical Garden at its northern edge is a feasible taxi ride. The rickety but charming old streetcars were scrapped in the 1970s, but the remnants of their tracks follow a rectangular route, demarcating the edges of the city proper. They run down Higashi-Ōji (Great eastern boulevard) on the east side, Nishi-Ōji (Great western boulevard) on the west, Kita-Ōji (Great northern boulevard) on the north, and Kujō (Ninth avenue) on the south. I always felt that to go outside these streetcar tracks was to make an excursion out of the city, although the official municipality of Kyoto takes in more area.

If, despite the smallness of the city and the straightness of its streets, one still feels unsure of direction, then Mount Hiei, towering in the far northeast corner of the basin and visible from almost any spot in the city, can be used for orientation. People who have trouble locating themselves spatially are, in

Japanese, *hōkō onchi* (tone-deaf to directions). Kyoto is the ideal city for people like me, who lose their way at the slightest jog in the map, whose "directional ears" never seem to be attuned. The faraway lights dotting the top of Mount Hiei were familiar and reassuring.

PONTOCHŌ REUNION

Tsunehiko let us off in front of the Mitsuba Ryokan, the traditional Japanese establishment that his mother owns and manages. Although technically a *ryokan*, an inn, the Mitsuba derives little of its income from lodgings. Most of its business depends on renting the one large or several small banquet rooms for parties to which geisha are called. The Mitsuba is one of a limited number of establishments in the area licensed by the city government to have geisha entertainment on their premises. The occasional overnight guest will almost always be a personal acquaintance of the proprietress.

Although guests pay for lodging, the mistress of the Mitsuba Inn lets them stay more as a favor than as a matter of business. In fact, the maids complain about all-night guests because they have to roll out the bedding, make breakfast, and keep the television turned down lower than they like. They work hard in the evenings when banquets are taking place, but they don't like their daytime routine invaded by lingering customers.

The Mitsuba is fronted by a slatted wood and clay wall with a sliding-door gate right at the street. This gate is never left open. The appearance is that of a private house, except for the discreet black on illuminated white sign reading "Mi-tsu-ba" in flowing syllabic script. Strangers are unlikely to walk in looking for lodging.

The tiled roof of the Mitsuba's gate affords shelter against the rain just wide enough to set down an umbrella while pulling letters out of the mailbox. Inside the gate, before the building itself, is an artfully planned narrow garden that frames the path to the main entrance. An inconspicuous wooden shrine sits off to one side.

The sharp-tongued "auntie" of the Mitsuba Inn.

On their return from a journey, the residents of the house stop a few seconds before the shrine and clap their hands three times to acknowledge its spirit. The principal resident servant of the Mitsuba, a crochety old woman, splashes water on the garden stones in the morning and then fills the crude porcelain cups in the shrine with water. A professional gardener is engaged to restore the original shape of the shrubbery once in the spring and once in the fall, although the garden usually needs attention weeks before he arrives. A slightly overgrown feeling clings to it. The old servant used to grumble about this as she swept up the leaves.

This woman, whom I never heard addressed as anything but *obasan* (auntie), lived in one of the several tiny, musty maids' rooms off the main part of the building. Occasionally she mentioned her grandchildren, and once a month she would return to her ancestral home, but she never did tell me where home was. She ate and slept at the Mitsuba, doing the laundry, sweeping, and simple family-style cooking for the other maids. She also walked Wanko, the Maltese terrier once a day.

When I lived there, I would get up very early on the days I did my laundry and hook up the tiny, old-fashioned washing machine just outside her room. If I had not returned to remove my things the minute they were ready, this "auntie" would have plucked them out and hung them on the line, making snide comments as I rushed in to get them. Once, during hot weather, she held a pair of nylon bikini underpants between her thumb and forefinger. "How can you wear these? They must be so hot." She wore heavily starched cotton drawers. "How can you wear those things?" I asked. She looked at me with narrowed eyes. "What do you know? Starching makes them stand away from your skin. It's much cooler." She had a low opinion of anything done differently from the way it is done in Kyoto – that is, when she had any opinion at all. Mostly, she was uninterested.

Just in front of the stone-floored front entrance of the Mitsuba is an electric eye, about three feet off the ground. Anyone passing through it sets off a bell in the kitchen. The ringing brings Wanko to the front steps, where she barks madly while skittering back and forth on the polished wood at the edge of the vestibule. No banquet was being held at the Mitsuba the night I arrived (the summer months are generally slow), so Wanko was loose, a frenzied wad of white fluff in the entrance hall. Auntie poked her head out of the kitchen, gave a perfunctory "welcome back" and, as I picked up the dog, reminded me unnecessarily that Wanko tended to lose control of her bladder when excited.

My room, for the two weeks of this reunion, was the four-and-a-half tatami mat room used by the kouta teacher once a month for singing lessons in this part of the city. In the winter, the eight-by-twelve-foot room was easy to heat with a portable kerosene stove because it was small and protected from the wind coming off the river. This made it less attractive in summer. An air conditioner had been installed, though, and five minutes could turn it into an icebox. I set my bags in a corner and went to the large guest bath to recover from twenty-four hours in transit.

All the guest rooms in the Mitsuba have a tiny sink inside the first set of sliding doors. A few even have a toilet in an attached closet, but there is only one bath. Unless extremely pressed for space, Japanese homes do not have the toilet and bath in the same room. The toilet is given as little space as physically feasible, whereas the luxurious bath is given as much as money and room will allow. Shower attachments off to one side are popular as aids in the process of soaping, scrubbing, and rinsing before getting into the tub itself, but an American-style shower *instead* of a tub is unthinkable in a home and especially in a traditional inn. Baths are taken as hot as bearable and as close to every day as possible.

The tub at the Mitsuba was full but tepid by the time I got there. The maids had heated it for themselves earlier, and they certainly would have reheated it had official guests been present, but as I was not a guest by their lights I had to take it as it was. After my bath, feeling light-headed from jet lag, I knocked on okāsan's door. She suggested a walk through Pontochō, past the charred ruins of the Hatsuyuki teahouse. We went out into the street, still full of people although it was close to midnight. As we walked, it seemed to me that okāsan had something on her mind. Taking a guess, I asked her when they had purchased the beautiful new car Tsunehiko was driving. She sighed.

"If you should see Tsunehiko's father in Tokyo, please don't tell him about the car, all right?" I had no plans to visit him, but agreed, slightly mystified.

"He said he would pay for a car but he doesn't know that Tsunehiko picked out such an expensive one. I'm going to tell him, of course, but only when the time is right. So it would be better if you didn't say anything about it."

"I understand."

Tsunehiko, okāsan's only child, was acknowledged by her patron as his son. This man had provided financial support throughout Tsunehiko's twenty-two years. The young man kept himself in British suits, silk ties, and imported cigarettes with this money, but it is doubtful that his father ever knew exactly how it was spent. His mother indulged his every whim and was often pressed into making excuses to his father. She had fallen into the habit of rationalizing his behavior even to herself.

"You know, it may look like pure luxury, but in fact we need such a car for business. Sometimes we meet guests at the station, or take them home, and this car will make a good impression on behalf of the Mitsuba. Tsunehiko's father should think of it as an investment and be glad that his son is showing concern for the business."

It was hard to imagine Tsunehiko willingly driving his mother's customers anywhere. Still, I agreed once again not to say anything about the car. I mentioned that Tsunehiko had changed somewhat since I saw him last. He had lost weight and had his hair crimped in a permanent wave. A gold chain around his neck, tinted glasses, and an Aloha shirt completed the new look. Well, said okāsan, it seemed that was the fashion now, and though she didn't care much for it personally, she was glad he was in style. His father took a dimmer view.

"Actually, I'm a little worried about Tsunehiko," she finally admitted. "He has a girlfriend. You know I'm very tolerant about such things, Kikuko – I wouldn't fuss even if he said he wanted to marry a foreigner – but he's spending all his time with a bar hostess who's twelve years older than he is. Far be it from me to say anything because she works in a bar, but she's not the type who could run the Mitsuba after I retire, and she's almost too old to have children. Tsunehiko doesn't even think of these things."

I sympathized with her, saying that he would undoubtedly come around and that things would work out, but silently I wondered how far his willfulness would go. He would have had to try perversely hard to find a woman so totally displeasing to his mother, whose one blind spot (which may perhaps one day cause the bankruptcy of the Mitsuba) is her fond devotion to her irresponsible, spoiled son.

We had come to a crumbling wall and some charcoal beams: the remains of the Hatsuyuki. A drunk in the shadows was urinating on the side of the wall. Pontochō seemed like a row of polished teeth with an ugly blackened cavity in the center. We went on. Several doors down, there was a tiny bar I remembered going to with customers once or twice, and we pushed open the door to see who was there.

THE LAST COGNAC

Every summer, this bar, the Sawada, covers one of its walls with numerous flat, round fans called *uchiwa*, which the geisha have had printed with their names and crests. The red characters on

Early twentieth-century photograph of three geisha friends.

the white fans make an intriguing design, and as we sat down I kept glancing at them for familiar names and new ones. The other customers were mainly geisha relaxing after work. On one of the bar stools sat a maiko I didn't recognize. She was introduced to me as Sumino, younger sister of the geisha Sumika, whom I knew. Okāsan said that I had in fact met this maiko once before at the Mitsuba, at a party for the Kabuki actor Tamasaburō last year. Although I didn't recall her face, I remembered a giggling young girl in a pink kimono who helped carry trays at that banquet. She was pointed out to me then as a maiko-to-be.

"What will you have, Okāsan?" asked the woman behind the bar. We called for the bottle of Rémy Martin VSOP bearing Ichiume's name. This elegant little bar had personalized bottles of cognac lined up on the shelf. Rémy Martin has replaced other liquors, especially Johnny Walker Black Label, as *the* status drink in Japan, so bars like Sawada are well stocked with it. Since I was Ichiume's younger sister, it was only appropriate that we should have some cognac from the bottle on which she and her patron had written their names. Okāsan, not supposed to drink because of a heart condition, diluted hers with water.

I greeted old friends as they came in, and the news of changes in the past year continued. Okāsan spun toward me on her stool and whispered, "I forgot to tell you – Ichiteru's pregnant." Not certain whether this was desirable for Ichiteru or not, I whispered back, "Congratulations or condolences?" "Oh, she's very pleased," was the response. The bar was now filled with gossiping geisha. Suddenly the door opened, and a customer about to enter did a double take at the scene. The roomful of women turned their heads to look at him – completely nonplussed, he bowed and stepped back outside. We all laughed.

The conversation eventually turned to the fire. I asked about Midori, Ichiume's younger sister. There was a low murmur in the room. "She quit," said one. "All her kimono were destroyed," said my okāsan, "and she had no choice." I asked where she was and was told she had gone back to her natural mother's house, where she was "recuperating." Someone had spoken to her recently on the telephone. Apparently she had called to protest rumors that she was going to work in Gion, the rival geisha community across the river. There seemed to be general sympathy for her in Pontochō, but also a firm sense that it would be impossible for her ever to work there again. From the various exchanges I overheard, I gathered that she should have called for help sooner, rather than trying to put out the fire herself.

On our way home, okāsan told me about the maiko's sneaking a cigarette late at night, and the dropped ashtray. Nothing of the kind had appeared in the newspapers, nor were police informed in their investigations. In such matters, Pontochō closes ranks. But I thought of seventeen-year-old Midori, banished from the community where she had worked less than a year, living with the memory of her older sister, to whom she was tied in a bond said to be closer than blood. It was three in the morning and suddenly chilly.

THREE

TIES THAT BIND

Sake no hitotsu ga　　　One cup of sake,
En no hashi . . .　　　　The beginning of
　　　　　　　　　　　　A relationship . . .

Opening phrase of a kouta

NAMES

AMERICANS ARE USED to having one "real" name. Of course we may have a nickname or two, either standard ones (Jack for John) or the Poopsie and Binky variety we'd all prefer to forget. And once in a while, a particular name does in fact substitute for a "real" name because it is a publicized convention: Duke, for instance, meaning John Wayne – whose *real* real name, by the way, was Marion Morrison. Ultimately, though, despite the blurring around the edges, our culture sees naming as a fairly straightforward procedure.

In Japan, by contrast, one may have several or even many different real names, depending on what capacity is being exercised under that name. Thus, as a calligrapher an individual may be known as Shumpō, as a dancer Kikufumi, as a shamisen player Yaeha. A potter has his name in pottery, a tea master his tea name. Similarly geisha have geisha names.

About the closest equivalent we in the United States have to all these names of capacities is the nom de plume, but there are several revealing differences between our custom and the manifold names of Japan. First, pen names are often pseudonyms, names deliberately meant to conceal or confuse one's "true" identity. In the Japanese case, by contrast, the possession of multiple names not only is not secret, it is the very essence of a public concern, in which so-and-so is indeed recognized by all as So-and-So, often to the total eclipse of his "true," natal name.

Then too, a pen name, or even a stage name, is, in American culture, the emblem of autonomy and individualism. It can be concocted at will, fiddled with and abandoned without a moment's reflection. Art names, pottery names, Kabuki actors' names, and so on are not chosen; they are given, generally in a ceremony of some sort. The intention is that the new name will remain attached to its bearer, in that particular capacity, until he or she either dies or "transcends" this name and is given yet another. The honor involved in name changes – or the dishonor, if, for example, one who is expected to succeed to a name does not – is anything but an individual prerogative in Japan.

People have names appropriate to their stages of life, and they even have Buddhist posthumous names that they bear in death.[1] Names can be passed on publicly and triumphantly, as in the case of Kabuki actors, for instance, who may be known not only by bequeathed stage names but actually even by their places in the order of inheritance. In the theater – but on the street as well – you can hear Rokudaime discussed: "the sixth generation" literally becomes his name, referring, as everyone knows, to Kiku-gorō VI, the famous actor of the Onoue line, who is talked about publicly in what at first seems an impenetrable shorthand.

Finally, the orthography of the Japanese language, notorious as one of the world's most beautiful and most complicated writing systems, contributes its share of subtlety to Japanese naming conventions. This is because single characters (there are usually three to five in the ordinary name) still are not completely standardized in pronunciation, despite repeated attempts at script reform. One result of the tangle of orthographic variations is a great sensitivity on the part of Japanese to the way characters are used to represent names, or parts of names. The same character can be used in a series of names to express the connections and continuity between the bearers. In short, capacities, stages of life, written representations, and above all, a sense of the public nature of names are the cultural points to bear in mind when one inquires of a geisha what she is called.

Ichigiku, Younger Sister of Ichiume

Ten women in the Pontochō community of sixty-five geisha have geisha names that begin with a character pronounced *ichi*.[2] This is not a coincidence, nor was my own geisha name, Ichigiku, chosen at random. The element *ichi* as the unvarying first part of their professional names graphically represents the interconnections within one particular group of geisha here. Like a family tradition, the Ichi-name can be traced back to one woman, the original Ichiko, who founded a teahouse called the Dai-Ichi in 1916.

Ichiko is in fact the single most prestigious and powerful name within this line. This name is passed on as one holder retires or dies, and the geisha currently known as Ichiko in Pontochō is actually Ichiko III. One meaning of the word (as opposed to the name) *ichiko* is shamaness. In primitive Japanese religion the shamaness revealed the will of the gods after entering a trance induced by dancing. The name Ichiko, not completely bereft of these mysterious overtones even now, can be held only by a dancer.

The original Ichiko started the Dai-Ichi teahouse as a branch of an older house called the Daimonjiya. She adopted the first character, *dai* (meaning large, or great), from the name of the parent establishment, and she used *ichi* from her own name to create the name for her house.[3] It so happens that *dai-ichi*, written with different characters, means "first," or "number one," and Ichiko took advantage of this homonym in naming her establishment. Indeed, the Dai-Ichi may well be the number one teahouse in Pontochō. Many geisha were trained on its premises, myself among them.

As a geisha, the original Ichiko had thirteen younger sisters: Ichiyō, Ichifuku, Ichiyū, Ichiyumi, Ichiyakko, Ichiryō, Ichiei, Ichimaru, Ichikō, Ichizō, Ichikoto, Ichigiku, and Ichitarō. There may have been more, but if so they are not remembered by their sororal namesakes of the present. No one really keeps track of

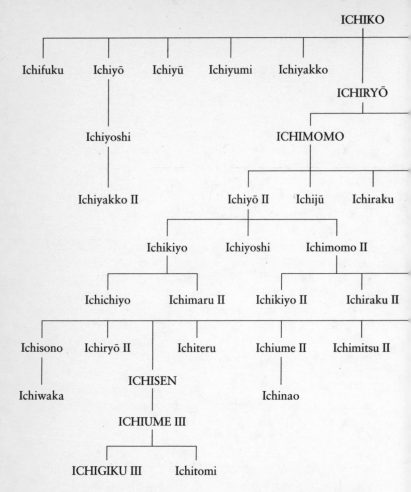

ICHIKO

Ichifuku   Ichiyō   Ichiyū   Ichiyumi   Ichiyakko

ICHIRYŌ

Ichiyoshi   ICHIMOMO

Ichiyakko II   Ichiyō II   Ichijū   Ichiraku

Ichikiyo   Ichiyoshi   Ichimomo II

Ichichiyo   Ichimaru II   Ichikiyo II   Ichiraku II

Ichisono   Ichiryō II   Ichiteru   Ichiume II   Ichimitsu II

Ichiwaka   ICHISEN   Ichinao

ICHIUME III

ICHIGIKU III   Ichitomi

these lines of "descent." They can only be reconstructed through the memories of old geisha, most of whom have long since retired to manage teahouses, although a few still appear at parties as grandmotherly coquettes. Nobody can remember any geisha having as many younger sisters as the almost legendary Ichiko. Today, a geisha is fortunate to have even one.

From Ichiko's thirteen younger sisters, only one line continued past two "generations." The geisha Ichiryō had two younger

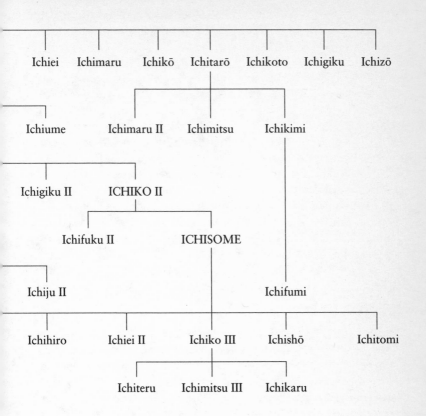

*Lines of sisterly descent for the Ichi- "family"
of geisha in Pontochō.*

sisters: Ichimomo and Ichiume (Ichi-peach and Ichi-plum). Ichiume (this was Ichiume I) had none, but Ichimomo had five. One of these was Ichiko II. By this time, the original Ichiko had retired from geisha life to manage the Dai-Ichi; thus the name Ichiko became available to another geisha. It was given to an apprentice who showed great promise as a dancer.

Ichiko II in turn acquired two younger sisters. One of them, Ichisome, had eleven ceremonial siblings, almost as many as the original Ichiko. One of these women became Ichiko III, once Ichiko II had retired from geisha life in her early twenties to marry a government official in Tokyo. Another, named Ichisen, became the older sister of Ichiume (by this time, Ichiume III). And it was she – a rambunctious young geisha given to undignified outbursts of laughter when amused – who was deemed an appropriate older sister for the unorthodox new geisha from America.

When I am in Japan, I ordinarily go by the name of Kikuko (*kiku*, "chrysanthemum" + a common feminine suffix, *-ko*), a name I was given when I first lived there as a teenager. When it was decided that Ichiume would be my older sister, the first part of my geisha name was determined as well. Ichi- it would be for certain, and because no one was currently known by the name Ichigiku (Ichi + kiku), I became as a geisha Ichigiku (III, as it happened), the younger sister of Ichiume.

ELECTIVE AFFINITY

Sisterhood is basic to Kyoto geisha society. What does it mean to be sisters? First of all, one is never just a sister, but specifically an older sister or a younger sister. Far from having the overtones of equality implied by the English word "sisterhood," in Japan this relationship primarily indicates hierarchy. A new geisha becomes the younger sister of a more experienced geisha in this web of relationships expressed in terms of the family. She and her older sister form a pair, but an unequal one.

Not only do geisha take on the capacity of sisters to one another, but they call the women who run teahouses "mother." In Japan, the parent–child relationship is also hierarchical: an unequal pair, with rightful expectations on the one side, obligations on the other. The use of kinship terms does not necessarily call into play the sentimental notions about family that we of Western European cultural heritage have come to presume are natural. Instead, the terms older sister and younger sister, mother and daughter, define the unequal but complementary sets of categories that are the basis of geisha society.

Geisha are by no means the only Japanese who live and work in a social group defined by kin terms, but this phenomenon does appear most explicitly in traditional occupations: among carpenters, miners, sumo wrestlers, and gangsters, for example.[4] The geisha sisterhood, however, differs from all these other groups in a distinctive way.

In the more usual form of these so-called ritual kinship groups, the *oyabun*, or the "one in the role of parent," is the linchpin of the entire organization. He (in almost every case it is a he) has a following of several *kobun*, "those in the role of child." Such groups are tightly knit, hierarchical, and to some degree authoritarian. Here, the roles of ritual brotherhood are merely extensions of the main parent–child tie.

The difference for geisha is precisely the primacy of sisterhood. Although the many "mothers," as the mistresses of teahouses, are powerful figures in the day-to-day work of the geisha world, they are not equivalent to the single, all-powerful position of the oyabun. Geisha communities have nothing resembling the pyramid of authority seen in other ritual kinship groups. Geisha mothers, daughters, and sisters participate in separate relationships, each created on its own terms, rather than as parts of one overarching whole. As with Ichiume and myself, a pair of sisters often have different mothers.

Although the key element in the relationship of sisterhood is hierarchy, geisha nowadays feel that there should be empathy, loyalty, and camaraderie between sisters. An onēsan expects deference from her younger sister, but tyranny is not supposed to be her style. Ideally, the older sister is at once mentor and friend. One has no say in who one's blood relatives are, but there is an *en*, an affinity, between two geisha who choose one another as sisters. Whatever else may enter into the considerations of this choice, compatibility between the two women is essential today.

A young woman embarking on the career of a geisha is similar to a bride leaving her natal family for her husband's home. Obviously the comparison does not hold on every point, but in general the "older sister" is similar to the bridegroom and the "younger sister" to the bride. The new geisha leaves her home to live in a place where she calls the proprietress "mother." She enters a sub-

41

ordinate relationship with a previously unrelated person who then becomes kin, her "older sister." Finally, she is expected to put her old family behind her in her devotion to the new group.

The similarities between new geisha and bride are not just incidental. They are quite explicit in the ceremony that creates the bond of sisterhood.

THREE CUPS THRICE

The traditional Japanese marriage ceremony reaches its culmination when the bride and groom take three sips of sake from each of three lacquered cups. This exchange of nuptial cups is called *sansan-kudo*, "thrice three, nine times," and the phrase can be used to mean a wedding. Most people think of sansan-kudo only in connection with the marriage of a man and a woman, but its meaning and use are broader than that. The sharing of ritual sake creates a deep and solemn bond between two people whom we and the Japanese ordinarily consider unrelated. Thereafter, they are kin. This is basically what marriage is about, of course, but the tie can also bind the older and younger sisters of the geisha world.

In Kyoto, when a new maiko or geisha joins the ranks, she and her older sister-to-be enter sisterhood by performing the ritual of sansan-kudo. "The tying together of destinies" signifies marriage in Japan, and geisha use the same term, *en musubi*, to talk about their special sister ties.[5] An en is a connection between people, usually a created connection rather than a "natural" one.[6] The Buddhist meaning of en, karma, lies behind the notion of human connections; but in everyday usage, when Japanese say that two people have an en, they are not necessarily thinking of the metaphysical reasons for it. If you have an en with someone, there is some sort of special affinity between you. One step further is the "tying of en" (en musubi), which creates a bond not easily loosened. In fact, if such a bound pair should separate, the tie cannot simply be undone, but is said to be "cut" (*en o kiru*).

Because this bond is not to be trifled with, Ichiume and I did not actually go through the sisterhood ceremony. My own rea-

*Ichiume (left) fixes the hair of her
new younger sister.*

sons for becoming a geisha were clear to everyone, but it was also
clear that I was not making a long-term commitment to the
geisha life. For practical purposes Ichiume was my older sister,
but for us to have exchanged the ritual cups of sake would have
been a sham. During the time I was in Pontochō, no new geisha
made her debut, so the one such ceremony I witnessed was in a
different community.

Early in June I had been invited as the only guest to one of
these quiet, private ceremonies in the hanamachi of
Kamishichiken, which is tucked away in the northwest corner of
Kyoto, behind the Kitano Shrine in the Nishijin weaving area.
Far from the center of town Kamishichiken contains no bars with
their flashing neon to compete with the subdued old teahouses.
The atmosphere is that of a century ago. In the opinion of many,
the geisha of Kamishichiken are more demure than geisha in
Gion or Pontochō.

I went to see the geisha Katsukiyo tie the knot of sisterhood
with a new geisha who was to take the name Katsufuku. Too old
to become a maiko at twenty-two, Katsufuku was making her
debut as a full geisha. Her father, I heard later, was an official in
the police department. He had opposed her entrance into the
geisha life at first, though she finally secured his grudging permission. Katsufuku's home was near Kamishichiken, and she had
first become friends with some of the geisha of that area through
her dance lessons. From them she got the notion of becoming a
geisha herself.

The rites of sisterhood were to be held in the teahouse where Katsufuku had gone to live a month earlier, taking one of the small rooms upstairs for her quarters.[7] Only two other women participated in the ceremony of sansan-kudo: the proprietress of the teahouse (whom Katsufuku called "mother") and a young geisha in her twenties named Katsuhana, who represented all the other geisha whose names begin with the character *katsu-*. Later, Katsufuku would be introduced at parties with customers, where her debut would be celebrated, but the actual ceremony of sisterhood was conducted in private solemnity by the geisha alone.

The room was bare of all furniture except for three large, flat cushions. As the older sister, Katsukiyo sat on the cushion in front of the alcove. She wore a pale blue silk summer kimono and darker blue obi with a small fan tucked into its folds. Her hair was up, in a smooth, simple bouffant style. She was about forty years old. Katsufuku was dressed in a summer version of a geisha's formal kimono with dipping collar and trailing hem. She wore an elaborate wig, and her face was painted and powdered to a porcelain white. She sat across the room from her sister-to-be. The third cushion, positioned at the edge of the room, was for the okāsan.

The three sat quietly with folded hands and lowered eyes for a few moments. Then a maid stepped into the room bearing a tray. Without saying a word, she set it down and with both hands took up a small lacquered stand holding the three nested cups. She placed it in front of Katsukiyo, who took the smallest of the cups, holding it with the fingertips of both hands while the maid poured a bit of sake into it from a long-spouted silver kettle. Katsukiyo emptied the cup in three sips. Wiping the rim with a tissue, she returned it to its place. The maid then carried the stand over to Katsufuku.

Katsufuku repeated these motions, and as she lifted the cup to drink, I noticed that she closed her eyes. Though it was bright outdoors, the room was shadowy, and her silhouette outlined against the dark screen was the profile of a classic Japanese beauty. When she held the cup to her lips, however, her suntanned unpainted hands looked as if they could not belong to that alabaster face.

*The new geisha Katsufuku receives
a cup of sake during the geisha
sisterhood ceremony.*

The cups were returned to Katsukiyo, who then drank three sips from the middle one. Just as the bridegroom, in the position of master, drinks from each cup before the bride, here the older sister, as superior, takes each cup first. The middle-sized cup was then given to Katsufuku, and finally the largest cup was exchanged in the same order.

Katsukiyo then relinquished her cushion in front of the alcove to Katsuhana and joined her new younger sister on the opposite side of the room. As sisters then, the two exchanged cups with the okāsan and with Katsuhana.[8] The whole ceremony took less than fifteen minutes. Through the sharing of three cups of rice wine, Katsufuku was absorbed into this community of geisha.

After the ceremony, the geisha and the okāsan invited me to stay for a lunch of *sekihan*, the special "red rice" served on felicitous occasions in Japan. We went upstairs to a bright, airy room, where the maid brought lacquered boxes of cold rice and delicacies. The noon sunlight streamed through the open window, which framed a view of azaleas and a pomegranate tree in the garden below. Once the solemnities were over, everyone could relax. We drank beer now instead of the ceremony-saturated sake.

Pulling Out: The Hiki Iwai

Because there is a ceremonial way into sisterhood, it makes sense that a ceremonial way out exists as well. In the past, a *hiki iwai*, or "pulling out celebration," took place in the licensed quarters when a courtesan's debts were finally paid off (either by her own efforts or by the largesse of a patron), and she could then re-enter ordinary society. Today the phrase refers to a geisha's departure from her profession for whatever cause. Marriage, different work, or a patron are some of the more common reasons for leaving.

How does one undo the ties formed by nine sips of rice wine? With cooked rice. According to geisha etiquette, a woman who leaves the community should present a small box of boiled rice to her older sister, to her okāsan, to her teachers, and to all those to whom she owes gratitude for training or for past kindnesses.[9] This gesture will undo the ties that sustained her as a geisha.[10] Unlike a marriage (which is an en that can only be cut, never undone) geisha custom recognizes the more likely possibility that one or the other sister may depart, marking the fact gracefully, in ceremony.

MINARAI: LEARNING BY OBSERVATION

As a model to her younger sister, an older sister is responsible for teaching the niceties of proper geisha behavior. Though any other senior geisha is free to instruct the new member about manners, the older sister provides the main example for minarai. In Ponto-chō, a new maiko will become affiliated with a particular teahouse. Her *minarai-jaya*, or "teahouse for learning by observation," is the same house that sponsored her older sister.

This is one of the many results from the choice of a particular onēsan. Almost every geisha of the Ichi-line in Pontochō has been trained at the Dai-Ichi teahouse.[11]

Learning by observation once meant gradually becoming accustomed to the geisha world by the simple fact of being around other geisha. Girls of ten to twelve years old, laboring in the teahouses as maids (*shikomi*), were thought to be learning by observation for their eventual careers as geisha.[12] They often suffered in the process, but a little suffering was thought to help them become stronger women and better geisha. Long hours of arduous work and strict shamisen and dancing lessons were the rule. Most places drew the line at out and out cruelty, at least.

How different things are now! Mothers of the teahouses are acutely aware of the difficulty of finding young girls who are serious about becoming maiko or geisha. They bend over backward to make the early experiences pleasant for apprentices. A girl who is preparing for her debut as a maiko, far from suffering, is coddled by everyone – the mothers, the customers, and the older sisters. Even before she has formally joined the community, she may be dressed up in the maiko's costume and sent to parties the mothers think will be interesting to her, a party where a movie star or a famous Kabuki actor is being feted, for example. Mothers hope the girl will be star-struck, and that any reservations about geisha life will evaporate in the glow. The mothers comment that the girl will have time enough later to experience boring parties and obnoxious guests; best to show her the attractive parts of geisha life first.

Ichitarō, a geisha brought up in the old school, thinks this modern pampering of maiko is scandalous. Now eighty years old, she is the retired proprietress of the teahouse Nakagawa in Pontochō. Under the geisha name Ichitarō, she was one of the younger sisters of the original Ichiko. So far as she is concerned, in the present-day geisha world manners have disappeared, artistic accomplishment is hardly worth the name, polite language is no longer spoken, and the young geisha have no sense of responsibility or proper sympathy for their elders. "They think only of themselves," she told me, tapping her long pipe emphatically on the edge of an ashtray. The young geisha privately regard her as

After the bath.

a harmless old curmudgeon, even a curiosity, with her old-fashioned *kiseru* pipe and her complaints. Suffering in the name of art is not quite so fashionable these days.

If a middle-aged Japanese woman has a perfectly round little bald spot on the crown of her head, then chances are good that she was a maiko in her youth. My okāsan, the mistress of the Mitsuba, has one. The "maiko's medal of honor" is how she refers to it. It is the result of pulling tight a small bundle of hair for the basis of the maiko's hairstyle. Over the years, that section of hair falls out and does not grow back in. My okāsan's everyday hairdo now hides the spot so completely that only her hairdresser ever sees it. When she happens to visit a beauty shop in another city in Japan, she never fails to impress the beautician. The bald spot is understood as a mark of the hardships of the training she undertook. The only time she ever felt embarrassed by it, she said, was once when she traveled in Europe and had no way of explaining it to the French hairdresser. She was mortified that the woman could only have thought her to be going bald.

In the future it will be a rare former maiko who will carry such a medal of honor. Because today's maiko begin their work at age

48

Maiko, *1954 watercolor by Okumura Togyū.*

seventeen rather than at twelve or thirteen, their scalps are probably safe. Although old Ichitarō sees this as another example of
how the geisha profession has gone soft, from the point of view
of most modern Japanese the discipline of the maiko and the
geisha is still redoubtable.

FOUR

PONTOCHŌ OF LONG AGO

A moonlit evening in Pontochō:
On the bamboo blinds of the cool verandas
The beckoning shadows of paper lanterns.

From Pontochō kouta

BRIDGES AND RIVERS

PONTOCHŌ IS A NAME that sounds vaguely odd to Japanese ears. There is a decidedly non-Japanese ring to the word, which has sparked much discussion and speculative etymology. One of the more plausible theories is that *ponto-* derives from the Portuguese word for bridge, *ponte*, as bridges are such a prominent feature of the area. Pontochō is located on the east bank of the Kamo River. The two great bridges of Sanjō and Shijō, where Third and Fourth avenues span the wide but shallow current, define its northern and southern boundaries. The Takase River, really a small canal, runs along Pontochō's west side, and here, too, alleys and narrow streets turn into small bridges as they cross it. One can hardly take ten steps out of Pontochō and not go over a bridge. But why Portuguese?

In the late sixteenth century, Portuguese missionaries conducted a brief but influential mission in Japan. They converted some of the country's most powerful samurai and provincial barons to the Christian faith. But because evangelism often brought colonialism close on its heels, the suspicious shogun, Tokugawa Ieyasu, finally banned Christianity from the country in 1614. Before their expulsion, the Portuguese fathers traveled freely throughout Japan. Their exotic dress and manners made quite an impression on the local folk. It is not impossible that they could have supplied the modish sobriquet that eventually came to overshadow the official name of the area designated on maps as Shinkawaramachi. The Japanese fondness for adopting foreign words for novelty was not much different then from what it is today.

The odd pronunciation "pon" applied to the first of the three characters used to write the word Pontochō is totally idiosyncratic. Even Japanese sometimes make the mistake of pronouncing the name of this area as Sentochō. Without seeing the characters, the spoken name Sentochō could be understood as "street of the boatmen." And this is not implausible either, for Pontochō has always been associated with water trade in one way or another. Before the area became popular as an entertainment district it was the home of charcoal makers and of the bargemen who poled the charcoal to Osaka in flat-bottomed boats.

Because the Kamo River has never been easily navigable, the Takase canal was built parallel to it for the purpose of transporting goods. During the 1600s, all the houses and shacks between Third and Fourth avenues faced the Takase canal where the barges were loaded, an eminently practical orientation that suited the people who lived and worked there. But these houses turned their backs on the beautiful Kamo River and the view of the Eastern Mountains beyond.

If the Takase canal was purely practical, the Kamo River was essentially aesthetic. Though unsuited for navigation, the Kamo-gawa became associated with tasks such as rinsing long, unfurled bolts of freshly dyed silks. The pattern of the brightly colored kimono cloth rippling in the clear waters was a favorite subject for poetry and painting. Another image associated with this river is that of the small water birds called *chidori* (plovers) that once skimmed the shallow ripples with their poignant cries. The chidori was adopted by the geisha of Pontochō as their special mark or crest, just as their public dances are called the Kamo River Dances.

Geisha on a veranda in Pontochō, circa 1890.

The transformation of the street of the boatmen to the street of the geisha involved, first, a reorientation of the houses away from the Takase canal and toward the Kamo River. By the early 1700s the area of Pontochō came to harbor a "water trade" rather different from that of the boatmen. The entertainment world in Japan is broadly referred to as the *mizu shōbai*, literally, the water business. The mundane water trade of bargemen on the Takase River was gradually replaced by the glamorous water business of the geisha and the teahouses facing the Kamo River.

All the houses located on the east side of Pontochō have wooden platforms in back, extending out over the wide river bank. These square verandas are strung with paper lanterns in warm weather for geisha entertainments. Summer has traditionally been thought the best season to appreciate Pontochō. Bright lanterns swing gently in the breeze off the river, and at dusk the Eastern Mountains look like an ink wash painting in which each receding mountain pales to a lighter shade of gray. Every Pontochō teahouse has invested in air conditioning, which does a more thorough job of cooling than a river breeze, so the verandas are not used as often as they used to be. But if the summer heat is not yet unbearably steamy and sticky, the lanterns go up, mats are put down, and parties still take place there.

Woodblock print (ukiyo-e), Evening Cool on the Riverbank, *by*
Utagawa Toyohiro, depicting a geisha holding a shamisen, a maid with
a kettle of sake, and a lady of pleasure on a wooden veranda over the
Kamo River in the early 1800s.

*Liza Dalby's okāsan as a maiko, photographed on a veranda
over the Kamo River, around 1930.*

*A sixteen-year-old maiko-to-be,
photographed on a Pontochō
veranda, 1978.*

Pontochō's location, on the bank of a clear, beautiful river, with a view of the mountains as they change from misty pink in spring to vibrant summer green to the vermilion of maples in the fall, helps explain why it was such an ideal place for an entertainment district to develop. Further, the huge Gion Shrine is nearby. The Gion geisha district takes its name from the shrine and is located next to it; but Pontochō, just over the Shijo Bridge, is within easy walking distance. Japanese shrines, especially famous ones like Gion, attract pilgrims, and these visitors were not likely to return home from their devotional trips without sampling the more worldly entertainments found close by. Many of the areas that later became famous geisha districts were originally places near shrines where pretty girls in teahouses served food and drink to travelers.

LEGAL PROSTITUTION

Entertainment in Japan during the Edo period (1600–1867), especially entertainment involving women, was considered to require close supervision by the government. Prostitution was legal, but only if properly licensed and controlled. Illegal – that is, underground and amateur – ladies of the night posed a constant problem for the authorities. As seems to be the case almost anywhere, however, illegal prostitutes took the risk and continued their work. The government cracked down on their activities arbitrarily; but depending on how the winds of official morality were blowing, individual women who were not licensed, or, occasionally, great numbers of women from areas where the license had been suddenly revoked, might be rounded up and deposited in Shimabara, the one great official licensed quarter of Kyoto.

Both Shimabara and its counterpart in the city of Edo, called Yoshiwara, were areas on the city outskirts where prostitution was contained and regulated in a finely graduated hierarchy until 1957. The containment was literal: these districts were fenced in by real walls as well as government regulation. In this way the shogunate tried to keep a rein on public morality. Besides the prostitutes, who were registered as such, a number of other classes of female entertainers and waitresses were permitted to work in designated entertainment areas. Geisha belonged in this category. For them, engaging in sex with customers was officially prohibited.

The question of geisha and prostitution arose almost as soon as women entered the profession. Although technically geisha were not prostitutes, reality has never been wholly determined by official dictates. "First, will she spread – second, how's her voice?" says an epigram referring to geisha of a disreputable area. Yet geisha entertainment usually did not entail sex as a foregone conclusion, and geisha did not count a knowledge of the "forty-eight positions" as part of their repertoire of skills.

The sex professionals were the *yūjo*, the women of pleasure. As her initiation into *toko no higi*, bedroom esoterica, a young yūjo was instructed with the aid of a dildo on how to pleasure a

A yūjo or woman of pleasure.

man – as well as how to make him climax quickly and how to fake a convincing orgasm. She had to learn to conserve her strength, after all. Yūjo were proud mistresses of technique. They kept their pubic hair carefully plucked and clipped, and an experienced rake could supposedly tell the degree of a woman's sexual skill by a mere glance at how she pruned her shrubbery.

For the Japanese male of the seventeenth and eighteenth centuries, sex with wives was for procreation, sex with yūjo for recreation. "The caged bird [the yūjo] who sings out in the night will sell well" ran a modish phrase, whereas "night crowing" by the chicken in the home garden was positively discouraged.[1]

Yūjo were supposed to know that charred newts, eels, and lotus root were aphrodisiacs, and that dried rings of bêche-de-mer (the sea slug, ugly in English and in reality, too) could be fitted over a penis like a French tickler. Yet from the standpoint of common knowledge of sexual techniques in America of the 1980s, the substance of the yūjo's secrets is not particularly amazing. One of the items in her treasure chest of foreplay was an outrageously exotic practice of touching mouths, called *seppun*. We call it kissing.

Of the numerous hours men spent in the Yoshiwara pleasure quarters, however, relatively few were devoted to sex. Most of the time was engaged in partying – sociable banter, poetry, preening, singing, dancing, eating, drinking. The lure of Shimabara and Yoshiwara was the romance, elegance, and excitement of that one place in feudal society where money, charm, and wit made more of an impression than rigidly defined social class.

Male Geisha

The first geisha sauntered into these parties of the yūjo and their customers in the 1600s. These geisha were men. They were also called jesters (*hōkan*) or drum bearers (*taiko-mochi*), and their lively, risqué patter made the guests and the yūjo laugh. Comedians and musicians, these men made all-around good company for parties. In 1751, some customers in a Shimabara brothel were surprised when a female drum bearer (*onna taiko-mochi*) pranced into their party. She was referred to as a *geiko*, the term still used in Kyoto instead of geisha. A few years later, in Edo, similar female entertainers appeared. They were called *onna geisha*, female geisha.[2] By 1780, female geisha outnumbered the men, and people began to say *otoko geisha* when they meant the latter. By 1800, a geisha, unmodified, was a woman.

Even after the novelty wore off, female geisha remained in high demand in the demimonde. By the 1750s, the licensed quarters had already been in existence for 150 years, and yūjo were not as skilled in the arts, broadly defined, as they had once been. In fact, the entertainments of the pleasure quarters had probably gone a little stale. The new female geisha took the quarters by storm. They sang popular tunes, not stuffy ballads; and they came in and out of the quarters freely and were in every sense worldly, unlike the caged and sheltered yūjo. In the official hierarchy of the licensed quarters, geisha, both male and female, stood near the bottom; but this must have been little consolation to a high-ranked yūjo whose customer was attracted to the fresh-faced geisha with her shamisen.

The term geisha, literally, "artist," was an element in numerous terms for different professional women in the latter half of the eighteenth century: *shiro* (white) geisha were purely entertainers, as opposed to *korobi* geisha, who "tumbled" for guests; *kido* (gate) geisha stood at the entrance to carnivals, playing their shamisens to attract business, whereas *jorō* (whore) geisha were probably not hired for their musical skills. Around 1770, the former dancing girls (*odoriko*) of the feudal towns began to be called *machi geisha*, "town geisha," as opposed to the geisha who appeared within the licensed quarters of the more sophisticated cities. Machi geisha in turn had other nicknames, such as *neko*, "cat," a word that could be written with characters implying the possibility of pussy from these cats.

The geisha in the licensed quarters were forbidden to sleep with the yūjos' customers. In 1779 geisha were recognized as practicing a distinct profession, and a registry office (*kenban*) was set up to provide and enforce rules of conduct for them. Geisha were not to wear flamboyant kimono, or combs and jeweled pins in their hair. They were not to sit next to guests, or otherwise insinuate themselves into the place of the yūjo. When a yūjo accused a geisha of stealing a customer, the kenban would conduct an inquiry. If the geisha were found guilty she could be suspended for several days, or even for good.

The status of the machi geisha was less clear. Among them were those who would "grant the pillow" and those who would not. The question of geisha and prostitution has always been complicated. Japan's feudal government certainly found it so, and considerable administrative effort was expended on trying to preserve a distinction between the two groups of women. Frequent reiteration of the law indicates the difficulty of enforcing it. At the same time, the fact that legal prostitution was abolished in 1957, but geisha were untouched, indicates a basic sense that geisha – in some true or best sense of the word – are not prostitutes.

Pontochō's Water Business

During the Edo period, licenses were required not only for prostitution, but for anything that smacked of the salacious. The gradual development of Pontochō's status as an entertainment district can be seen in the connection between tea, women, and song. In 1712 the authorities granted a petition allowing the establishment of *chaya*, teahouses (which meant, essentially, bars), in Shinkawaramachi, that is, Pontochō. Waitresses known as *chatate onna* (tea-brewing women) were permitted to serve customers in these places. This was the beginning of Pontochō's new "water business." Other, similar areas were licensed at about this time, including the Gion district and Kamishichiken. A century later, each of these areas would be famous for its geisha.

By the 1770s, flourishing Pontochō teahouses had set up branches in the area of Nijō Shinchi, just to the north. This expansion may also have been a maneuver to hide illicit prostitution from watchful government eyes in Pontochō proper. There was a gradual rise in illegal prostitution along both sides of the river in the late 1700s – so much so that the licensed brothels in Shimabara complained to the authorities that they were losing business because of it.

Shimabara had a monopoly on authorized prostitution in Kyoto. Naturally, many people stood to profit from permission to operate brothels in other areas of the city. Such entrepreneurs petitioned continuously for this privilege. In 1790, the government granted licenses for brothels in four areas outside Shimabara: Gion, Nijō (which included Pontochō), Kitano, and

Nighthawks *is the title of this woodblock of prostitutes setting up shop on a riverbank during the Edo period.*

Shichijō. In 1813, these four areas were further permitted to employ the services of the immensely popular female geisha as entertainers.

Despite continuous government restrictions, Pontochō flourished, and the combination of yūjo, geisha, and a growing number of so-called amateur prostitutes (*hakujin*) made it a rake's paradise. This class of "amateurs" is said to have originally consisted of the wives and daughters of the boatmen who lived in the area. While their men were away poling their barges down to Osaka, the women took a few customers of their own. Because they spent most of their time making charcoal and bundling up firewood in their homes, to attract customers they had to powder themselves thickly to cover the smudges. Their white (*haku*) powder is purportedly the reason why they were called hakujin, but this word also works on a more extended phonetic pun having to do with the dichotomy between *kurōto* (professional; *kuro* = black) and *shirōto* (amateur; *shiro* = white). Whatever their origin, such women formed a group of lower-class, probably part-time ladies for hire, and the term hakujin, unique to Pontochō, lingers in registries and advertisements from dance programs up through the early twentieth century.

From about 1800 to 1840, Pontochō and other similar areas created a style of living for the Kyoto city dweller that, while undeniably licentious, was also a fertile ground for the growth of numerous new styles in literature, music, and art. The same thing occurred in other cities as well, most brilliantly in Edo, the feudal capital.

Takizawa Bakin, a writer of the early nineteenth century, described the open atmosphere of lasciviousness in the pleasure districts along the Kamo River: the tiny shacks that sprouted like mushrooms every night on the wide river bed, shacks that would disappear at dawn after their occupants had concluded a night's business. About Pontochō in particular, Bakin noted how women could be rented by the month at the inns. For twice the price of a room, a man could obtain food, drink, sewing, mending, and "pillow service." The women who provided pillow service were not licensed, however, and Bakin said that, whereas the *tayū* and *tenjin* (higher-ranking women of pleasure) wore under-sashes of silk crepe, these raffish ladies of the month wore no underclothes at all! "One soon tires of their appearance," he claimed.[3]

A lady of pleasure with child attendant.

This open atmosphere of sexual indulgence finally provoked the government into bringing down the curtain on the lively play. In 1842, a series of edicts known as the Tempō Reforms were leveled at the problem of public morality. Racy literature came under heavy censorship, and yūjo were disenfranchised in one terse official statement: "All ladies of pleasure are enjoined to seek proper employment." Public morality, it seemed, had fallen to an all-time low. The unemployed brothel keepers petitioned continuously during the succeeding decade for reinstatement of their licenses, but to no avail.

The 1840s would have been exceedingly slow years for the inns and teahouses of Pontochō had it not been for a clever serving girl named Haizen. *Haizen* means "table service." In those days men were hired by the teahouses to provide and set up the table service required for a banquet. A serving girl decided to learn that occupation, and in so doing, she started a vogue for the service by women. When customers would "call for Haizen" (literally call for the table service), women would appear and provide them with companionship during the meal – and perhaps later as well. In such ways Pontochō was able to keep on attracting customers.

Politics and Patronage

Finally in 1851 the government relented and allowed the reopening of the four entertainment areas it had originally licensed. The decree stated that anyone operating outside these sanctioned areas would be strictly dealt with. The arbitrary granting and rescinding of licenses seems to indicate that the authorities were torn between the dictates of an official morality that would have suppressed the pleasure quarters completely and a more relaxed recognition of human desires that could be (and therefore might as well be) regulated and taxed.

Perhaps more important than the issue of public morals, however, was the government's desire to control the movement and whereabouts of suspicious characters. The entertainment areas were notorious hiding places for outlaws and, increasingly in the 1850s and 1860s, for political dissidents as well. It is often remarked that the scheme for the overthrow of the Tokugawa shogun, which led to the restoration of the emperor, was primarily sketched out by rebel samurai in the teahouses of Gion.

63

Two geisha.

Among those in this ultimately successful anti-shogunate group were several men who eventually married their loyal geisha sweethearts from Gion.[4] Later they brought the women along to Edo, by then the renamed city of Tokyo (Capital in the east), where the ex-geisha held sway as the wives of the country's new leaders. The Pontochō geisha, it seems, mostly backed the status quo supporters of the shogunate during this time. This perhaps says less about the political proclivities of Pontochō than about the way political factions tend to patronize different geisha areas. The political conversations that take place in front of geisha even today make it unlikely that rival factions would visit the same teahouses. A geisha's unwritten code of honor theoretically prevents her from divulging what she overhears, but why take chances?

In any case, the cautious granting of limited licenses for running houses of pleasure in 1851 was partially revoked again in 1855. All denizens of Pontochō were summoned to a nearby temple and told that, although the local magistrate was sorry to inconvenience the geisha, the prostitutes were to pack up and prepare to move to Shimabara, where they belonged. Again, prostitutes had just two choices: go to Shimabara or go underground. Both options were exercised. Four years later, the Nijō Shinchi area received permission to operate again, and new teahouses were established in Pontochō. One that dated from this time was the Daimonji-ya, the mother house from which the present Dai-Ichi branched off in the first decade of the twentieth century.

THE GOLDEN AGE

The 1860s were, in a way, the golden age of the geisha. The relatively informal ambience of a teahouse to which geisha were called was an atmosphere very different from a brothel in Shimabara. Already the yūjo were seen as slightly old-fashioned compared to the geisha, who dressed in – and indeed often initiated – the latest fashions for women. Whereas money was the only thing a prostitute supposedly understood, geisha had heart and a reputation for being loyal and responsive to gallantry.[5] In those days, socially speaking, the last word was style, and the geisha had it. In Kyoto, they also proved their mettle and daring by risking their lives to protect their politically dissident lovers. They were valiant heroines (especially after their side won) who created a dashing and romantic image invoked later by the term "Meiji geisha."

In 1870, the third year of the reign of the newly installed Emperor Meiji, Pontochō was designated an independent hanamachi, or flower district, that is, "geisha community." The city of Kyoto, which had been a hotbed of political activity during the preceding years, when loyalists to the imperial cause rallied around the emperor, became suddenly quiet as the emperor and the new government took up residence in Tokyo, the new capital

Portrait of Gion geisha Ikumatsu,
wife of Meiji oligarch Kido Kōin.

of the country. If the city of Kyoto as a whole experienced a loss of verve, the entertainment areas felt the new ennui particularly sharply.

In 1875, the mayor of Kyoto devised a plan to revive the flagging spirit of the city with a Spring Festival aimed at drawing tourists from all over Japan and even from foreign countries. One of the main attractions was public dances performed by geisha from three of the renowned areas of the city. The most famous of these dances is the Miyako Odori of Gion, which was advertised in English brochures at its inception as the Cherry Dances, as it was performed in the cherry blossom season. Pontochō's contribution to civic pride was the Kamogawa Odori, the Kamo River Dances. The geisha of Kamishichiken performed a program called the Kitano Odori. All three areas have maintained the tradition of yearly (and for Gion and Pontochō since 1952, twice yearly) public dance performances under the same names.

This was the beginning of a new and somewhat different role for geisha: as public entertainer, promoter of local color, star. The first time the Kamogawa Odori was staged, there wasn't even a suitable building to accommodate it. A raconteur's hall in the area was turned into the dancing platform, and the yard of a

Buddhist temple next door became a makeshift dressing room. The 112 geisha of Pontochō divided themselves into four groups that performed on alternate days; those not performing would pursue their usual rounds at teahouse parties, where customers waited to be entertained. The whole project was a smashing success, and the auspicious title of Pontochō's first program, Prosperity in Kyoto (Miyako no Nigiwai), seemed to be fulfilling itself. This was March 1872.

Emancipation

It was a great surprise to the geisha and their aficionados, therefore, when in October of that year the Meiji government announced a Proclamation for the Emancipation of Geisha and Prostitutes. Although it echoed the feudal proscriptions of thirty years earlier (in both cases women were "encouraged" to follow more proper pursuits), in fact the rationale behind the familiar-sounding order was rather different from what it had been during the Tempō Reforms.

The fledgling Meiji government was having to deal not only with the various internal problems of a newly unified nation, but also with its new position as an independent country within a world community. Japan was acutely aware of the eyes of foreign nations, especially Western nations, upon her and was extremely anxious to appear up-to-date, competent, and, above all, civilized. The fact that Japan had a system of legalized prostitution raised Victorian eyebrows, as well as doubts about how really civilized a nation with such practices could be. Today one might look back at the elaborately stylized world of the Japanese licensed quarters of the nineteenth century and see a form of cultural sophistication and civility rarely matched in the history of the world. But "civilization" had a different meaning then, and Japan was ready and willing to modify all sorts of cultural traditions that did not seem to fit in with what the West defined as civilized.

Although, in dealing with international society, the Meiji government was able to point proudly to its new legal statute, many of the women affected by the emancipation ruling were at a loss

"Of the numerous hours men spent in the pleasure quarters, relatively few were devoted to sex. Most of the time was engaged in partying."

as to what to do. A great number of them petitioned the government to be allowed to return to work. The practical result of the "liberation" of the geisha and prostitutes was not to abolish the system, but to put a number of theretofore legitimate working women out of jobs. On the positive side, for the first time an official channel was opened to the women for the airing of complaints and abuses.

All debts of geisha or prostitutes to their houses were canceled, and contracts for apprentices were limited to seven years, subject to renewal only by agreement of both parties. The city governments acquired the authority to license and register all women working as geisha or yūjo. Geisha were seldom in the state of bondage that many prostitutes were, however, so the limited protection and avenue of redress afforded by the new law were less important to them. Geisha who still wanted to pursue their profession went to City Hall and registered themselves. There was definitely a change in the wind, however, amounting to a government-sponsored and -encouraged nation-wide "practicality" campaign aimed at raising Japan's status in the world to that of a modern industrialized power. This new anti-frivolity atmosphere was to have a distinctly dampening effect on the geisha of Pontochō.

REGULATION

The Women's Handicraft Workshop

As a result of the Emancipation Law, geisha were free to return to their parents' homes. But most of those in Pontochō did not want to go home, so in 1874 the local government was persuaded to modify the edict to allow them to work. But a monthly tax was imposed on their wages to be used for the financing of a Women's Handicraft Workshop (Nyokōba), where they would be taught the practical skills that would enable them to find other work, should they so desire. It was also taught that they should so desire. Class attendance was compulsory, and if a geisha missed classes she was not permitted to do her "geisha work," either.

Descriptions of this workshop make it sound more like a sweatshop than a school. In any case, it is somewhat difficult to imagine a workroom full of industriously spinning geisha. The Nyokōba was comprised of eight divisions, most having to do with the making of clothes: a sewing department, a weaving department, spinning, knitting, and embroidery departments, and departments of silkworm cocoon unraveling and silkworm feeding. The women produced useful items as they learned the various skills, and the income from sales was reinvested in the enterprise. There were also classes in reading, accounting, dance, and music.

Women of the pleasure quarters had once passed the time waiting for customers by grinding tea. That phrase, *ocha o hiku*, then became a metaphor for an idle geisha or yūjo. Now, instead of the homely grinding of tea, they were told to occupy them-selves with the more salable weaving of cloth.

When a geisha was wanted at a teahouse, a messenger was sent to the registry office to report that geisha X was requested to appear at teahouse Y by customer Z. The registry office then sent a message to call the woman from the workshop, and she could drop her cocoons, pick up her shamisen, and enjoy a reprieve from classes. If the engagement at the teahouse ended before the close of the day at the workshop, though, the geisha had to go back and finish up. Rather than enticing women with the satisfaction of honest labor, the policy of the handicraft workshop probably had the opposite effect, making the geisha life seem all the more interesting. The experiment in training "practical geisha" lasted for seven years. In 1881, the governor of Kyoto declared that attendance at the Nyokōba would be voluntary and immediately all "lessons" in Pontochō, except music and dance, were abandoned.

STANDARDIZATION

This was not the end of the regulatory hand of government in the geisha world, however. As we have seen, the various categories of pleasure quarters were subject to outside control from their very inception. In fact, the character of these places was in large part shaped by their being special areas, set apart. But within the bounds set by the authorities, there was a degree of spontaneity, freedom, and play found in no other area of feudal society. Precisely because the quarters were so carefully bounded, they offered a safe zone (both geographically and socially) for fantasy, frivolity, and luxurious display.

One of the main concerns of the various feudal reforms was to preserve the boundaries of social discretion through the periodic cleaning up of sources of licentiousness. The notion that the very nature of the pleasure quarters could be changed – indeed, turned to government purposes – never occurred to the shogun's administrators.

This was the fundamental difference between earlier forms of government regulation and the sorts of measures promulgated by the Meiji regime. Some historians have characterized the most crucial aspect of Japan's early process of modernization as the creation of a modern efficient bureaucracy, able to marshal and rationalize social resources in an orderly and systematic way. Rather than leaving things up to chance, tradition, or the dictates of one privileged class, the meaning of rationality in this sense is that goals were decided upon, and those means deemed most efficient in reaching the goals were systematically put into practice. This process of "rationalization" pervaded many areas of society, and the geisha world was no exception. One example was the standardization of geishas' fees.

A fixed fee was determined for Pontochō geisha services in the year 1886. Before that time, the matter of a geisha's wage had been decided arbitrarily between the teahouse and the customer. Different geisha commanded different fees according to their popularity, and customers paid to some extent according to the fatness of their wallets. It would have been uncouth to shop around, so there was a wide variance in the economic aspect of engaging geisha. The standardizing of fees changed this: not only would all customers be charged the same price, but all geisha (regardless of beauty, experience, or popularity) would receive the same wage for the same amount of working time. This system still prevails today.

A move like this may seem merely sensible, if not trivial, but in fact it tended to set a very different tone. This was one of the first steps leading to the creation of a more businesslike atmosphere in the geisha world. Also in 1886, a new set of regulations was instituted for the purpose of both supervising and taxing the "five vocations" defined as the working elements of an area like Pontochō. The geisha houses, the prostitutes, and the go-betweens who introduced customers to the latter were three of the groups, and the banquet halls and houses of assignation were the others. Those two were required to keep a record of all customers who visited their premises, including the guest's name, age, address, and how much money he spent. The house was to report this information to the administrative office by nine o'clock the following morning. Any customer staying longer than twenty-four hours was to be reported to the authorities.

Were the Meiji officials transplanted Victorians, primarily interested in excising moral corruption from the social body? It seems not. The evidence from diaries, memoirs, and popular literature of the time points to a group of men who themselves played as hard as they worked, and who certainly showed no inclination to cast a jaundiced eye on the system of geisha and prostitutes. In this social climate what was reprehensible – if not morally, then socially – was profligacy with money, idleness, and shirking of responsibility. As long as one's comings and goings in the pleasure districts were conducted with moderation, they would be viewed indulgently by society as a whole. If they showed a tendency to get out of hand (something that the new regulations were designed nicely to reveal, and probably by that very fact to prevent), then some sort of admonition to the offender was in order.

The Meiji government, instead of focusing on the pleasure quarters as a source of negative social influence, recognized them as legitimate areas of relaxation and release from humdrum everyday life. Further, the quarters could be required to help support society through taxation. With an internal system of surveillance and a systematic keeping of records, the pleasure quarters could also provide officials with potentially useful information on the activities of citizens.

This sort of government intervention into the affairs of the hanamachi was qualitatively different from the regulatory efforts of the old regime. The shogunate had been concerned with making the appearance of a rigidly stratified class hierarchy congruent with official doctrine. In fact, the concern with appearance was quite literal: feudal sumptuary laws prescribed (and proscribed) a wide range of things, including articles of dress, style and material in clothing, hairstyles and their decoration, and items that were used in the home, for the various stations of life that comprised the social order. For example, *chōnin* (non-samurai townspeople, like merchants and artisans) were not to wear padded silk clothing. Their wives were forbidden fancy dyed silks and heavy embroidery. Farmers were not only forbidden to wear silk, but also striped, patterned, or brightly colored materials. And the samurai themselves were not to outdo the daimyo in finery. In short, the entire social code of dress, which people in all cultures have used to demonstrate social differences, was regulated and clarified by the authorities of Edo Japan to provide clear signs of a person's status within the hierarchy. Detailed rules governed the kimono and hairstyles of the geisha. Generally these were plain and simple, as opposed to the gaudier styles that marked prostitutes.[6]

At the same time that Edo period officials legislated matters like dress in minute detail, they were also likely to condemn the entire system of the pleasure quarters with large-scale crack-downs. Their policies embraced the picayune and the ultimate, with little in between. Yet they made no attempt to change the basic nature of the quarters. In contrast, the policies of the Meiji government went to neither extreme but, consciously or not, effected small yet fundamental changes in how the system was integrated with the larger society. In the Meiji period (1868–1911) can be seen the beginnings of the modern geisha world.

THE PARADOX OF MODERNITY

The 1890s were a decade of popularity and prosperity for the geisha. Novelists like Ozaki Kōyo and Izumi Kyōka wrote stories that fixed geisha in the public mind as daring romantic heroines. Already nostalgia for the Edo period, so recently left behind, had begun to spread, and geisha, women of "true Japanese spirit," basked in public adulation. Some geisha became stars whose portraits were collected by adoring fans. Adolescents mooned over these beauties as, in another generation, they would idolize movie actresses. In 1898, there were close to twenty-five thousand geisha in Japan.

The Tokyo hanamachi of Shimbashi was one of the communities that blossomed. Shimbashi was patronized by the increasingly influential militarists in the government. In 1895, when the entire country was intoxicated with the victory of the Sino-Japanese War, what better place for the military leaders to celebrate than in the teahouses and geisha restaurants? Not surprisingly geisha were fervent patriots. The memoirs of politician Katsura Tarō, who became prime minister in 1902, mention a party where a young Shimbashi geisha performed a dance of her own invention for which the main prop was the Rising Sun flag. The geisha was named Okoi, and she later became his mistress, but at this first meeting what most impressed him was her patriotic spirit.

Confident after having successfully beaten China in 1895, the Japanese declared war on Russia in 1904. This too was a popular war, and most Japanese tried to contribute to the military effort in some way. Again, geisha were no exception. Only weeks after the declaration of war, the geisha organized themselves into a group called the National Conference of the Confederation of Geisha Houses, the purpose of which was to coordinate their war support activities into a geishas' auxiliary. Thus it was as a united group that geisha nobly and patriotically gave up wearing the customary three layers of kimono for the duration of the war. They limited themselves to two – the outer two, of course.

Confederation

Originally a rallying point for one specific cause, this wartime geisha organization became the nucleus of the National Confederation of Geisha Houses. The confederation was promoted primarily by geisha and geisha house owners from Shimbashi and Yanagibashi, then the two most prestigious and progressive hanamachi in Tokyo. All but one of the twenty-five established Tokyo hanamachi eventually joined the confederation, and there were efforts to solicit members from areas outside Tokyo as well.[7]

The confederation formalized rules of conduct, a standard for the profession, and by common consent had the power to enforce sanctions for transgressions. Each member hanamachi was represented by one to five persons, either geisha or owners of geisha houses. Meetings were held in response to specific problems that arose. A twelve-article charter was drawn up by the board of representatives, the key provisions of which were that the board's approval would be required of newly entering geisha, the board could expel any geisha guilty of misconduct, and the board could require notification of all details of any such problems, so that official internal records could be kept. These records could then be used as documentation to prevent a miscreant geisha from trying to obtain employment in some other confederated hanamachi. Despite the severe tone of the document, a clause at the end provided leniency for an outcast geisha who sincerely repented, permitting her return into the fold.

In essence, the National Confederation of Geisha Houses was a professional guild organization – similar to that of the traditional carpenters, for example – where standards and codes of conduct were fixed by those within the profession. Since the Edo period, such organizations have been powerful and extensive enough in Japan to create blacklists of undesirables who then find it impossible to obtain work. The geisha world had been required throughout the two centuries of its existence to order the conduct of its members according to outside, government-created rules. Here was its first attempt at self-regulation.

During the first two decades of the twentieth century, geisha were still required to obtain licenses from the municipal governments, and taxes were still levied on their wages, but at least an influential group representing the inside interests of the profession had taken shape. In some sense, then, geisha themselves came to define what a geisha was, and who was qualified to be a member of the geisha ranks.

The effectiveness of the confederation began to wane in the 1920s, however, partly because of the sheer increase in the numbers of geisha. In 1905 there were about twenty-three hundred geisha in Tokyo; in 1920 there were closer to ten thousand. Besides struggling with this unprecedented rate of growth, the confederation had difficulties in coping with various early experiments at "modernization" in the hanamachi. The identity of an ideal geisha, especially the nature of her *gei*, or art, and of the way she ought to relate to customers in the rapidly changing Japanese society of the 1920s, became problematical in a fundamental way that could not be arbitrated by a board of representatives from a confederation of the geisha houses. On the contrary, the various hanamachi all tried their own answers to the problems posed by the modernization question. The erstwhile unity of the confederation dissolved in the absence of the sharper focus provided by war support activities.

*A yūjo (lady of pleasure) in the Yoshiwara licensed
quarter of Tokyo, about 1890.*

A Nagasaki geisha, circa 1890. She holds a Western-style umbrella,
a new-fangled item that was all the rage at the time.

Old Vogue

To be considered up-to-date was definitely desirable in early twentieth-century Japan. And being modern was almost completely identified with the adoption (and often the creative adaption) of things Western. "Western style" meant modern, and "Japanese style" tended to be identified with old-fashioned. This raised an interesting problem for geisha, who were thoroughly accustomed to being in the vanguard of all the latest trends in fashion, the arts, and social graces.

Modern-day geisha in full formal attire.

Eishosai Choki woodblock print of geisha, circa 1900.
The verse at the upper left is a kouta: "Parting, regretting,
reuniting again. Left waiting, still meeting – such is life."

Geisha and Kabuki actors were the fashion innovators in the latter part of the Edo period. A novel of the 1830s, called *Geisha tora no maki* (Geisha: the tiger volume), by Ryūtei Tanehiko, mentions that if a geisha were seen wearing a honeycomb-patterned kimono, the wives of townsmen would all rush to copy it.[8] The popular tunes and lyrics heard around the cities were sung by – and, as often as not, about – geisha. The well-known woodblock prints of this era (which, like Toulouse-Lautrec's graphics, were popular poster-like depictions of the contemporary scene) often pictured geisha and scenes from the pleasure quarters.

Whereas the prostitutes locked in the licensed quarters continued to purvey a relatively fixed style of dress and manner, geisha vied with one another for novelty and chic display – within the traditional Japanese mode. All this changed, however, when Western dress became another option for ladies of style. When geisha started cutting their hair and demanding permanent waves they may have been in vogue with the latest fashion, but for some people at least, they didn't seem quite like geisha any more.

For a decade or so geisha tried to keep their position as fashion leaders, even as the forms of fashion were changing radically. This era of experimentation, the 1920s and early 1930s, finally led them to the realization that, in trying to be modern, they were in danger of losing that which made them special as geisha. During this period, then, their profession underwent a crucial change in its nature and social meaning: geisha ceased being fashion innovators and became curators of tradition. This conservative function has been vital to the existence of their profession today.

FIVE

GEISHA RENOVATION

Consorting with geisha is an old man's pastime.
Young men of style nowadays dismiss geisha as
utterly boring.

Hagiwara Sakutarō, "Shin Geisha Ron" (1927)

It is generally recognized today that geisha are
absolutely necessary as mainstays of social life.

Hayashida Kametarō, Geisha no Kenkyū (1929)

GEISHA IN RIVALRY

AT THE NORTHERN edge of Pontochō on the east side of
the street stands a large, yellow-brick turn-of-the-century building called the Kaburenjō. It was completed in 1902 with funds
obtained through systematic deductions from the geishas' wages,
matched by equal amounts from the teahouses where their
engagements took place. The ground floor houses an auditorium,
and dressing rooms and classrooms are upstairs. The basement is
used as office space by the officials of the geisha association. The
Kaburenjō was originally built in order to give the geisha a
decent place to perform the Kamogawa Dances. As the most
commodious building by far in cramped Pontochō, it quickly
became the center of community life. Singing, dancing, shamisen,
and drum lessons took place here; and around 1915, when Japan
was hit by a craze for Western-style ballroom dance (*dansu* in

Japanese), the Pontochō Kaburenjō became the first place in the country to give the geisha lessons in that skill, too. The geisha community of Pontochō could then boast women known as *dansu geisha*, who counted social dance as one of their artistic specialties. With their traditional Shimada-style coiffures jiggling, they were wildly popular as they tangoed with their equally modern customers in Pontochō.

Pontochō has always been innovative and daring. Even today this reputation lingers in the inevitable comparisons made between it and Gion, just across the river. Both areas are considered high-class (although Gion perhaps has a slight edge), and it is probably their similarity that makes the urge to contrast them so irresistible. Gion's Miyako Odori, done in a unique style of traditional dance, is much the same year after year.[1] People expect it to be the same, and it has almost attained the status of a ritual performance. Pontochō's Kamogawa Odori, in contrast, is always a new program. The geisha perform a Kabuki-style

GEISHA RENOVATION

In 1912, geisha were chosen for a poster advertising Japanese beer. But the glamour of the girl depicted in the 1922 poster for Akadama Port Wine is a far cry from the geisha idea of sex appeal.

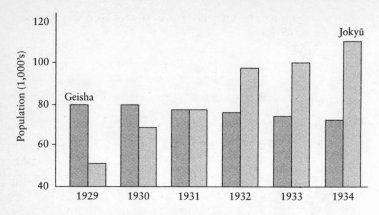

The rise of the jokyū and fall of the geisha.
Source: Naimushō Keisatsu Torishimari Tokei [Department
of the Interior, Police Regulation Statistics].

drama, as well as individual classic dance numbers. I once over-heard a Gion geisha disparaging the spectacle of the Kamo River Dances. Those who favor Gion will put down the more ebullient Pontochō in this way. Others, naturally, find Pontochō much more interesting than Gion for the same reasons. As early as the 1920s, customers who looked for novelty in Kyoto headed for Pontochō.

At that time geisha and the still legal but increasingly passé licensed prostitutes were by no means the only form of female entertainment and companionship available to men. This was the period of the rise of the café girl, the *jokyū*, the direct precursor of the modern bar hostess. For the first time, geisha faced real competition for the attention of customers. The prime attraction of these café girls was their modernity. They had no feudal or old-fashioned associations, as did the geisha by virtue of their long history; and the ranks of jokyū were swelled enormously by young girls from both city and countryside looking for a few years of glamorous nontraditional employment.[2]

This was Japan's equivalent of a jazz age, and the café girls were at center stage. Geisha tried to keep up with the times by expanding their repertoire of talent in the arts, but from the

1930s on there was increasing dissonance between the shamisen and the saxophones.

Cocteau in Kyoto

Pontochō pursued the modern experiment further than most geisha communities. By 1930 the entire top floor of the Kaburenjō had been turned into a dance hall. Besides dancing with customers, the Pontochō geisha worked up routines not unlike those of the Folies-Bergère for performance alongside such traditional pieces as "Pine and Bamboo." Meanwhile, the teahouses, the original sites of geisha entertainment, were losing money and customers to the extent that they could not provide more modern facilities to accommodate the changing tastes of the times. Often their response was to build an attached dance hall – exactly as they try today to have an attached cocktail lounge – in order to keep the paying customers within the realm of the establishment. Because many potential young customers were unfamiliar with the etiquette of patronizing teahouses, a sign was posted outside the Kaburenjō to make it easier for them. It read: "First-time customers may obtain introductions to the teahouses at the registry office." A young man could meet a geisha at the Kaburenjō Dance Hall and then continue the evening in Japanese style at one of the ochaya.

The culmination of Pontochō's artistic innovation was perhaps the Kamo River Dance of 1936, a program entitled "Dancing Down Tōkaidō Road" (Odoru Tōkaidō). Its interludes of Rockette-style revue numbers brought rave reviews from, among others, French artist and film director Jean Cocteau, who was in Japan at the time. Charlie Chaplin, who also viewed this extravaganza, was rather more laconic: "Interesting," he is reported to have remarked. Undoubtedly, the geisha dance hall revue was "interesting," but certainly by the late 1930s the novelty had palled. Tokyo, too, had been experimenting with such original items as violin-playing geisha and geisha who posed semi-nude in Grecian style drapery, as well as various gimmicks to attract customers such as bargain-rate banquets for end-of-the-year celebrations.

GEISHA ARE THE NAVEL OF SOCIETY

"Why does our body have a navel?" asked journalist Tanaka Iwao in 1935.

> Why do we have eyelashes? These things may appear to serve no useful function, but could we be without them? The eyelashes keep dust out of our eyes, the navel was the route of nourishment from our mother's womb. According to doctors, the navel is the center of the belly, the center of our strength. If we had no navel, how would we concentrate our energy? Geisha are the navel of society, in my opinion. Those who say their usefulness has disappeared would just as well try to get rid of their navels.[3]

One could see in the geisha world a condensation of the problems of modernization and Westernization that affected all of Japanese society in the late 1920s and early 1930s. Contemporary intellectuals, critics, and journalists often used the example of the geisha when airing opinions about what was happening to traditional Japan and traditional values. Debates raged over the fate of geisha in the modern world, and the implication seemed to be that, as go the geisha, so goes traditional culture.

One position, ruthlessly progressive, maintained that geisha were already anachronisms, and that the profession should be allowed to die a natural death. A more moderate view held that geisha should by all means try to update themselves and adapt to the changing times. Finally a few nostalgic writers suggested that Japan would lose something valuable if geisha were to change or to disappear. They thought society at large was responsible for maintaining a place for geisha as they were.

Few Japanese intellectuals had no public opinion about geisha. Whether they reviled them as feudal remnants or sought to preserve them, those people concerned with the direction of change in society used the geisha as an example in their arguments. At the time, the karyūkai was beset with problems. The geisha themselves may have wondered what, precisely, their gei was to be in modern times. But because of its importance to the Japanese sense of cultural identity the geisha world was not about to wither away unnoticed.

THE GEISHA READER

A Mirror of Social Opinion

In 1935, a book called *The Geisha Reader* (*Geigi tokuhon*) was published in Tokyo.[4] Including essays by businessmen, restaurateurs, poets, politicians, and actors, as well as numerous literary dilettantes, the book gives a dramatic picture of the problems facing the karyūkai at that time. It gives the impression that its compiler gathered a contribution from anyone who ever had an opinion about geisha, except geisha themselves. The 74,200 geisha of Japan in 1935 were, rather, the ostensible audience for this collection of opinions and advice.

Geisha were exhorted to read the volume carefully and to regard it as a "mirror of social opinion." They would then be able to correct their public image as easily as they straightened their collars. Dozens of prominent people were sent questionnaires asking their thoughts on geishas' merits and faults. The results, not surprisingly, presented a jumbled picture indeed. Under "Geishas' Faults" we find that they were "limited and uninteresting," that they had become no different from prostitutes or jokyū. Geisha had "gone modern, forgotten the old ways," "lost their manners." In the book, writer Kojima Masajirō faults geisha for not reading books. But under "Geishas' Merits" are the opinions that they are "much better read than they used to be," "it is more convenient to sleep with them now," that they "uphold the codes of duty and honor," and that they "preserve valuable tradition." Because one man's notion of a geisha's faults consisted of precisely those things another saw as laudable, one can imagine the confusion of the poor geisha who seriously tried to read this section in the quest for self-improvement.

Geisha Are Happy

Yet the overall concern of the book was plainly to infuse new life into the drooping flower and willow world. Several articles paint a bright and cheerful picture of the geisha profession as a wonderful occupation for women. In chapter six, "Why the Geisha Have Reached an Impasse," Osaka restaurant owner Sakaguchi Sukesaburō writes:

> With today's economic situation it is difficult for men, not to mention women, to make a living. A girl is not likely to find a decent job even if she graduates from one of the top women's colleges. And if she *should* manage to find employment, she can barely support herself, let alone have a bit extra for her parents. If she decides to become an actress, a jokyū, or a dancer, then no matter how good her intentions may be, a girl is in danger of coming under bad influences. This is unfortunate but true. The more I see of these "new occupations" the more I am confirmed in my opprobrious opinion of them.
>
> Keeping this in mind, all of you geisha, yours is truly a marvelous occupation. You get to enjoy yourselves taking artistic lessons – dance, song, shamisen – and then have people listen to you perform. If you were amateurs, you would go to untold expense holding recitals to draw an audience like this, but as geisha you get an audience for free, and are paid for it to boot.
>
> Once you have mastered your artistic skills, they are your most important possessions. Such skills are unscathed by fire, unmoved by earthquakes, and make you employable for the rest of your life. You should guard such treasures by keeping them polished!
>
> The actual work involved in being a geisha is nothing like the hard labor required in other jobs. Mostly it consists of being a companion to prominent people you would otherwise never have a chance to associate with. Again, you are actually paid for this opportunity to learn all sorts of interesting things.
>
> Anyone who thinks the occupation of geisha is a lowly one is mistaken. Look at the word itself – a woman who lives by art. Think of this, you geisha, and take pride in yourselves. Don't fall in love with fickle characters, fall in love with your gei instead![5]

Society's School

A geisha, inspired by reading this, would be further heartened to learn that her profession had always had an important social function. Kawamura Tokutarō, director of the Shimbashi Association of Geisha Houses, stated that, of all the working women

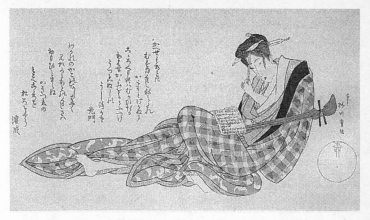

Woodblock print by Yanagawa Shigenobu (1787–1832).

of Japan, geisha had the most comprehensive knowledge and artistic skills and should therefore be accorded the highest social position.

> Along with Fujiyama, cherry blossoms, and the samurai's hara kiri, are not "geisha girls" one of the main symbols of Japan to Europeans? And like these other things, should not geisha be admired and respected in their own country as one of the distinctive glories of Nippon?

According to Kawamura, not only was the karyūkai traditionally Japan's sole instrument of public sociability but it also served to educate society. Geisha were the leaders of fashion and the most knowledgeable people about social goings-on:

> In the Edo period it was not strange at all for geisha to be seen entering the houses of people of good family. When a wealthy merchant invited people to his house, of course he would call geisha to attend his guests. Samurai families did so too, and geisha freely associated with the ladies of these households. Through such experiences geisha knew more about society than most of the guests they entertained.
>
> In an age without newspapers or magazines, the teahouses were the centers for social communication. Parents brought their adult

sons here, not for sex, but for a social education from geisha. And in the countryside, geisha displayed the only bit of cultural refinement farmers were likely ever to see.[6]

Geisha were encouraged to see themselves as having what amounted to a social mission. Their role in feudal Japan as purveyors of style, information, and social skills was upheld as the goal to which they should still aspire in the 1930s. The consequence of this premise was that geisha would have to be worldly-wise, 1930s style. Thus we find geisha being urged to learn modern arts, wear Western clothes, cut their hair, and read the newspapers to keep abreast of things. In the view of some, these were ways that geisha could preserve their profession through changing times.

UPDATING THE GEISHA

In Japan of the 1920s and 1930s geisha were not automatically regarded as traditional with a capital T. They remained sufficiently a part of the current social world for people to argue seriously about their function and style. In the 1980s the idea of a geisha in a Halston gown dancing to a disco beat is ludicrous, but the 1930s equivalent was not, at the time, utterly unthinkable.

Poet Hagiwara Sakutarō had strong opinions on this subject. His essay *Shin geisha ron* (A discourse on the new geisha), written in 1927, was reprinted in *The Geisha Reader*:

> "Fun with geisha" is something for old men. Young men of style nowadays are of the opinion that geisha are dull and boring, and they turn their steps toward the cafés, not the teahouses. The reason for this is perfectly clear. They prefer shingle-cut bobbed hair to the once fashionable *tsubushi Shimada*. They like Western music, not the shamisen. Young people don't even understand the plays of the Kabuki stage any more – they like Paramount pictures at the movie theater. Geisha are a part of these old-fashioned things youth just isn't interested in.
>
> In the Edo period, of course, the situation was different. Geisha were then the pioneers of popular fashion – clothes, accessories,

music, songs, novels – all these things revolved about geisha as the center of the world of style. Geisha were truly the "flower of civilization" of the Edo period.

Now, geisha have become a prime example of what it means to fall behind the times. Who originated the shingle-cut and the pageboy hairstyles? Not the geisha; coeds and movie actresses set the fashions now. Yesterday's flower of civilization is faded and left by the wayside.

Hagiwara tells the geisha in no uncertain terms why their profession is languishing. Dull, boring, behind the times – it is no wonder geisha attract no young customers. Ultimately, though, the problem with geisha is that they are no longer able to perform the function that is the raison d'être of the profession: to be companions in conversation and comfort for men. Hagiwara continues:

> Our wives at home are engrossed in cookery and children, and our conversations with them are quietly serious, mostly concerning household affairs. Outside of this, men need a totally different sort of companion: a woman with whom we can talk about affairs of the world, about the arts, about ideas. We need someone who is entertaining, knowledgeable, educated. This is what a geisha should be.
>
> And how do the geisha of today measure up? Very badly indeed. Ignorant and illiterate, most of them. How can they expect to be companions to men who have even a smattering of knowledge? If I hear someone say he is going off to see a geisha, that can only mean one thing nowadays – geisha are not companions of the mind, they are companions of the body.
>
> It's too bad if geisha are called high-class prostitutes, but that, in fact, is what they have become. There is much I have resented about Japan's feudal age, but in this case, I feel, the geisha of the past were more admirable than what we have now – they were not so quick to offer their bodies. Those geisha were creators of new forms of beauty, and they could match their customers in education, taste, and wit. Truly, they were "comrades of the opposite sex" – qualities one does not see at all in modern geisha.

The corruption of the karyūkai, so mercilessly described by Hagiwara Sakutarō, appeared total – yet he did not advocate doing away with geisha altogether. On the contrary, his answer to their problems lay in their realizing the original meaning of the profession and then recreating it for themselves. Specifically, the answer was education followed by modernization:

> All geisha should have at least the equivalent of a women's high school education. With this basic knowledge, understanding of the civilization of the new age will follow as a matter of course . . .
>
> Just as the geisha of the Edo period long ago were the most up-to-date, the most avant garde in their tastes, so also geisha should now become the most modern, the most stylish members of our civilization. From now on geisha should wear Western clothes; but before anything else, they must get rid of their shamisens and learn to play piano or the mandolin. Before too long we should see tea-houses being turned into bistros.
>
> As long as the entire society is changing to Western styles, if geisha persist in clinging to old-fashioned ways they will ensure their own demise. The only true geisha in Japan now are the dance geisha of Osaka. They wear dresses, not kimono, but more than that, most of them have been exposed to higher education. They can truthfully be called intellectual companions to their customers. They are the ones who have translated the real meaning of the Edo period geisha into modern terms.[7]

COST BENEFIT

Working Women

For every critic who encouraged the geisha to modernize or face extinction, however, another warned that they were ruining themselves to the extent that they adopted newfangled ways. One point drawing strong opposing opinions was whether geisha should be considered *shokugyō fujin*, working women. This term has overtones of organized labor, of career, business, and profes-sional consciousness. In Japan of the 1920s and 1930s it was very modern, and somewhat daring, for a woman to be a shokugyō fujin.

To have such a businesslike attitude toward one's work was contrasted with the traditional notion of *ninjō*, human feeling.

Proponents of the "new geisha" said they must think of themselves as shokugyō fujin, but others pointed out that as working women they would lose their romantic appeal. A factory girl as a "working woman" was fine, but it was not quite the same thing for a geisha. Many parts of Japanese society were becoming more businesslike, but some people preferred to draw the line at geisha parties. "The age is changing. It makes me feel I've missed something when there are so few women like the plucky and stylish geisha one hears about from the past," wrote actor Ichikawa Kyūzō. "And this 'job consciousness' of geisha, too, makes me feel melancholy."[8]

Set Service

Some men who wrote articles for *The Geisha Reader* concentrated on schemes for revamping the geisha system. If it were made more accessible, cheaper, and straightforward, they reasoned, more people would want to engage geisha. These reformers turned their attention first to the expense involved.

The matter of geishas' wages has always been camouflaged. This is undoubtedly because it is awkward to admit that one side of a festive gathering is paid to be there. No one would deny the fact, but no one wants his nose rubbed in it either – hence the euphemistic terms for geishas' fees: flower money, jewel money, incense money, and *shūgi*, literally, an honorarium (in effect, a tip) on top of that.

The reformers wanted to sweep all these flowery terms away and standardize geishas' wages – for the customers' benefit, of course. So much per geisha per hour. Any differential should follow rational principles. One proposal called for the creation of a system of ranks: the more a geisha could do the more she should earn. Tipping should be abolished, all hanamachi should charge the same, teahouses and menservants should get no cut of a geisha's pay.

Another plan to make the karyūkai more democratic was the proposal that geisha be engaged in "sets." The teahouses (not the customers) would call each set, and every geisha would be assured an engagement. The price would be fixed at 1 yen for one geisha for one hour. The advantages of this plan were that the overall price would be cheaper for the guest, and all the geisha would be kept busy. (This system was tried briefly in Yanagibashi but soon dropped because the geisha there opposed it. They had been accustomed to earning closer to 5 yen for a two-hour party, and they preferred to decide on their own which banquets to attend.)

Other writers attributed the high price of geisha to pernicious middlemen: the owners of the restaurants, the managers of the *okiya*, or geisha houses, and the various hangers-on. On an unintentionally macabre note, newspaper reporter Suzuki Bunshirō wrote, "Geisha must first be rescued from those who exploit them. Is there no Hitler for the karyūkai?" – meaning, in Japan of 1935, is there no savior who will sweep away the social injustice perpetrated by exploiters of the weak?

Everything about geisha was examined to see if there were not something that could be changed to be more cost-effective. Why should geisha work only in the evenings? Why not have "matinee geisha" for the afternoons? Kimono seemed a wasteful expenditure – why not replace them with uniforms, or at least scale down the number of kimono required. Abolish the custom of changing garments midway through a formal party.

The feeling of many was that, if geisha were to be called by that name, then gei should be their function. There was a desire for clear-cut, fixed-price categories. A prostitute is a prostitute, a waitress is a waitress, and a geisha is an artist. One should visit a restaurant without geisha when interested in serious eating and patronize a theater or dance hall when looking for entertainment. As strange as many of these proposals look today many were tried out in the 1920s and 1930s. Most were total failures. It seemed that, of the people who appreciated geisha in the first place, many liked precisely those aspects of the karyūkai that were irrational, sentimental, inefficient, and old-fashioned.

HELPFUL HINTS FOR THE PRUDENT GEISHA

Yet even customers who more or less liked the geisha system the way it was could still find ways to urge self-improvement on geisha. One of the last chapters in *The Geisha Reader* is a didactic piece called "Geishas' Day-to-Day Work," which lays out proper behavior from "rising in the morning through an evening's work." The specificity of the proffered advice makes a modern reader smile, but it was hardly proposed in jest at the time. "How To Get Ahead with a Professional Attitude" might have been the subtitle of this lecture. Where is the place of ninjō, where is there room for romance, human foible, spontaneity – all those things that had been part of the very human appeal of the geisha to writers like Nagai Kafū in the first two decades of the century?[9] Sentimentality was relentlessly excised if a calculating geisha were to follow these precepts:

First. You should get up by no later than ten o'clock in the morning, straighten your clothes, clean your room, wash up (paying special attention to your teeth), smooth your hair, make obeisance to the deities' altar, greet the others of the house (especially the master or mistress), and then have breakfast. Never forget that you are what you are because of your parents and the people who raised you, and you have a great debt of gratitude to them.

Second. Your work involves staying up late drinking at parties, so it is very important that, during the morning at least, you remain serious.

Third. Again, I emphasize cleaning your teeth. You must never be embarrassed to give customers a bright smile.

Fourth. Unless you yourself have the desire to learn, your lessons will never progress. Unfortunately, the interest in learning usually arises only after age twenty – by which time it is too late. Ideally, one should start lessons at age eight. Children want to play, but you must take them firmly by the hand and force them to attend lessons. This is how they absorb the proper form. Gei is something money can't buy. The stricter your teachers are, the more you have to thank them for.

Fifth. When you go to the hairdresser don't gossip with other geisha, bad-mouthing customers or your superiors. Don't be munching snacks you buy on the street. Sloppy geisha who waste their time like this will never succeed in life. Practice your singing or poetry while you wait instead.

Sixth. When you go on an outing, I beg of you, don't wear your hair in poufs or chignons or fancy new styles you see the actresses wearing. You will be mistaken for a jokyū or god knows what. At least always have your hair done up in a geisha-like style.

Seventh. In the hot summer weather you can't help perspiring, but please keep your hair clean so it doesn't smell. Smelly hair is a geisha's disgrace.

Eighth. Always take your bath by three in the afternoon.

Ninth. When you have finished bathing, put on your makeup and be ready waiting for any calls. Be careful there is no caked face paint under your fingernails or splotched on your earlobes. If you rush because you are not prepared when you get a call, it will show in your hasty makeup.[10]

Following this prudent advice, a geisha would spend her daylight hours in an attitude of respectful studiousness, mindful of her appearance, methodically disposing of her chores. These nine helpful hints bring a geisha to the beginning of her working day. The remaining twenty-five pointers concentrate on her attitude and professional conduct. She is enjoined to accept every engagement and not wait to hear who else is going to attend it. On her way, she is not to speak familiarly with her *hakoya*, the manservant who carries her shamisen – for who knows who might be watching and forming a bad impression? Someone on the street might be a future customer, so a geisha must be careful to advertise herself accordingly.

The first thing she must do at the banquet is greet the proprietress with deference and find out from her exactly what sort of party it is to be. Who is the host, whom is he entertaining? Then, she should be especially solicitous of the guests in the seats of lower prestige, for they are usually the ones who are paying and who are likely to be of future use to her as customers.[11]

"Be on time, pay your bills, don't beg treats, be respectful, live within your means, buy Japanese"; such a serious and conscientious geisha would go far. This was 1935, two years before Japanese leaders began mobilizing society for war. Yet there is already more than a whiff here of the flavor of the new ethics texts that would soon be introduced to schools, of the antifrivolity campaign that would soon be pressed upon the whole nation.

WARTIME GEISHA

The infatuation with things of the West, so apparent in Japan of the early 1930s, cooled considerably in the face of growing nationalistic fervor later in that decade. English was labeled the language of the enemy and even long-accepted foreign loan words were officially erased from Japanese. "Japan's unique civilization must be promoted," read a 1937 pamphlet from the army news office.[12] The voices that had urged geisha to modernize in 1935 were nowhere to be heard two years later. Because geisha were such an obvious example of "Japan's unique civilization," the fickle wave of public favor swept them up once again.

Tokuda Shūsei's novel of 1941, *A World in Miniature* (*Shukuzu*), contains a passage that illustrates this change nicely:

> At times it had seemed as if the flower and willow world sheltered on the back streets of this district would be carried away by the tides of change accompanying each successive period. At one point, the polished manners and Japanese hair-styles of its denizens had been all but overwhelmed by the Western fashions and permanent waves that swept in with the flood of modernism after the First World War. In the harsh light of day, the geisha had appeared by contrast faintly laughable, shabby anachronisms as they strolled down the Ginza.
>
> Yet as the darling of political potentates and financial tycoons during the Meiji era this demimonde had developed deep roots; along with Mt. Fuji, cherry blossoms and Kabuki, it had come to be extolled even by foreigners as one of the glories of Japanese civilization.
>
> Recently, with the reassertion of truly Japanese tastes, it had regained its former prosperity, benefitting greatly from a booming war economy under strict government controls, and from the busy socializing of the upper classes, who favored its establishments with their banquets and parties. Even if the renewed prosperity proved to be a purely temporary phenomenon, it was clearly indicative of the inextricable ties linking this institution to the structure of the society and the fortunes of the nation.[13]

Geisha continued to cater to customers right up through the last years of the war. In Tokyo alone, close to nine thousand geisha were still entertaining guests in 1944 when teahouses, geisha houses, and bars were ordered closed. Geisha then became eligible for conscription into factory work. According to Kishii Yoshie, many of them wangled their names onto the employment lists of their patrons' companies.[14] On August 15, 1945, the emperor of Japan announced the fact of defeat to his war-weary subjects, and on September 2 the treaty of surrender was signed on the U.S.S. *Missouri* in Tokyo Bay. On October 25, the bars, teahouses, and geisha houses were permitted to reopen.

Retrenchment

Geisha in the postwar flower and willow world have relinquished any claim to being avant garde. The question of whether geisha should seriously include modern, Western art forms as part of their gei has been answered, and the answer is no. The image of the geisha was formed during Japan's feudal past, and this is now the image they must keep in order to remain geisha. A fully decked-out geisha in 1975 looked much the way a formally dressed geisha did in 1875 – but this very fact means that the social import of geisha has changed considerably. They are no longer innovators, they are curators.

There is a period bar in Kyoto, carefully decorated in 1920s style, with a jukebox that plays exclusively music from that era. Customers are served by kimono-clad women wearing cotton aprons in the manner of the old jokyū. The café girls of the 1920s are reenacted here in this one Kyoto bar, but one could hardly say that they have maintained a tradition. The real descendants of the jokyū are bar hostesses, who now outnumber geisha by at least twenty to one. They are the ones who have taken over the banner of modernity and up-to-date style, which the geisha finally relinquished in the late 1930s. Had geisha continued in their initial attempts to stay in the social and artistic avant garde, they would today be indistinguishable from bar hostesses. Then there might be a bar somewhere which took as its theme the old teahouse atmosphere, with women dressed up as geisha.

For over fifty years, geisha have been used by others as convenient symbols of Japanese tradition. But they have come to

Geisha wearing a shawl, circa 1890. Photograph by Ueno Hikoma.

realize from within their own ranks as well that this is where their hope lies, hope not only of survival as a profession, but also of success. The preservation of a unique tradition is the social contribution of the geisha, and it is one that cannot easily be threatened by new forms of art and entertainment. "As long as there are tatami in Japan," wrote one contributor to *The Geisha Reader*, "there will be a place for geisha."

On an early May evening, the narrow street of Pontochō is lined with round red lanterns decorated with flying plovers. The lanterns are hung out when the dances are in progress. Geisha and maiko slip between buildings on their way to different parties, ignoring the staring tourists with their cameras. The customers inside the teahouses are mostly businessmen, mostly well-off, and mostly on expense accounts. But some are there on their own money, by themselves rather than with a client who needs to be impressed, who come because they truly enjoy the geisha atmosphere.

The tourists would never dream of actually venturing into one of the teahouses; that they can still see a painted maiko on the street is quite enough, and they feel relieved and vaguely satisfied somehow to know that traditional Japan is alive and well, at least in this little enclave. The wealthy and the cultured who actually engage the services of the geisha world and financially support it sit in the teahouses overlooking the Kamo River when they could just as well have made the choice to go to an expensive modern bar. In fact, they don't really have to make the choice, for what they will most likely do is proceed to such a bar later – taking the geisha along.

SIX

THE BEGINNING OF THINGS

Isasaka no   A lingering speck of dust
Chiri mo medetaya   Auspicious now,
Koto hajime   When things begin.

THE SENSE OF beginning afresh in the New Year season is almost a religious feeling for Japanese. The sensation of newness is most concentrated on the first day of January, but the season and its ceremonies precede and follow the special day itself. People take a holiday from work at the beginning of January to visit friends and relatives. Much ceremony attends the various "firsts" of the year: the first sunrise, the first bath, the first mirror (putting on makeup), even the first sparrows observed chattering in the eaves. Food consists of cold delicacies, prepared in the busy last days of December so that the women can have respite from cooking for a few days.

The quiet that descends upon the geisha quarters at the beginning of January is uncanny, following, as it does, the crescendo of activity that peaks on December 31 when "forget the old year" parties fill the bars and teahouses. The lull is brief, however, and the revelry starts up again after January 3, when the "first parties" of the year begin.

In order for Japanese to be able to appreciate fully the feeling of purification and renewal cultivated on the first few days of the new year, a tremendous effort to clear up all unfinished business of the old year consumes its final week. Housewives do a thorough cleaning, people try their best to pay off lingering debts, and department stores have their biggest bonanza of the year while everyone shops for *oseibō*, year-end presents.

In Kyoto, in the geisha communities, the whole process starts weeks ahead of time. December 3 is called *koto hajime*, the time, literally, when "things begin." On this day, every geisha visits her teachers and the mistresses of the teahouses to pay her respects. The entire community rolls up its sleeves in preparation for the hectic days ahead. Although rehearsal season for the Kamogawa Dance may be more intense, no other time of year matches December 13–31 for sheer activity.

GREETINGS

Kyoto people in general are notorious for their attention to the customs of the yearly round, and the strict observance of formalities is even more pronounced in the geisha world. Nearly every time a geisha turns around she is likely to be paying her respects to someone. A geisha will make a brief visit to thank the proprietress of a teahouse where she worked the previous night. She need do no more than open the sliding door at the street and poke her head in to say "Senjitsu wa ōkini, okāsan. Yoroshū otanomōshimasu" (Thank you for yesterday, mother. Please think of me in the future). For Kyoto geisha, such formalities are like the air they breathe, and become so ingrained as to require next to no special effort.

The social obligations of the beginning of each month echo the ceremony of the first month itself, and geisha make a point to greet the mothers of the teahouses at this time. Generally, the more formal and important the occasion, the further into the house one comes to pay respects. On the first of the month, geisha usually step off the street into the vestibule.

The events surrounding a geisha's change of status are of greater importance. A maiko pays her respects at her debut, her passage to full geisha status, her independence, and (perhaps) her departure from the geisha world. She is required to announce such facts ceremonially to all the teahouses. Geisha conduct these ceremonies for themselves and for the community, not for the benefit of customers. Everyone living in each of the sixty tea-houses in Pontochō comes to the edge of the vestibule to sit in formal posture and receive greetings from the new maiko or geisha.

But the greeting that geisha perform on December 13 is the most significant of the year. Each woman brings two large, round cakes of pounded rice, topped with a citron, to the house that sponsored her training.[1] The total assembly of smooth, rock-hard lumps of white rice and orange fruit is displayed on low shelves inside the house. All afternoon, the mistresses of these teahouses receive the visiting geisha in their own quarters. The geisha bow the most formal of bows for this greeting; but when offered tea they usually relax and stay to chat for a while.[2] By coincidence, my own debut as one of the geisha of Pontochō occurred on December 13, this day of koto hajime, when "things begin."

ICHIGIKU'S DEBUT

I had been living in Kyoto for three months. A fortunate intro-duction to the mistress of the Mitsuba Inn had induced me to move from Tokyo, where I had begun my study, down to the old capital, which everyone agreed was the place to find the most authentic geisha. (In fact, the geisha communities in Tokyo are just as old as Kyoto's; but the popular image of the Kyoto geisha, especially that of the doll-like maiko, stands out in people's minds as being somehow more traditional.) Living at the Mit-suba, which was used for geisha banquets two or three nights a week, I met the Pontochō geisha as they came to work in the evening and also when they came by in the daytime to greet the proprietress.

I began to accompany the mistress of the Mitsuba on her own visits to the other houses of Pontochō – the block where she had been born, brought up, appeared as a maiko, and found a patron, and now where, as owner of an inn, she held sway as one of the okāsans of the community. She had no daughter of her own, nor were there geisha or maiko attached to her establishment. Before

*Display of rice cakes at the Dai-Ichi
teahouse, December 13, 1975.*

I came to live at the Mitsuba, she had always been alone on her visits to the houses of friends and peers.

After a few months, people became accustomed to seeing us together, and later, when I went to interview any geisha for my research, I would announce myself at the door by calling, "It's Kikuko from the Mitsuba." Thus it seemed quite natural when I began calling the proprietress okāsan, "mother," just as the other geisha did.

On December 13, okāsan knocked on my door and said, "Today is koto hajime. I think you'll be interested in the display of rice cakes over at Dai-Ichi. Why don't you come with me when I go to visit this afternoon?" In her geisha days, okāsan had gone by the name of Ichiraku. Like all the other geisha whose names began with the *ichi* character, she had been affiliated with the teahouse Dai-Ichi. Thus, even though she was now one of the mothers, she still went to pay a courtesy visit to the okāsan of the Dai-Ichi.

The narrow street of Pontochō echoed with exchanged salutations. The geisha greeted one another and the mothers with the phrase "Omedetōsan dosu," a purely Kyoto way of saying congratulations, bowing as they passed. The weather was chill but not yet the penetrating dankness of full winter. Women wearing kimono didn't really need a shawl yet, although my okāsan had a silver mink stole draped over her shoulders. The mothers often wear fur stoles over their kimono, although I rarely saw a geisha do so.

"What I would really like," okāsan was saying, "is a chinchilla." She had acquired her mink through a customer who was

*Liza Dalby (second from left) with a group of older geisha
and mothers in Pontochō.*

able to get it for her cheaply on a trip to the United States. She was
now musing about taking a trip abroad herself, with some of her
friends, to see the sights and snap up bargains in jewelry, leather,
and furs. "Isn't Mexico where they raise chinchillas?" she asked.

Several pairs of *zōri* (sandals) and shoes were already lined up
in the vestibule of the Dai-Ichi when we arrived. "Gomenyasu,
Mitsuba dosu e," okāsan called out as the maid, a wisp of an old
woman, hurried to meet us. We slipped off our shoes before step-
ping up to the wooden floor, leaving them for the maid to arrange
with the other footgear. A three-level tier displaying rows of powdered rice cakes stood inside the vestibule. Geisha names, written
in bold ink strokes on wide tongues of paper, hung from each
contribution. The younger the geisha and the more recent her
debut, the closer to the bottom were her rice cakes. The okāsan
of the Dai-Ichi, a corpulent yet sharp-chinned woman, was holding court in the large downstairs room that served as her private
quarters. Several geisha sat by the wall, compactly and stiffly,
their legs tucked under them.

My okāsan made a deep bow on the floor, bouncing up almost immediately to turn and nod to the younger geisha. They smiled, for they all genuinely liked the mistress of the Mitsuba. Ceremony is said to be a Kyoto characteristic, but my okāsan, though a Kyoto-ite to the marrow, seldom concerned herself with it. On the contrary, she added warmth and humor to any gathering. It was easy to imagine how popular she must have been as a geisha.

The mother of the Dai-Ichi was sitting at a low table, chain smoking fashionable imported Kent Lights. She had inherited this house only six months before. Her bluff and somehow slightly too loud manner may well have been an attempt to assert her position as the new mistress. The room where we were gathered was dominated by a tall mahogany *butsudan*, the household Buddhist shrine, with its doors opened wide, surrounded by small offerings of food and flowers. A black and white memorial photograph draped in black dominated the center.

The gray-haired lady in the picture had been the previous okāsan of the Dai-Ichi. She was a woman respected by society at large and practically venerated by the geisha of Pontochō. When she had died suddenly of a heart attack the past June at age eighty-two, just after returning home from dinner with friends at the finest French restaurant in Kyoto, Pontochō was thronged with geisha in somber black mourning clothes. Everyone said it was the passing of an era. This renowned okāsan, eulogized in the newspaper as a living encyclopedia of Kyoto geisha customs, died before I first saw Pontochō. Although I never met her, her presence was still tangible six months after her death.

It was unorthodox in the extreme for people to come visiting with the felicitous greeting "Omedetō," bearing rice cakes symbolizing abundance and life, to a house still technically in mourning; but the geisha of Pontochō had decided to hold the usual ceremonies of koto hajime there because, they said, the old okāsan would have wanted to be remembered by happy activity, not by silent ceremony. In fact, the deceased woman, not her nervous successor, seemed to preside that afternoon. In the eyes of many of the geisha, the grand doyenne of Pontochō had committed but one lapse of judgment in her long life in the geisha world: her choice of heiress.

The new okāsan, perhaps unaware of these sentiments, set about making the Dai-Ichi her own and in so doing seemed further to alienate many of the community. Whether the geisha liked her or not, however, she was still the okāsan of one of the largest and most prestigious teahouses in Pontochō. I was supposed to attend my first banquet as a geisha soon, so during our visit my okāsan adroitly brought up this matter in order to forestall any criticism from the main house if I were to prove an embarrassment.

During my first two months in Kyoto, I had pursued my study through interviews, as I had in Tokyo. I also continued my shamisen lessons, but with a new teacher, the woman who taught the Pontochō geisha. One day in late November the okāsan of the Mitsuba had said to me, 'You know, you'll never really understand geisha life unless you try it. I could find some kimono for you, and Ichiume could be your 'older sister.' What do you think?"

The longer I lived in Pontochō, the more fascinated I had become with the geisha life. I found myself attracted to both the glamor and the discipline, so I had to hide the excitement I felt at her suggestion. Okāsan would talk to a few people and arrange to get the clothes. It would take a week or so. "One thing, Kikuko," she added. "You will hardly ever be asked to play *nagauta* [long songs] at a geisha banquet. If the customers want to sing, they will mostly know kouta. Why don't you take some lessons from the kouta teacher who comes to the Mitsuba once a month? Since you already play the shamisen, I'm sure kouta will be easy for you." It wasn't easy at all to learn this new style of music, but after a few lessons I determined that I would make kouta my gei.

With characteristic enthusiasm, the mistress of the Mitsuba outlined our plan to the okāsan of the Dai-Ichi. "Kikuko here," she said, "can play the shamisen better than any of the young geisha. She has started taking kouta singing lessons too, and can sing while playing – it's really quite something." I demurred while okāsan continued her efforts to interest the proprietress of the Dai-Ichi in the experimental American geisha. Finally, the other woman showed a spark of interest. "But what will she wear?" she asked somewhat dubiously, referring to my five-foot seven-inch height.

Taking this as a favorable sign, my okāsan launched into details. "We've got some hand-me-down but still nice kimono and obi from Ichimitsu and Hisaroku," she said. "Those two are almost as tall as Kikuko here." Lifting up my long dark hair, she showed the mistress of the Dai-Ichi how the girls at the beauty parlor could arrange it in an upswept smooth chignon of the sort geisha wear. "Also," continued okāsan, "her Japanese is quite fluent, but she can speak English too – that could come in handy when there are foreign guests."

The other okāsan acknowledged that this was probably true. She began to warm to the idea. "Well then, what about her name?" Turning to me she said, "Is your name really Kikuko? That sounds rather old-fashioned." "No," I replied, "it's Liza." "Riza! That's very good – rather exotic," she said.

One of the foremost dancers in Pontochō was a geisha in her mid-forties named Raiha (pronounced rīha). There was some talk of my becoming Raiza, younger sister of Raiha. But, as my okāsan pointed out, I really had more connection to the Ichi- line of geisha trained at the Dai-Ichi. Since there was no Ichigiku at present (the last holder of that name had died years ago) would-n't "Ichigiku" be more appropriate? It certainly seemed so to me. If I were to have a new persona as a geisha, then I wanted a new name to go with it. "Liza" did not strike me as very geisha-like. Besides, Ichiume was slated to be my older sister.

Ichigiku it was, then. My okāsan had succeeded in involving the mistress of the Dai-Ichi in the plan to give me real geisha experience. My debut would take place the following evening, when I would accompany a group of Pontochō geisha and several of the mothers to a banquet at a mansion just outside the city. The mistress of the Dai-Ichi was going and would thus have an opportunity to judge the reaction of customers. Ichigiku's debut held the possibility of great embarrassment for all concerned. I began to get nervous early the next afternoon at the beauty parlor where okāsan had instructed the beautician about my hair.

MY FIRST BANQUET

American college women who came of age in the late 1960s have had relatively little experience in beauty parlors. Our hair was long, herbal-shampooed, "natural." Until the day of my geisha debut, in fact, I had never had my hair "done" at all. First it was washed and rolled, then I was put under the helmet to dry. Rollers out, the next step was to construct a perfectly smooth dome. In order to make the back full, small wads of soft nylon filaments (what my grandmother used to call rats) were inserted as stuffing under my own hair. The final result was shellacked with a heavy spray to keep each hair in place. Feeling as if I were wearing a strange new hat, I came home to the Mitsuba to be dressed. Okāsan and the maids there, never much taken with the natural look in the first place, heartily approved.

As I had done the first few times I wore kimono, I put on a fresh pair of white split-toed socks (*tabi*), purposely wearing one size too small in order to achieve a perfectly smooth fit. Geisha, especially the dancers, go through tabi at the rate ballerinas wear out toe shoes. They have them custom made and order them by the gross. Geisha think nothing is so tacky as wrinkled or faintly grayed tabi.

Geisha do not wear underpants.[3] This is a perennial topic of conversation among drunken customers. Since the kimono is pulled fairly tightly over the hips, geisha think the line made by the elastic looks lumpy. Also, answering nature's call in kimono is difficult enough without struggling with panties. Instead, the most intimate layer of underwear is the traditional *koshimaki*, a yard-wide, two-yard length of thin cloth, silk or nylon, that is simply wrapped around the waist.

I put on my koshimaki and a cotton gauze front-wrap under-shirt and was ready for help in lining up the collars and sleeves of the yellow silk under-robe and the pale pink damask kimono I had received from Hisaroku. Okāsan and one of the maids together tied a brocade obi of gold and silver chrysanthemums around my waist, securing it with a tightly woven red cord. Feeling breathless, I walked over to the Dai-Ichi, where the other geisha were gathering. Okāsan accompanied me. As we left the

Mitsuba, the old auntie called out, "You're flapping your feet," poking fun at my clumsy steps.

When geisha go to a banquet outside Pontochō, the engagement is still routed through one of the local teahouses. This is a rule of the Pontochō Geisha Association. That evening the Dai-Ichi was in charge of a group of six geisha including Ichiume and me – Ichigiku. We were to wait there for the limousines to take us to Sekison, a mansion of exquisite traditional architecture originally built by writer Tanizaki Jun'ichirō and used by him as a literary salon in the 1920s.

Sekison is now owned by the conglomerate Sumitomo Incorporated, and it is made available to the firm's highest executives to entertain themselves and clients. The chief of the Osaka branch of Sumitomo had reserved the main banquet room that evening. The light was fading as we drove up the long gravel driveway, and stone lanterns flickered on the moss amid twisted pines. It was six o'clock in the evening, the time for a geisha's workday to start.

The party of guests had already arrived. Ten of them, all men, were drinking Scotch and talking business in the banquet room overlooking the garden. We geisha were shown to a small side parlor with sofas and a television, to wait until our presence was called for. Momizuru had brought her shamisen and the younger women their dancing fans. They briefly discussed the musical pieces they would perform if the guests requested something. Momizuru could play almost anything, so the choice really depended on what Ichiume and Ichiteru, graduated from maiko to geisha a year ago, were able to dance. They quickly reeled off their as yet rather short repertoire. Two numbers were decided on: "Matsu no Midori" (The Green Pines), and a pas de deux from "Ishibashi" (Stone Bridge), both compositions in the nagauta style. The one maiko in our group, Ichiwaka, would dance the ever popular "Gion Kouta" (Ballad of Gion), a folk song enumerating scenes associated with Kyoto and maiko.

Momizuru tightened the three strings of her shamisen and, plucking them softly with her finger instead of the large ivory plectrum used for performance, gave the two young geisha a quick rehearsal. She then turned to me and asked whether I could

Group of geisha and maiko in front of Dai-Ichi teahouse,
January 1976.

sing anything yet. I said I could probably sing "Mizu no Debana," one of the two kouta that I had so far mastered at my lessons. The geisha had heard that I supposedly could play the shamisen and was studying kouta, but they didn't quite believe it. Behind Momizuru's offer to lend me her shamisen in order to practice lay the curiosity to see for themselves whether what they had heard about me was true.

I accepted her shamisen, a beautifully made instrument with cat-skin belly, gold fittings, and ivory pegs that was much finer than the sturdy but dull dog-skin, wooden pegged instrument I used for practice. When I twisted the pegs to the *honchōshi* tuning, an octave with the middle string tuned to a fourth above the lower fundamental, the geisha let out small gasps. "You really do play!" one of them exclaimed, falling into the Japanese habit of professing great astonishment if a foreigner exhibits the barest rudiments of competency in anything Japanese. "I've studied nagauta since I was sixteen," I told her, and that seemed a satisfactory explanation for my ability to tune the instrument.

111

In fact, although the shamisen technique for kouta is quite simple compared to the nagauta I was already able to play. I had not studied singing before. The lyrics, which appeared to be the easy part for the geisha, were quite difficult for me. I had to spend hours practicing with a tape recorder to get my voice to slide between notes that themselves seemed to fall between the keys to my piano-trained ears. Kouta in general should be performed in a much looser manner than nagauta, but their casualness is deceptive and required much hard work on my part.

An hour passed before the guests called us into the banquet room. The geisha had soon grown bored with rehearsing and begun to gossip. When a maid finally came to fetch us, the mother of the Dai-Ichi told me to stick close to Ichiume and do what she did. Maids handed each of us a small porcelain bottle of warm sake outside the banquet room.

Ichiume entered. She stopped in the center of the lower part of the room, swiftly knelt and bowed with her hands on the floor, then picked up the sake bottle, and, bearing it like a vial of holy water, went to sit at the side of a guest. The proprietress of the Dai-Ichi gave me a small shove as Ichiume was getting up from her bow, so with one eye on where she went, the other on where I was going, I followed her in. The guests, who had been fore-warned, all looked at me and then at each other, then at the pro-prietress. I bowed and said, "Minarai dosu e. Yoroshū otanomōshimasu" – in Kyoto dialect, "I'm a novice [literally, learning by observation], begging your favor, please." They smiled, scratching their heads.

Ichiume poured sake for the man next to her, so I did the same for the guest on my right. They downed their small cups in one gulp and offered them to us. "My" customer asked the mistress of the Dai-Ichi, "Does she drink sake?" uncertain as to how to address me. "Of course," I answered him directly holding out the small cup to be filled. "Did you ever hear of a geisha who didn't drink sake?"

A teetotaling geisha is a contradiction in terms.[4] I had passed my second test in the eyes of the other geisha. I was beginning to be accepted in a legitimate role of geisha society: the watcher and learner. Once I had demonstrated that I could observe and mimic the behavior of my older sisters, then the customers, the mothers, and the other geisha began to treat me as Ichigiku. And once I overcame my initial nervousness, I began to enjoy being Ichigiku myself. What is the mysterious training a new geisha goes through in order to attend banquets? None other, I discovered, than gaining the experience and ability to converse and joke with men, mostly older men.

Young Japanese women by and large do not have this ability. Girls are not encouraged to speak easily and freely with men who are their seniors; quite the opposite, in fact. Much of a young geisha's "training" in this sense consists of helping her overcome this socially inculcated reticence. Maiko are usually shy. As seventeen-year-olds this is their prerogative. They are taking everything in as they sit there demurely, however, and by the time they graduate to geishahood their glib skill at repartee has become quite remarkable. This ability improves with age. Often the geisha in their fifties or even sixties are the most entertaining at the table.

Thus my own background, as an American middle-class college-educated young woman, had prepared me in an unexpected way for this aspect of geisha life. Women of my generation in America are not expected to be shy. We were not socialized to be tongue-tied in front of men, nor have we received social approval for humble modesty. Much time and effort are needed before maiko and young geisha can sustain easy conversation with guests, but the American geisha took to the work of geisha banter like a duck to a pond.

THE DEFLOWERING ARRANGEMENT

At one point during the evening of my debut, the okāsan of the Dai-Ichi felt obliged to explain my presence to a curious customer. "She's come to Japan to learn about geisha. Foreigners don't know anything about us except 'Fujiyama, cherry blossoms, geisha girl,' so she wants to study what a geisha is. She's even taking shamisen and singing lessons."

Aside to me: "What did you say you are, Kikuko?" "An anthropologist," I whispered. The okāsan announced bombastically, "She's an anthropologist who wants a geisha Ph.D. from the Pontochō school of life!"

The guests laughed. One man stated that it was about time somebody studied geisha, and the okāsan thanked him, taking this as a personal compliment. Once my presence had been explained and accepted, several guests, with mock solicitude, decided to see to it that my education would not be wanting. "Do you know what *mizu-age* is?" inquired the *shachō*, the company chief who was playing host that evening. The young geisha all giggled, while the older ones feigned to look shocked. "Only from books," I replied, remembering that in the argot of the pleasure quarters this was the term for a woman's first sexual experience.

Delighted at the opportunity to expound his knowledge of the subject, the shachō asked, "Shall I tell you about mizu-age?"[5] Sensing a good story, we geisha egged him on. "Well," he started, "I don't know how it is now, but mizu-age used to take seven days. The okāsan of a girl's house would choose the man who would have the privilege. This was a great responsibility, mind you. Not a young man – a young man would be too rough. It should be an older gentleman with money and sincerity."

"Like you, shachō-san," piped up Ichiume.

"That's right," he continued, "I am your ideal mizu-age patron. Any of you in need can talk to me later." Squeals of laughter erupted from the geisha.

"This mizu-age patron was something like a male honeybee, you know. After his initial function was served, he had no further relation with the lady." The younger men in the group, unfamiliar with the more exotic customs of the geisha world, were fascinated. One of them ventured, "What took seven days then, shachō-san?"

"The okāsan or one of the experienced geisha prepared a chamber. They placed three eggs on top of the coverlet by the pillows and then withdrew to an adjoining room. Once in a while they would cough or rustle, just to reassure the young girl that they were nearby."

"Oh, how embarrassing," exclaimed Ichiteru, fully imbued with more modern notions of privacy.

"The man would tell the maiko to lie down; then, breaking the eggs, he swallowed the yolks and rubbed the whites between her thighs. 'This is mizu-age. Good night, my dear,' he said, and turned out the lights. The next night the room was readied in just the same way and again he cracked the eggs, consumed the yolks, and applied the whites between the girl's legs. 'This is mizu-age. Sleep well, my dear.' Again the next night, and the next. Each time, however, he wiggled his fingers in a little deeper with the slippery egg whites. By the end of the week, the maiko had gotten used to this little ritual and she was very relaxed. And at that point, fortified as he was with all those egg yolks, you see, mizu-age was easily accomplished."

The older women roared with laughter. "I had my mizu-age when I was sixteen," said the mother of the Dai-Ichi, recalling her maiko days. "Some years later, comparing notes with my friends, we were amazed at how similar our experiences had been. Then we discovered we had all had the same mizu-age patron!"

"What about now?" I asked, seeing this as a chance to find out more about sex in the geisha world – a topic that geisha are understandably touchy about. "It's all changed now," said the okāsan. "There's no mizu-age ceremony any more, with or without eggs. All the maiko have been through junior high school, so they aren't as ignorant as we were – right, Ichiume? They pretty much pick their own boyfriends and patrons when they're ready. That's not the same as mizu-age."

I sensed a faint embarrassment in a few of the older geisha as the curious young ones listened. Today geisha and women in general have more control over their sexuality. Older geisha automatically say how wonderful it is that their daughters do not have to submit to mizu-age. Yet this means that their own experiences, far from being a useful guide to the younger women, are dismissed as "feudalistic" – a term used in Japanese not only in a political sense, but also to refer to any practice considered passé, unenlightened, or simply unfashionable. I often found that the older geisha spoke more freely about sex when the young women were not present.

For Love of a Geisha

Sex undoubtedly used to be simpler in the geisha world. A maiko was a maiden, and her sexual initiation was part of becoming a full geisha. Ordinary girls put aside their swinging sleeve kimonos when they married; maiko put aside theirs when they graduated into geisha. In both cases, adulthood presumed sexual experience. A virgin geisha would have been as odd as a virgin wife. Now, however, freedom of choice has muddled these once straightforward categories. I know a maiko who has stolen away to meet her young boyfriend in one of the hotels that offer special day rates. On the other hand, Ichiume and Ichiteru passed into geishahood with maidenheads intact.

Geisha generally know more about sex than housewives do, but a man who thinks of a geisha's gei as rampant eroticism will be disappointed. Even in the long-gone era of the licensed quarters, geisha were not the foremost sexual adepts. The appeal of a romantic entanglement with a geisha has always embraced more than sex.

From a man's point of view, sleeping with a geisha is not to be undertaken lightly, for he will not be able to extricate himself easily if his passion cools. With this in mind, some customers who enjoy geisha banquets in Pontochō avoid becoming too intimate with any one geisha. They know that if the intimacy should sour, reproachful eyes will ruin relaxation at their favorite teahouses. Men who do take a geisha mistress must be prepared for everything that the relationship entails, and they are expected to show their patronage by continuous magnanimous gifts.

A geisha is not necessarily infatuated with her *danna*, or patron, but if he is a good provider and a comfortable companion she may well be content with him. A *boifurendo*, or lover, is a different matter. A boyfriend does not give opal rings and perfume to his geisha inamorata; he gives her a good time. A geisha may even keep a lover as she herself is kept by a patron. A geisha's dream may be to find a rich, handsome danna she can adore, but like everyone who dreams, she usually settles for less.

On the questionnaire I distributed among a dozen or so communities, one item asked geisha their reasons for wanting a patron. Almost half checked column (b), "needing someone to be close to." A third of them marked (e), "it makes no difference," and a quarter (c), "needing enough money to live." A few replied (a), "to have money for luxuries," and even fewer (d), that having a danna "gives high status in geisha society." I realized that my survey technique had been too bounded when I began to tally one brandy-splashed sheet where my columns had been obliterated by a bold scrawl: "In my case, it's because I love him."

FOOD AND DRINK

Geisha are not waitresses. Carrying trays of dishes is the job of maidservants, although once the food is set on the table a geisha may deftly remove the bones from a trout, or peel a muscat grape the size of a kumquat. At my first banquet, I marveled at the parade of elegantly prepared dishes brought in sequence by the maids. Sliced raw fish, tuna and bonito in a glistening green nest of seaweed strands was followed by clear soup in individual lacquered bowls. The entire head of a red sea bream gazed up through the broth. Pottery and porcelain dishes shaped like fans, gourds, and baskets were presented, each holding a few morsels of some delicacy: six roasted gingko nuts skewered on pine needles, thin slabs of soy curd brushed with sweet bean paste. A square bowl with glutinous boiled yams was brought in with an oblong flat plate holding a salt-baked trout. The fish had been fixed in position with a bamboo stick before cooking, to appear as if it were swimming upstream. A shoot of red pickled ginger lay under its tail. Small gold-rimmed bowls containing a vinegared mound of tiny white fishlings, each the size of a shred of coconut with pinpoint black eyes, were set out, and some of the empty dishes were cleared away.

Geisha are never served food with the guests at a banquet, so they either eat early or very late. I often saw maiko in full dress, napkins tucked into their collars, eating a hurried bowl of cheap curry and rice before being escorted by limousine to some of the most elegant restaurants in the city. When cuisines of the world are compared, it is often said that Japanese food is more a feast for the eyes than for the palate, so even if I didn't get to taste the banquets I witnessed, I at least got to view the beautifully orchestrated composition of dishes.

At last, *misoshiru* soup, pickles, and tubs of steaming white rice, signifying the end of the meal, were brought in and passed around. Japanese food comes in two categories: "rice" and "everything else." No matter how much a Japanese eats from the profusion of dishes preceding the rice, he always has room for rice. He might even say he hasn't really eaten unless he has had at least a small bowl of it. The maids waited to give more on request. Finally pale green tea was poured.

The tea traditionally marks the end of a formal banquet. But now the Western custom of dessert is usually appended to the meal in the form of fruit of some kind: if not seasonal, then the more unseasonal (expensive) the better. The fruit that evening was melon wedges the color of a luna moth, on glass plates, served with small silver forks. I had seen such melons selling in the fruit stores for nearly thirty dollars apiece.[6]

The banquet was winding down, and people were discussing where to go for the rest of the evening. The melon disappeared in three or four careless bites. Once the host had stood up, everyone else left the table. It was nine o'clock, and cars were waiting to take the guests back to Osaka. Geisha helped those who were weaving slightly to get their arms into the sleeves of their overcoats. We went as far as the vestibule with them, kneeling as a group while they fumbled for their shoes, bowing as they drove away.

Having been too excited to eat before we came, and having watched the procession of delicacies at the banquet, I was famished. The geisha were shown back to the parlor where we had first waited. We received individual boxed dinners of cold rice, fish, and other tidbits that the skillful Sekison chefs had prepared for us. Ichiume grumbled that we should have been fed before the banquet because we were kept waiting for an hour anyway. She was in a hurry to get back to Pontochō, where more guests were waiting in one of the teahouses.

Besides our dinners, the host had also provided several cars, "hires," which are a notch more genteel than taxis, to transport us back to our various destinations in and around Pontochō. On the way home it suddenly occurred to me that we had not performed any of our diligently rehearsed entertainments. I asked Momizuru, the shamisen player, if this was unusual. "Not at all," she answered. "Sometimes the guests simply aren't interested. But you have to be prepared just in case." I asked to be dropped at the Mitsuba. As I got out of the car she said, "Goodnight, then. You really did quite well this evening – it was very interesting."

I was exhilarated. Praise from Momizuru, the warm sake, a fancy envelope with a tip from the mother of the Dai-Ichi – all had gone to my head. I slipped the envelope into the breast of my kimono, as I had seen the other geisha do, and went to look for the okāsan of the Mitsuba. A party was in progress upstairs in the big banquet room, and okāsan was attending to that, so I asked the maid to tell her that I was home. Immediately word came back for me to come up and join the party.

NEW GEISHA IN TOWN

With more confidence now, I opened the sliding paper door with my fingertips, entered the room, and bowed. "Ichigiku dosu e. Yorōshū otanomōshimasu." With a gleam of mischief in her eye, okāsan announced, "Everybody, there's a new geisha in Pontochō – for the first time one belonging to the Mitsuba, training at Dai-Ichi."

"Oh, Mitsuba-san," said one guest, "I didn't know you had a geisha in your own house. Congratulations! 'Ichigiku,' you say?"

"Younger sister of Ichiume," beamed okāsan, hardly able to contain herself.

Another guest looked a bit quizzical. "She's awfully tall. Must have really been something when she wore maiko clogs."[7]

My okāsan couldn't take it any longer. Three geisha who knew what was going on burst out laughing. "Ichigiku isn't Japanese," she finally gasped, "she's American." The kimono, my dark hair done up, and my pale complexion had not roused a whit of suspicion. Although my features are not Japanese, with the proper attire and body language it was remarkable the number of times

119

Liza Dalby's okāsan as a maiko in the 1930s.

I could enter a room of new customers and not be perceived as other than a somewhat taller than average geisha. Once I was seated there was no problem, since my very long legs could be tucked under my relatively short-waisted torso. Seated, I appeared the same height as a Japanese woman who might only come to my shoulder when standing.

"Is this one of your jokes?" a guest inquired of okāsan. "It's not a joke. She's learning about geisha. This is practical experience," said the mistress of the Mitsuba. One guest ventured that the outer appearance looked authentic, but he wondered whether I could handle any of the arts. There was nothing to do but fetch a shamisen. I strummed the accompaniment for a kouta that okāsan sang, then I played and sang the piece I had rehearsed before the earlier banquet. The guests applauded wildly, enjoying the novelty of the situation if not the artistic merit of our performances.

By eleven o'clock, the group, about a dozen of us, decided to move en masse to a bar two blocks away. Spilling noisily into the street, geisha and guest arm in arm, we took up most of the narrow sidewalk. Venders of cheap snacks – noodles and octopus pancakes – had stationed their wooden carts on the corners along our way, and they shouted their wares as we passed. One of our number was tempted, but the thought of the teasing he would have to endure from the rest for indulging in such low-class eatables made him hurry on. I think he hoped the maiko with us would beg for a treat, giving him an excuse, but she wrinkled her nose at the pungent odors.

Bar Satomi, our destination, was run by the ex-geisha Satomi, a woman the same age as the okāsan of the Mitsuba and a close companion since their childhood together in Pontochō. A phone call had given her a few minutes to prepare for our arrival. We burst in, jarring three or four quiet customers already well into their cups. This evening was the first time I saw my okāsan as she must have been as a geisha, flirting with guests, bright-eyed, utterly charming. She pulled a small booklet of *papier poudré* "powder papers," out of the fold in her obi, tore off a sheet, and handed it to me. "Powder your nose, Kikuko, it's shining," she whispered.

At about 1.30 A.M. okāsan and I walked one of the guests back to his hotel, then turned our steps home. The main gate of the Mitsuba had been locked by the maids at midnight, but a small side door was left unlatched for us. "Come have a bowl of *ochazuke* with me." Okāsan invited me in to her private quarters. The hot tea poured over leftover rice sent up spirals of steam in the cold kitchen. We carried our bowls to a small table with a heater underneath and tucked our knees under the coverlet.

"What did you learn at the banquet?" she asked me. "I learned about mizu-age," I replied. She looked up. "Were you surprised?" "No, it didn't sound so horrendous, actually. A lot of American girls have their mizu-age in the back seats of their boyfriends' cars – often neither one knows what they're doing. I could see the advantage in one partner, at least, being experienced." She blinked. "The maiko are all so embarrassed about the subject of sex. I don't understand it. Nowadays it's all right for young people to do it with each other, quite irresponsibly, in my opinion, but the mere mention of mizu-age makes everybody squeamish. Next time you see the new maiko Ichiwaka, would you please tell her that it didn't sound so awful to you."

"Yes, Mother," I said.

SEVEN

GENERATIONS

Haru kaze ga	The spring wind whispers
Soyo soyo to	Bring in fortune!
Fuku wa uchi e to	Fragrant plums breathe
Kono yado e	Drive out devils!
Oni wa soto e to	Is it rain?
Ume ga ka soyuru	Is it snow?
Ame ka yuki ka	I don't care –
Mama yo mama yo	We'll go on this evening
Kon'ya mo ashita mo	and tomorrow too,
Itsuzuke ni	Drinking
Shōgazake	Ginger sake

A Kouta

SETSUBUN: THE SPRING NEW YEAR

THE SEASONS ARE somewhat out of step in modern Japan. The lunar year, flexible and finely tuned to an agricultural society's observations of nature, was scrapped in 1872 in favor of the Gregorian calendar. Holidays that previously had wandered within a range of possible dates are now fixed, pinned down, their stability more suitable to a bureaucratic mode of life than to an agrarian one. Yet certain holidays and seasonal phrases based on the old lunar system still linger in Japanese life, creating an odd sense of disjunction between the natural and the cultural orders of things.

123

A maiko throws soybeans to the crowd at the conclusion of her Setsubun dance. Photograph by Hamaoka Noboru.

For the New Year, which now occurs in the dead of winter on January first, one of the most common greetings proclaims joy at the beginning of spring. Before the calendar change, the new year actually did begin with spring. Even though the *weather* may still have been cold in early February, the three-month-long season of spring (which would reach its peak of "springness" about six weeks later, at the equinox) commenced to signal the stirring of new life in the round of activities of the agricultural year. This first day of spring, called *risshun*, is now fixed as February 4.[1] It is also called the old new year (*kyū shōgatsu*), that is, new year's day according to the old calendar, and is still celebrated as such in rural Japan, as well as in many other Asian countries.

124

The day before the first of spring by the old calendar is known as Setsubun, the day that "divides the seasons" winter and spring.[2] All over Japan on February 3, people can be found throwing roasted soybeans out their doors, shouting "Devils out! Fortune in!" Or they nibble roasted soybeans and talk about how people used to call "Devils out, fortune in," slamming their doors after routing the evil spirits. Throwing beans was originally a household custom at Setsubun, although it is now part of a festival celebrated at temples and shrines. One shrine that is especially famous for its Setsubun festivities is Kyoto's Gion Shrine (Yasaka Jinja), in the heart of the city.

Itinerant peddlers set up wooden stalls along the edges of the paths inside the shrine compound. They hawk balloons, cheap toys, and snacks. A sweet, milky, fermented rice brew seasoned with grated ginger root is served from vats. This *shōgazake* is drunk only at Setsubun, as we usually drink eggnog only at Christmas. Young geisha from Pontochō and from three other hanamachi in this part of Kyoto perform votive dances to the deities on a wide open-air stage. After each performance, the dancers toss packets of soybeans into the crowd, causing a scramble among observers anxious to obtain them as good luck charms.

These religious dances only make sense when one remembers that Setsubun was originally the day before the new year. Throwing beans was meant to exorcise the spirits that caused sickness and misfortune and the dances were intended as homage to the deity of the new year.

The juncture of old year and new is a time when the spirit world is felt to be closer to manifest reality. People once fasted and undertook other rituals of purification on Setsubun eve. In some parts of Japan, tools normally left outside would be brought indoors lest a wandering spirit mark them for destruction by fire. Sardine heads attached to branches of holly were hung outside the door as talismans. Rice cakes were balanced on the lintels of doors and windows to bribe a devil to go elsewhere.

Setsubun was a day set apart from ordinary time. As in many cultures, such days are marked by customs of ritual inversion: high becomes low, old becomes young, women play men and vice versa. Though modern Japanese hardly remember, on Setsubun

*Setsubun silliness. An elderly geisha
dressed as a maiko with a guest in
wig and ascot.*

young girls once did their hair in the *marumage* style of adult women, and old ladies rolled theirs into the "split peach" *momoware* style of girlhood.

A class of people known as *tabi geinin*, traveling entertainers, played an important role when the year changed. Having no fixed abode, they wandered from town to town, where, like gypsies, they were both shunned and courted by established society. They dressed up with masks to dance and perform morality plays, and they were welcomed in the villages and towns because of their power to chase away evil spirits who may have hunkered in during the old year. The tabi geinin could do this precisely because they never did settle in one community but always moved on, sweeping the devils away with them.

This dressing up, changing of appearances, is almost forgotten as part of Setsubun now – except in the geisha world. The custom of *obake* (disguise), where geisha dress up to be characters like Western brides, Meiji period schoolgirls, and heroines from novels, is carried out with great hilarity by geisha and guests on the evening of February 3. The geisha seem mostly unaware of the roots of obake, which almost certainly go back to ancient customs and superstitions that accompanied the changeover from old year to new.

PONTOCHŌ'S BIG THREE

Geisha, especially the older ones, take custom, omens, and religious observances seriously. At Setsubun, besides devising imaginative costumes for parties, they undertake a pilgrimage to four shrines in the environs of Kyoto. This ritual tour, called *shihō mairi*, is another custom aimed at starting the new year off on the right foot, through the observation of spiritual proprieties in each of the "four directions." All four shrines are crowded with stalls, children, and merrymakers. Blessings accrue as one spends a lighthearted afternoon. I made this pilgrimage in the company of my okāsan and her two best friends, Korika, who runs a teahouse, and Satomi, the mama of the Pontochō bar of that name.

"Pontochō's big three," these ladies are sometimes called. They were all born in the same year of the dragon, thus they were all fifty-six when I was conducting my research in Kyoto. All were daughters of women who had been geisha in Pontochō, all became maiko the same year they turned thirteen. When they were in their twenties they had gone their separate ways and for more than two decades had little contact with one another. Then, time and karma brought them all back to Pontochō in middle age. These three women share their pasts and their customers, and, in the case of my okāsan and the bar mama-san Satomi, they share a business venture – a small restaurant called Rokudan, which serves Kyoto-style home cooking.

The three women are in that rare position in Japan of being almost precise equals: none is older or younger sister to the other, so they always address one another by their given names or nicknames. In the geisha world kinship terms are almost always used in preference to names, emphasizing the hierarchical nature of relationships. In contrast, the equal camaraderie of these three women is delightful, and I looked forward to the pilgrimage with the three mothers. At each shrine we made sure to get a ticket from the priests to take home and hang up for luck, but once that was accomplished we were free to stroll about, sampling the ginger sake.

Outside the Yoshida Shrine, Korika tugged my okāsan's sleeve. "Look, Mi-chan, an old-style candy maker." She pointed to a wooden cart where an old man was deftly spinning barley sugar into various animal shapes. We gathered around him to watch. A brown crystallized syrup octopus, a snake, a monkey, and many other fanciful sugar creatures came to life on sticks. Satomi bought a dragon because that was the trio's animal, my okāsan bought a boar, saying, "Stubborn, just like me." I asked the candy maker to make a tiger, my year in the zoological zodiac, and he stretched a leaping tiger out of a shapeless blob of syrup.

"I didn't know there was anybody who could make these any more," commented Korika. "There are two of us in Kyoto," the candy maker informed her. "But the other guy is even older than me. Young people aren't interested in learning how. I had an apprentice once, but he quit. Not much money in it, you know." "You should really be a Living National Treasure," said my okāsan brightly. "Thanks," he said, "but the trouble is, my artwork all melts away."[3]

We continued at leisure in our hired car to the next shrine, the Kitano Tenmangu, on the other side of the city. Here the tight, round buds of the plum blossoms were just starting to open: pink, white, and my favorite, deep crimson. Students (or their mothers) visit this shrine, dedicated to the patron saint of learning, to pray for success on the crucial college entrance examinations. The cryptic written fortunes they obtain are tied to branches of the plum trees in the grounds of the shrine to gain the deity's attention. In earliest spring more fortunes than flowers flutter on the branches.

On the way to our third destination, Akiba Jinja, the threat of a traffic jam made the three okāsans decide against a visit there and to Mibu, the remaining shrine on the pilgrimage. We had to get home to prepare our costumes for the evening, so we headed back to Pontochō. "Remember the year I was Carmen?" my okāsan asked the other two. They agreed that the act had been a Setsubun tour de force. In a flounced Spanish skirt, clenching a carnation between her teeth ("It should have been a rose, of course, but the thorns . . ."), she had created a dance with what she supposed was a farruca flavor for the evening party. As the final flourish, she stamped her feet and got so carried away that she bit the carnation in two. The guests loved it.

Pontochō's "Big Three." Satomi, Korika, and Michiko as young geisha in the 1930s.

Today, however, she was going to put most of her effort into getting me dressed, so her own outfit would be a simple one: a pageboy-style wig with bangs and a bright, swinging-sleeved little girl's kimono. Satomi would let her hair down to her shoulders with a big bow in back and wear a dark red masculine-style skirt over a large print kimono: the outfit of a turn-of-the-century schoolgirl. Korika was not going to dress up this year. She had decided to stay home in her teahouse and watch the procession of characters as they passed through.

Korika

A faint aura of sadness surrounds Korika. Her face is long anyway, the face of a Kyoto beauty. Occasionally, when she is unaware of being observed, her whole body lapses into a melancholy pose as she gazes into the distance, her attention momentarily cut off from the lively chatter around her. Her friends call her the *shirōto okamisan*, the "amateur proprietress," because she spent twenty years away from the geisha world before taking over as mistress of a teahouse, the Korika.

Korika left Pontochō when she was twenty-one. She had become linked to a patron who was a high government official, and he had prevailed upon her to move to Tokyo. Korika lived there as his mistress for many years, and then, after his wife died, she moved into his house to care for him as a wife herself. He was proud of her and often brought friends and colleagues home, where she welcomed them and entertained them with her Kyoto manner. This in itself was a very unusual mark of his affection and regard for her.

Korika had been known as one of the top dancers in Pontochō at the time she left. Her geisha name had been Ichiko. Pontochō's customers in the 1930s had taken note of this group of three girls, always seen together: Ichiraku (my okāsan), comely and good-humored; Satomi, the so-called Western-style beauty because of her round eyes; and Ichiko (Korika), slim, elegant, the ideal image of a Kyoto geisha. She was proclaimed the true beauty of the three. Her patron had pulled quite a coup in winning her. The other two congratulated her on moving to the capital, and on the rich and famous patron she had acquired; but even more, they sighed and envied her happiness, because it was plain that this older man was crazy about Korika, and she was completely devoted to him.

Once in a while something will remind Korika of her patron – she refers to him as her husband – and tears well up in her eyes. An old customer who knew them both told me that he had died suddenly about ten years before, without having made adequate provision for her. She had thought they were as good as married by common law, or else she hadn't really thought about it at all, but his family was of a different opinion. It was a cruel blow to her. Never a particularly practical person, and all her life accustomed to being taken care of, she never thought to protest. She humbly accepted a small amount of money from his family and departed. There were no children.

Many people who had known them together over the years were outraged at this treatment. One of her patron's close friends suggested that she return to Pontochō, where he and a few others would help her settle down with her own teahouse. There she could be among friends, continue with her music, and make a living doing what she did best, keeping a house that people loved to visit.

So Korika came back to Pontochō, where her friend Michiko was the lively and vivacious proprietress of an inn and where Satomi, wearing evening gowns, presided over one of Kyoto's oldest hostess bars. She slipped back into the community she had left over twenty years before, and the newer customers now never suspect that she was not always there. Still, late at night when we had all been drinking too much, a sadness would steal over her. As a dancer, she is accustomed to punctuating her speech with gestures from the fan she always carries. She would move it rapidly, as if cooling her face, to hide her blinking eyes.

Satomi

Satomi and Michiko are much more practical than Korika, though Satomi, by some lights, has had a hard life. She left the geisha world when she was still a maiko, not to become some-

*Liza Dalby as Ichigiku (left)
with Satomi in old-fashioned
schoolgirl attire.*

one's mistress, but to marry. Hers was a love match, of course. No one arranges marriages for maiko. Her husband ran a small dry goods store on the other side of the city. He had first met Satomi when she and her two close companion maiko were hired to dance at his sister's wedding. Smitten, he wheedled his father into paying for almost nightly visits to Pontochō, where he made the geisha laugh because of his single-minded interest in Satomi and his lack of attention to anyone else.

In the etiquette of the geisha banquets, such intensity is somewhat uncomfortable. A party is an environment for flirting, jokes, aesthetic indulgence, and laughter. Serious passion may be permissible as an undercurrent, but it should not be allowed to surface in public. The more sophisticated geisha teased the young man. He was also scolded by his father, who was anything but happy at the prospect of a geisha daughter-in-law. On the other hand, Satomi herself seemed modest and sensible enough; and because his son, his only son, threatened to leave the business otherwise, the father finally gave in. He paid a sum of money to Satomi's house to cover her debts, and the two were married.

Satomi had a lot to learn as a wife. As a maiko, she had been told not to bother her pretty head about financial matters. A generation ago, maiko could walk into stores in the neighborhood, picking out this and that, and say, "Charge it to my house," never paying attention to the price. They didn't even handle money. Part of this cultivated ignorance of practical affairs was to give them an image that was a step removed from hard reality. Customers liked to think of maiko as charming dolls, spoiled and protected. As a shopkeeper's wife, however, Satomi suddenly had the responsibility for keeping track of the books and managing a household, something she was completely unprepared for. Her mother-in-law, true to form, was less than helpful.

Satomi was forbidden to see her geisha friends. She told me that once during this time when visiting the Gion Shrine with her new baby son, she saw a few of her Pontochō cronies. They knew not to speak to her and she of course, in the presence of her mother-in-law, turned her back. That night she lay awake, stifling sobs with her bed quilt.

Her marriage lasted for seventeen years, and there was another baby. When this second child, a girl, entered high school, Satomi obtained a divorce and came back to Pontochō. She never talks about her life as a housewife, and I don't know what finally soured her marriage so irrevocably. Her daughter is now married, with young children of her own, so Satomi, though she hardly looks it, is a grandmother. Her Bar Satomi draws on disaffected geisha, among others, for hostesses, and Satomi as mama-san provides a relaxed, Western-style drinking environment for customers who need a break from teahouse entertainment. Her customers are elderly and faithful, and parties that begin at the Mitsuba or at Korika's teahouse often end at Bar Satomi.

Michiko

On this evening of February 3, Satomi was to be one of the guests at a boisterous Setsubun party at the Mitsuba. The group was the Dragon Club, an assemblage of about fifteen wealthy, cosmopolitan Kyoto-ites – businessmen, a tea master, company presidents, a famous potter, and several ex-geisha proprietresses – who had all been born in the same year of the dragon. Every other month this club throws itself a party, choosing elegant and interesting banquet halls all over the city for its gatherings. Setsubun was a perfect excuse for a party, and they decided to hold it at the Mitsuba in case things got too silly. My okāsan, Michiko, as a member of the club, was delighted to be hostess.

My okāsan is primarily interested in hosting banquets, creating her own style of entertaining for a select group of customers and friends, and generally leading the life of a busy socialite. She chooses flowers for the alcoves, plans the banquet menus, and arranges for geisha to attend the parties held at her establishment. Like her two best friends, she left her geisha career early, but she did not stray far from the center of Kyoto.

Michiko was born in 1916 in Pontochō. Her mother ran a small teahouse, and her father, her mother's patron from her geisha days, worked for a trading company. Michiko could have inherited her mother's teahouse directly had she been so inclined, but she really wanted to become a maiko. From all accounts (including her own), she was the toast of the town. A large water color of Ichiraku in her maiko days now hangs at the landing of the Mitsuba's main staircase. It was painted by a well-known artist in the early 1930s who used her as a model of plump Kyoto beauty.

Her first patron, a man from the same company her father had worked for, made it financially possible for her to retire from the geisha life at age twenty. Her ambitions ran beyond her mother's little teahouse, however. When her patron's company needed a manager for the new inn they had just built for business entertainment, she happily accepted the position. She was given a free hand in running the inn, provided, of course, that she would keep some rooms always available for employees of the firm and arrange entertainment for them. The Mitsuba is a large, beautiful building, and it gave her precisely the kind of base she wanted.

In 1975, Michiko managed to buy the Mitsuba. She had been working toward ownership for many years and finally, triumphantly, made the last monthly payment to the trading company. The president of that firm remains a loyal customer. He allowed her to keep the name Mitsuba, which originally referred to the three-leaf design of the company trademark, although the connection between the firm and the inn is now only a sentimental one. When the last payment was made, Michiko threw a huge party in celebration, picking up the tab for about ninety guests who came in three successive groups for a full banquet meal with attending geisha.

The small teahouse her own mother had managed was taken over by a maidservant who had earned the right of inheritance after years of faithful service.[4] This woman is about the same age as Michiko, and the two are very close. In their early teens they shared the same living quarters, calling the same woman "mother": Michiko had been born to her, the maidservant in a sense adopted by her.

Michiko continued to operate the inn throughout the Second World War. Kyoto suffered no destruction from air raids, so places like the Mitsuba were in great demand by government officials and leaders of industry from nearby Osaka, which had been heavily bombed. The Mitsuba was used for strategic planning sessions, for parties – meager though the fare became in the later days of the war – and for geisha entertainment. Kyoto's geisha population even increased slightly in wartime because of the influx of geisha from Osaka.

With only the briefest lull at the beginning of the Allied occupation, a time when the whole country waited to see what would happen, the Mitsuba was soon thronged with customers again. For a time, many of the guests were high-ranking American soldiers. At the Mitsuba they were but a block from the Pontochō Kaburenjō, the geishas' dance theater. The theater had been converted, with the help of the capable okāsan of the Dai-Ichi teahouse, who headed the Pontochō Geisha Association at the time, into a Western-style dance floor for the G.I.s.

About that time, Michiko fell in love with a businessman from Tokyo, a man who had been invited as a guest to the Mitsuba by one of her old customers. This man had a wife and child in Tokyo, although he and his wife were not on good terms. Taking up with the ex-geisha Ichiraku in Kyoto did not improve his relationship with his wife. The affair blossomed. The mistress of the Mitsuba was thirty-two, he was in his early forties. When she was thirty-seven, she bore him a son, a spoiled baby boy and the pride of her life. Michiko's patron, by now divorced, asked her to move to Tokyo.

She thought about it. Her life in Kyoto was very full. There were always women around, friends and relatives to help her care for the baby, and she managed the Mitsuba with hardly a crimp in her style. Everything she knew was in Kyoto, and she was known there – fairly well-known, in fact, in precisely that circle of wealthy Kyoto-ites she most admired and loved to be part of. If she went to Tokyo to live, she reasoned, she would give it all up to sit in a small apartment with her baby. Her patron might visit from time to time, but she could hardly live in his house. The choice was not difficult for her, and she stayed in Kyoto.

Three or four times a year, she and her patron would go off for a long weekend at some seacoast or mountain resort. I watched her prepare for these excursions with some amusement because, though there were many details to be arranged in her absence from the Mitsuba, her mind was clearly elsewhere. It would drive the maids to exasperation. Finally she would go have her hair done, relax under the familiar fingers of her hairdresser, then come home for her suitcase, asking one of us to call a car to take her to the station. We would all wave goodbye from the curb in front of the inn. Once, the dour auntie made a comment about a woman her age acting like a dog in heat; and I found myself irritated by her sharp tongue. I told her she was just jealous, and that I at least thought it was very touching to see okāsan go off with the excitement of a young girl to meet the man she was still in love with after twenty-five years.

Of the trio of okāsans, the mistress of the Mitsuba is the only one who still has a man. "How lucky you are, Mi-chan," sighs Korika. Michiko's career in the geisha world has been a successful one by any measure – but it also seems to have been a happy one.

BLIND DOVES

The week before Setsubun, okāsan had taken me to the Kobayashi-ya, a shop that specializes in fine old kimono. Their garments are rented out primarily to dancers, mostly professionals like geisha, who call when they need a certain kimono for one of their performances. But amateurs who study classical dance as a hobby go there too when they need a costume for a recital. Okāsan had decided that because most of the geisha who were coming to the Mitsuba on Setsubun would not be dressed as geisha, I should appear in full regalia. The rental fee for a geisha's *desho*-style kimono was high: 30,000 yen ($90 in 1975) for the evening, but the price included two men from the shop to come to the house to help put it on. For a small surcharge, the sleeves would be resewn to fit. Any of four kimono would have been suitable, but among them one in particular struck us both as perfect.

On its glossy black background, a white spray of willow branches cascaded down one side from the hip, brushing a golden footbridge that was set among graceful bubbling waves at the hem. It was gorgeous, and it fit me exactly. We arranged for it to be brought to the house in the late afternoon of Setsubun. Pleased with our choice, we went on to the wig shop. There are only two such wiggeries in Kyoto, and they take care of all the geisha of the city, custom-making Shimada-style wigs for each woman, redoing them when they become mussed, and supplying specialized wigs for the various roles the geisha take in their dances.

If a geisha does not stay in the wig maker's good graces, he can drag his feet when she needs her wig styled in a hurry. This man is thus plied with tips, joked with, and sweet-talked by dozens of women all the time. He can be seen coming in and out of the teahouses during the daytime and backstage during dance performances when the geisha are in various stages of dress and undress, preparing to go on stage. He and the kimono shop men are the only males to share this unique position of intimacy with geisha. It is entirely unerotic.

At his shop I tried on several wigs till one seemed to fit comfortably. They are made of human hair (Korean, he said) attached to a metal frame. The hair is sectioned, dressed with

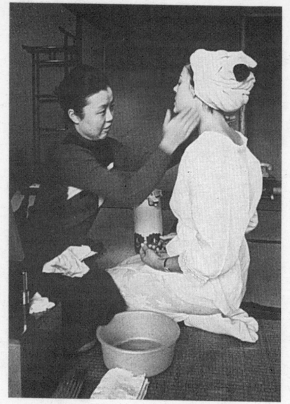

*Ichiume (left) prepares Liza Dalby's skin
for the white geisha makeup.*

camellia nut oil, and smoothed out with heated spatulas. The wig maker can re-do a wig completely in only twenty minutes, securing each loop of hair with hidden paper cords. As the final touch, a tortoise-shell comb and a coral hairpin are anchored securely in the heavy coils. We asked the man to bring the wig to the Mitsuba after the kimono men had dressed me.

Because putting on this paraphernalia is such an involved process, the mothers thought it best to cut short our pilgrimage on Setsubun. Ichiume, my older sister, came to the Mitsuba to help apply my makeup, which had to be done before anything

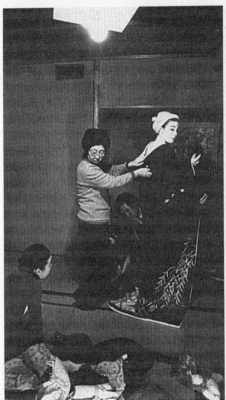 

*Left: The mistress of the Mitsuba (center) and Ichiume (left)
dress Liza Dalby in the formal kimono of the geisha.
Right: The mistress of the Mitsuba applies a final touch to
Liza Dalby's makeup. Note the unhusked rice and the dove
decoration in the wig.*

else. The first thing she did was to pat a sticky substance all over
my face and neck, so that the white makeup she painted on next
would adhere evenly. (Several months later, at a banquet we both
attended, she described this cosmetic procedure to a guest: "For
my face, I close my eyes and go fwa, fwa, fwa, with the brush and
it's all done. So on Kikuko's face I went fwa, fwa, fwa – but there
was this untouched spot on either side of her nose." She was

making fun of herself because her nose was very flat, and because one of the most common epithets for foreigners is "high-nosed" – even though, as these things go, the bridge of my nose is nothing out of the ordinary.) The white makeup is a nontoxic concoction like thick paint, a great improvement over the old type of *oshiroi*, which eventually gave lead poisoning to women who habitually used it.

Okāsan outlined my eyes in red and painted a crimson mouth, smaller than my own, onto my lips, which had been blotted out with white. I quickly saw in the mirror that having one's face the color of chalk places a constraint on smiling: teeth cannot but look ghastly yellow in comparison to that dead white. Suddenly I realized why the maiko were constantly told to hide their teeth when they laughed – accounting for the enigmatic close-lipped smile they often wear.

In the meantime, the men from the kimono shop had come with a large bundle containing the kimono and obi we had chosen, plus a special undergarment with a red silk slip (which would show when I held up the kimono train in my left hand), and a band of red silk at the collar, which would also show as a glimmer of vermilion between the white of my painted back and the black kimono. The effect of the total outfit would be of deep black (hair and robe), mat white (my skin and the lining of the kimono), and touches of brilliant red.

When I stepped out onto the street that evening, answering a summons to Korika's teahouse, I felt the eyes of passers-by swiveling to stare. I listened to some of the comments. Not one was a sotto voce exclamation at a foreigner dressed as a geisha. Yet because of my height, several seemed sure I was a Japanese man, a female impersonator dressed in drag for Setsubun. "Still, he's awfully glamorous," I heard one man comment.

Because it was the new year, I wore as a hair ornament a spray of unhusked rice gathered by a few buds of plum and a dove made of plaster. The dove had no eyes, and Ichiume told me that a man who would become a lover would draw in the eyes that evening. "My doves are always blind," she lamented.

Ichiume was hardly a compelling beauty. She was always ready to fend off teasing remarks by deprecating herself first. The other geisha knew that if they called her *kabocha*, pumpkin, they could make her furious or make her cry. I thanked her for helping me with my makeup, saying how glad I was to have such a kind older sister. Remarking that it felt strange to be called onēsan (among all the geisha, only Pontochō's four maiko were in a position to call her "older sister"), she packed up her makeup box and hurried home to dress herself.

THE LITTLE DRAGONS

Ichiume was a member of a trio that some people referred to as the "little big three" of Pontochō. Her two best friends were Ichiteru and Komachiyo, and just a year before these three maiko together had "turned their collars," graduating to the status of full geisha. Among Kyoto geisha, dancers have a more prestigious position than musicians, and dancers who have been maiko have more status than women who have not. Ichiume, Ichiteru, and Komachiyo were all dancers, and their four years of experience as maiko easily established their credentials in Kyoto geisha society. The three, all aged twenty-two when I knew them, were seen as the future leaders of Pontochō. The parallels between them and the trio of mothers, Michiko, Korika, and Satomi, were obvious to everyone.

It was almost too much of a coincidence that the younger women were also born in the year of the dragon, thirty-six years, or three zodiacal cycles, after the mothers. They were frequently called to entertain at the parties of the Dragon Club. People would ask, "Are the little dragons coming tonight?" For Setsubun, the three were planning to visit one party after another in Pontochō, performing a skit they had worked out with the help of Tōsha Sen, the old woman who taught drums and flute.

For this occasion, they dressed identically in mannish striped kimono with *haori* (jackets), low sashes, and hair swept back. Ichiteru carried a big drum, Komachiyo a smaller hand-held one, and Ichiume a small, shrill flute. Giggling and clowning, they had practiced a swaggering walk the previous afternoon after one last rehearsal with Tōsha Sen. Their obake disguise was Japan's version of the Three Musketeers – Edo period outlaws with panache. I ran into them later on Setsubun evening at Korika's teahouse.

A customer there, who had come all the way from Tokyo just for Pontochō's Setsubun, was trying to convince me that he should draw the eyes onto my dove, when a great commotion appeared at the door. Drumming and fluting, the young dragons burst into our room. "Ohikaenas'te," growled Komachiyo in a low voice, starting her pastiche of a classic *jingi*, the old-style gangster's self-introduction. Full of tongue twisters and word play, her spiel was in Edo dialect, reeled off with a completely straight face. As soon as she finished, Ichiteru began: "Ohikaeyasu," she drawled sweetly, delivering the same boastful jingi Komachiyo had done, but in exaggerated Kyoto dialect. The effect was that of a southern belle doing an imitation of Edward G. Robinson.

As Ichiume's turn approached, she covered her mouth – then, taking her hand away, revealed a pair of huge buck teeth made of paper. Her jingi was in *zuu-zuu* dialect, the Japanese stereotype of the backwoods hick. Ichiume was unable to make it all the way through without laughing. This was of course very funny, but it was a touch pathetic as well. Ichiume was known to drool when she got to talking too fast.

The okāsan of the Mitsuba took a special interest in Ichiume. I think she felt a motherly bond between herself and the young woman, one that went beyond the framework of kinship terms defining the relationships between women in the geisha world. She regularly called Ichiume to parties at the Mitsuba and took her along as a companion when she made a trip to Tokyo. Although she never said so, I had the feeling that she would have been very pleased if Ichiume had someday married her son and taken over the management of the Mitsuba. There would have been a nice sense of balance, of one generation recapitulating the other, if this had happened. Ichiume, however, was not the least bit enamored of the sullen young man.

Ichiume's good friend Ichiteru is also a bona fide Pontochō product. Like the three women of the older generation, she was born to a geisha mother who now has a teahouse in Pontochō.

Pontochō's "Little Dragons." Ichiume, Komachiyo, and Ichiteru joke as they practice their Setsubun skit in 1976.

Ichiteru's mother broke off with her patron when her daughter was born because, she said, she didn't want him to have any say in the girl's upbringing. A "single mother," she raised her child in one of the few places in Japan where she could do so with no social opprobrium: in geisha society. The little girl grew up and took the geisha name Ichiteru, Ichi plus "sparkling." Of all the young Pontochō geisha, she is probably the most striking, with her quiet voluptuousness and her skin as fine as a white Japanese peach. When I went back to Pontochō two years after I had lived there, I learned that Ichiteru was pregnant and taking a leave of absence.

Komachiyo was not born in Pontochō. I gathered that her mother had been the mistress of a wealthy man who frequented Pontochō teahouses. She had not been a geisha, but other than that, no one knew much about her. When the child had shown artistic leanings, the father sponsored her entrance into a Pontochō teahouse for training. She chose a geisha named Komako as her older sister, and Komachiyo became a maiko the same year as Ichiume and Ichiteru.

I didn't know Komachiyo as well as the other two, for as Ichigiku I attended banquets mostly with geisha from the Dai-Ichi house: Ichisen, Ichiko, Ichiteru, Ichiwaka, and of course Ichiume. Of the young trio that was regarded with such fond hopes by the Pontochō old guard, Komachiyo is the only one now left as a practicing geisha. Ichiume is dead, and Ichiteru may or may not return to the profession.

New maiko continue to appear on the scene in Pontochō, and there are still young faces among the geisha, but the mothers are slightly anxious. No one ever thought the little big three would fall apart in such an untimely way and there is now a gap in their age group. Pontochō has always been known for its home-grown, "born and bred" members, but they are fewer now. There is even a maiko-to-be from Nagoya, who is coached on the side to speak in Kyoto dialect.

The cycle of the seasons continues in modern Japan, but with a great deal of slippage, and with nearly total loss of the old fortnightly ordering of time and nature. Human generations continue to move on to interact and intersect, but with an even greater loss of continuity. There was such a temptation to see the old generation in the new. I could see it in the eyes of the mothers as they watched the three exuberant young geisha do their Setsubun skit that evening before the first day of the spring new year.

EIGHT

GEISHA PARTIES

Why, in the West, is politeness regarded with
suspicion? Why does courtesy pass for distance,
if not, in fact, evasion or hypocrisy? Why is an
"informal" relation (as we greedily say) more
desirable than a coded one?

Roland Barthes, L'Empire des Signes *(1970)*

THE ZASHIKI

A *ZASHIKI* IS a kind of drawing room. Whenever geisha talk,
the word crops up frequently because it also means engagements
with customers, the bread and butter of geisha work. "Konban
o-zashiki ga kakaru" (Tonight I've got a zashiki) means "I'm
working tonight."[1] Some geisha feel that their professional lives
have two aspects: gel, art, the source of their pride and self-defi-
nition as geisha, and zashiki, the night-to-night partying that
they are actually paid to do. The geisha who are happiest in their
work are of course those for whom these two aspects coincide.

Some zashiki are memorable, some quite dull. Some are elegant banquets where every detail has been executed with care,
some are spur-of-the-moment decisions to drop in on so-and-so's
teahouse. After my debut as Ichigiku, I began to receive calls
from the Pontochō ochaya to appear at their zashiki. For formal
banquets I was usually given a week's notice, yet often enough
the telephone would ring around nine o'clock in the evening:

"*Erai sumimahen*, Kikuko, but could you come over right away, please?" I would drop whatever I was doing, struggle into kimono, and in half an hour be ready to bow at the entrance to a zashiki.[2]

The customers did not pay for Ichigiku's time because I was not registered to receive wages, but the okāsans usually gave me go-shūgi, a tip. The tips covered my beauty parlor expenses – which were not trivial, as I had to go twice a week in order for my hair to stay in shape for last-minute zashiki. In the early days I answered the calls not knowing whom I might meet. Customers often prodded an okāsan to call me because they were curious. Later, after I had come to know the Pontochō regulars, I would receive calls more like those of the other geisha, from customers I knew, requesting me to join their zashiki.

THE BEER CEREMONY

I first met the headmaster of the Urasenke School of Tea at a zashiki. Cosmopolitan and urbane, the idol of millions of Japanese women who study tea ceremony, Sen Sōshitsu is also a habitué of Pontochō. At our introduction, he insisted on shaking hands instead of bowing. I thought back to my study of the tea ceremony at age sixteen. I had been living with a Japanese family, and, along with the other two daughters, attended lessons in music, cooking, flower arranging, and the tea ceremony. We belonged to a local branch of the Urasenke School of Tea.

Once, in the spring, our class had taken an overnight train trip from our small town in Kyushu (Japan's southernmost island) to Kyoto to make a pilgrimage to the Urasenke mansion. Hundreds of tea classes from all over Japan do this every year, and our group was hardly important enough to be allowed a glimpse of the master himself. Now, a decade later, here I was, being challenged to a beer-drinking contest by the grand master Sen. "If mother could only see me now," I thought to myself, remembering my first Japanese okāsan in Kyushu.

The point of the challenge was not how much beer one could consume, but how fast. Mr. Sen swallowed an entire tumbler-full in a single gulp, a trick that would have done a fraternity man proud. I conceded defeat immediately. This zashiki had started several hours earlier, and the only person still steady on her feet by the time I arrived was the maiko. It is impolite to be sober when others are not, so newcomers to a party are encouraged to get drunk as soon as possible. Fortunately, I have a high tolerance for alcohol, so I was in better shape than the others at the close of this zashiki.

By eleven, the mistress of the teahouse could no longer stand up. Ichiko, the maiko Ichiwaka, and I undressed her, pulled out her bedding, and covered her with a quilt. Two semi-sober geisha saw the guests out to waiting cars and then staggered home themselves. The teahouse was quiet then, except for the snoring coming from the okāsan's room. We three who had put her to bed sat in the adjoining parlor eating bowls of rice with tea. Ichiko had kept her composure as long as she was standing up, but as soon as she sat down it was plain that she was very drunk too.

"Why are you studying geisha?" she asked between mouthfuls of rice. "Geisha are no different from anybody else." Ichiwaka lowered her eyes and kept eating, a napkin spread over the folds of her magnificent maiko's kimono. Maiko don't drink because it is unseemly, not because they are under age; the fact that it is against the law is of minor consideration. Ichiwaka thus was sober and a little uncomfortable, both with the inelegant snoring rattling the paper doors and with Ichiko's belligerent questioning. The maid, looking worried, poked her head in. "You make sure Ichiko gets home all right," she said to Ichiwaka, and to me she said, "Are you okay?" I assured her that I could manage.

As I walked back to the Mitsuba I thought about Ichiko's insistence that geisha were no different from other women. This very evening she had danced an acrobatic folk dance, nibbled snacks from the tips of the tea master's chopsticks, and drunk herself silly. What "ordinary" Japanese woman ever does such things? I was reminded of a comment by a professor of religion I had met the week before. He had spent several years in America. "Japanese wives are generally uninteresting," he had said. "They're so confined to the home that they can't talk about anything. We have a real need in Japan for women who can interact with men socially." "That's why there are geisha in Japan," I reminded him. He was horrified. Never having met a geisha in his life, he had been thinking back to his student days in America, where wives routinely join their husbands on social occasions. "Well then, wives should be more like geisha, and geisha should all get married," he stated. "Maybe that would solve the problem." I thought to myself that most Japanese women I knew – geisha *and* wives – did not really see the problem he saw.

FUTAMI, THE LITTLE MOTHER OF DAI-ICHI

In mid-April 1976 the Japan National Railways went on strike, predictably. The rail workers always go on strike in the spring, and the ensuing transportation blockage ties up the entire country. I was called to a zashiki during the strike on a Friday evening. Ichiume, Ichiteru, and Ichiwaka were invited, too. For us, getting to the Dai-Ichi teahouse was a matter of walking a block, but the guests coming from Osaka were delayed two hours. While we waited for them in the Dai-Ichi, we watched television in the okāsan's quarters. She was drinking Scotch and stubbing out a series of half-smoked cigarettes. She wore a sloppy housedress and was obviously not planning to attend this zashiki. Sensing her bad mood, we were all very quiet. She was especially curt with Ichiume, for some reason.

The customers that evening were not hers, but Futami's. Futami had worked in the Dai-Ichi for six years. She had once been a member of the Pontochō geisha ranks under the name of Ichifumi, but she had dropped out to work permanently in this one teahouse. She would most likely be the next okāsan. The geisha sometimes call her the "little mother" of the house – as opposed to the "great mother," who had died recently, and the just plain "mother" who had taken over after that and was now sitting slapping cards onto the table in a game of solitaire. With some relief we welcomed the guests when they finally arrived.

The occasion of this zashiki was a birthday party. There were three guests: the host, who was one of Futami's loyal customers, his mistress, and his friend, whose birthday it was. There were five geisha including the maiko, Futami, and me. The guests had already eaten dinner in an expensive French restaurant in Osaka, but that was several hours ago, and the birthday honoree, a man of simple if not countrified tastes, was ready to give his birthday dinner its proper finish: rice.

Futami had planned the menu in advance, and the dishes had been brought in by delivery boys on bicycles. First there was bean curd – small tumuli of tofu, handmade in a temple in western Kyoto. Fresh and mild, each mound contained a dollop of biting Chinese mustard. There was sushi of a shellfish called *akagai*, the biggest I'd ever seen; sashimi of the first bonito of the season; and rice made festive for the birthday as *chirashi-zushi*. Of course everything was washed down by cup after cup of warmed sake. Ichiteru exhibited her talent for imitating famous Kabuki actors, and Futami played exaggerated renditions of various musical styles on her shamisen.

The birthday guest was having a great time. The more he drank, the more loquacious he grew. We became the audience for anecdotes about the genesis of his *vita sexualis*. He claimed to have discovered the intrigue of the opposite sex at the tender age of seven – that he would play doctor with a neighbor's six-year-old daughter, giving her a penny to show herself. Once, he said, he had tried masturbating into the hollow tube of a sea anemone, but it had stung him with its tentacles. "Naturally," said Futami, "it must have thought that was strange prey – a long, one-eyed fish."

Her birthday present for the guest, which she brought out with a flourish when he seemed about to fall asleep from sake, was a contraband Swedish pornographic magazine. Such items are hard to obtain in Japan, where obscenity laws ban the depiction of pubic hair. These laws are said to be rigidly enforced by a corps of middle-aged ladies with magic markers, hired to black over the offending areas of imported magazines.[3] The nudes in the issues of *Playboy* sold in Japan, for example, all wear discreet inky patches. Futami had gotten the Swedish magazine from a customer who had smuggled it back from a foreign city. The recipient of this treasure roused himself sufficiently to page through it, and he made a big fuss about protecting the innocent eyes of Ichiwaka, the maiko. Ichiume and Ichiteru, however, were teased about being virgins.

Finally the birthday guest fell asleep with his head on my lap, and this zashiki petered to a close. He had to be awakened to leave, which Ichiume did with glee. After sending off the guests, we geisha returned to the party room and finished off the remaining sushi. The okāsan, in a better humor, emerged from her room to have a bite, too. After the customers go home, geisha feel that they are entitled to a drink. Their workday over, they can relax. Even when their zashiki end by midnight, geisha are seldom ready to sleep before 2:00 A.M.

Futami has a ready smile. She is kindly and plump, looking more like a kindergarten teacher than anybody's idea of a geisha. She had, in fact, once wanted to teach children. In junior college she majored in home economics, but she dropped out to work in the karyūkai, skipping the maiko stage because she was already past twenty-one. Her mother had floated in and out of the mizu shōbai, her father was unknown, and, when Futami needed to work, becoming a geisha seemed a natural option. Her dream of working with children has faded, and she is childless at thirty-nine.

I liked Futami immensely, as did everybody else in Pontochō. She is good-natured, humorous, and sympathetic. The position of okāsan in the geisha world (which Futami did not technically hold) has two sides. "Mother" implies warmth and nurturance, as we think of the term "motherly," but also, and more important in geisha society, mother means someone who has authority and deserves respect. The mothers run the show in Pontochō, as the geisha and the regular customers well know. In the teahouse Dai-Ichi, the okāsan is given deference and courtesy, but I doubt that the geisha ever went to her with their problems. Futami, though not the okāsan, is more motherly. Though she is not a geisha any more, she has numerous customers who appreciate these qualities and enjoy her company. They often call to take her out to dinner.

As Ichigiku, I attended more zashiki at the Dai-Ichi than at any other single teahouse. Sometimes the maid would call me on behalf of the okāsan, but more often Futami would call, inviting me along to a party for one of her many loyal customers. The last thing one could call her is a prima donna, yet when Futami left the room for any reason her absence was felt immediately. She kept a zashiki going with stories that were really no more than chatter about everyday things – made entertaining because Futami was telling them.

At one of Futami's zashiki, a favorite customer had brought his old high school teacher. The teacher in turn had brought his wife. This was rather unusual, I thought, for I had seen a wife at a zashiki only when someone entertained a foreign client whose spouse had accompanied him to Japan. Then, conforming to the American notion of socializing as couples, the Japanese businessman might bring his own wife, and this would often be her first chance ever to attend a party with geisha. Still, I could not imagine that one of Futami's parties would be as stiff as the wife-attended zashiki I had been to before.

Everyone got very drunk and sentimental, as it turned out, including the wife. We went through several rounds of rock-paper-scissors, where the losers had to drink cups of sake and the geisha usually won. Futami treated the wife as she would any guest, making her feel welcome and comfortable. Ichiume and Mameyuki were not a bit inhibited from their usual flirting with the men; but an understanding seemed to exist among the women that this was the geishas' job.

At one point, the teacher's wife, emboldened by sake, said, "This is a bit immodest, but there is something I've always wondered about and would like to ask as long as I'm here." Her husband looked at her with mild surprise as she continued: "Those *rin no tama* I've heard about – were they for a woman's pleasure or for a man's?"

Futami cocked her head. "That's a good question," she said after thinking a moment. "What's a rin no tama?" asked Ichiume.

A rin no tama is a hollow metal ball a little larger than a quail's egg. Inside it is another, solid ball that makes a gentle click as it rolls about. Nestled deep inside the vagina, the rin no tama moves when a woman does, not exciting great waves of pleasure exactly but making her aware of that part of her body. "You know, I tried it once," said Futami, "and it was no big deal. It made me giggle every time I felt the 'clink.' My guess is that it's

151

really for a man's pleasure. A man would probably get a kick out of that little clink every time he entered."

"That reminds *me* of a story," said Mameyuki. "Once there was a lady who heard that kumquats were good for the same purpose, so she rushed to a nearby fruit store and asked the grocer for kumquats. 'Madam,' he said, 'I regret that I'm all out of kumquats, but I have some lovely oranges – how about those?' 'Don't be silly,' snapped the woman, 'oranges wouldn't do at all.'" "Kumquats!" exclaimed Futami, when she had recovered from her laughter. "I'll never be able to eat one with a straight face again!"

When the teacher and his wife left at midnight, the geisha all said goodbye with apologies to the wife for causing her any embarrassment. "On the contrary. Indeed, quite the contrary," beamed the lady.

During the course of this zashiki, two geisha from our number left to go on to other parties, and Ichiteru joined us. Any lengthy zashiki in a teahouse will have a changing of the geisha guard late in the evening. The mothers usually have a rough idea where everybody is working on a particular night, and if a customer wants to call a certain geisha on the spur of the moment, the mothers can find out quickly where she is. They may not always be able to get her to come, but an okāsan with clout will usually be successful. Even more than the actual guests, the mothers wield influence over the geisha in this respect.

At midnight, Ichiteru, Ichisen, Ichigiku, and Futami remained. After seeing off the teacher and his wife, Futami's customer took us out for yakitori, the grilled chicken mini-shishkebabs that can be a snack or a meal, depending on how many one eats. The bill is figured by the number of bamboo skewers piled up on the customer's empty plate, and by 1:00 A.M. the five of us had accumulated quite a few. Our benefactor paid for the lot, yawned, and had Futami call him a cab. We all saw him to the car, but Futami, Ichisen, and I decided to stay and drink a while longer. Ichiteru got into the cab.

After they had left, I asked Futami whether the two were having an affair. "Ichiteru?" she snorted, "and Kohda? Don't be silly. He's just giving her a ride home." "Oh, I see," I said. Then,

Pontochō's American Geisha, Ichigiku,
with a guest at a geisha party.

"But they could be headed off to a hotel right now, and nobody would know, would they?" "People would find out," said Futami. "Kohda's my old friend, anyway, so I would know." I hadn't meant to pry into Ichiteru's affairs, but I was curious about how and when a geisha would be able to arrange a rendezvous with a patron. It would be difficult to conduct a love affair in secret, that was certain.

We ordered a final round of beer and lingered over it. Futami was not particularly anxious to rush home that evening. I had the feeling that most of the administrative work at the teahouse fell on her plump shoulders, and that she also bore the brunt of the okāsan's ill-humors. She took such treatment with good-natured forbearance, but this night she seemed a little weary. She confessed that sometimes she felt in Kyoto that she was living in a fishbowl. "I might buy land somewhere," she said, "maybe in America. What if I started my own teahouse in America – there surely wouldn't be much competition." "It would never work," I told her. "American wives wouldn't put up with the sort of thing

153

that went on at tonight's zashiki." Ichisen nodded. "Americans get divorced at the least little thing, I hear. A woman can support herself in America on the alimony from three divorces. Is that true? Maybe that would be a good plan . . ."

"*Ahorashii* – that's ridiculous," said Futami. Ichisen claimed to look forward to running a teahouse of her own someday. "It's a real headache," Futami told her, "all the finances, arranging things for this guest and that – you've got it easy now as a geisha. I'd trade places with you in a minute." They disagreed on the difficulties of their respective positions for a while, until we noticed we were the only customers left. It was 2:15 in the morning. "Let's go," said Futami, finishing the last inch of beer in her glass. Outside, it was chilly and we huddled together on the corner watching for a cab. The cherry blossom season had peaked, and petals from some tree we couldn't see had blown into a little heap at the curb. Futami stirred them with her toe.

ALONE IN GION

I had come to Japan to learn about geisha in general but found myself identifying with Pontochō in particular. The more zashiki I attended as one of the Pontochō contingent, the more I felt like a member of it, and the more I was treated as such. When one of my okāsan's longtime customers invited me to a zashiki where some Americans would be guests, I accepted without a second thought. I had done this before because I was able to include interpreting as one of my "arts." This zashiki was to be held in the elegant Doi restaurant, one of the beautiful old mansions once built by wealthy families as summer homes in the hills to the east of the city. I was invited as a guest that evening; all of the attending geisha came from Gion.

Gion is roughly double the size of Pontochō: there are twice as many geisha, twice as many teahouses. It is probably more than twice as well known in Japan, for the name Gion has become synonymous with Kyoto geisha. I knew a number of Gion geisha from my shamisen lessons and from interviews, yet I didn't see any familiar faces that evening. But they all seemed to know about me; and as the zashiki progressed, several of them took the opportunity to sneer at Pontochō. One of the older geisha was extremely polite, itself a form of insult, as she commented on the kimono I was wearing.

This was the first time I had gone to a zashiki by myself. As a Pontochō geisha, I couldn't help taking umbrage at the subtle gibes. I had to remind myself that, as an anthropologist, I was acquiring insight into the larger geisha society of Kyoto. The maiko danced the Gion Kouta – "dear lovely Gion, the dangling obis" runs the refrain of this well-known song – with the maiko twirling around to show off their obis from the back. Later, when they had rejoined us at the table, the maiko too denigrated the way Pontochō maiko dance the piece. They had completely absorbed the superior attitude of their older sisters.

"Only Gion dances in the Inoue style," said one geisha whom I engaged in conversation. "You have to start dance when you are five years old to be a true Gion geisha." She was giving me the official line that portrays geisha from this area as artistic marvels, born and bred in Kyoto in an atmosphere of tightly controlled discipline. I knew from the other Gion geisha I had met that this was not strictly true. Gion, not Pontochō, recruits non-Kyoto girls for three- to five-year stints, shaping them into the required mold of Kyoto geishahood. One of my fellow kouta students was such a person. Her time in Gion was almost over, and she was gladly going back to her home city of Hiroshima.

At first this young woman had enjoyed being a geisha, but because she had not started out as a maiko, she was accorded only second-class citizenship by the geisha who had come up through the maiko ranks. By her third year she had grown tired of this treatment. Outsiders are seldom aware of these hierarchies within a hanamachi. To a certain extent Pontochō had the same inner differences, but not, it seemed to me, to the degree I saw in Gion.

Ichiriki

I had one other opportunity to attend a zashiki in Gion as the only Pontochō geisha. I had met one of okāsan's old customers, the president of a Tokyo publishing firm, in Pontochō, and he invited me to come to the teahouse Ichiriki the following night for a zashiki he was hosting.

Ichiriki is the most famous teahouse in Japan.[4] It is a large old building with attractive, dusky red walls, located a block from Gion's Geisha Theater and a block from the Gion Shrine. It is known as the ochaya where Ōishi Kuranosuke, the leader of the Forty-seven Rōnin, pretended to lead a life of debauchery while secretly plotting his revenge against the lord who had provoked his master's death. Although I did not look forward to another evening as the lone Pontochō representative in Gion, I was eager to see the inside of the renowned and exclusive Ichiriki.

I informed my okāsan of this invitation and told her my qualms about going to Gion. "Don't be such a coward," she said. "You've been especially invited, which is probably not the case for any of the Gion geisha who will be there tonight." Still I was nervous. "What shall I wear?" I asked her, low in confidence after the last time. She loaned me one of her unlined (hitoe) kimono and an obi with a dyed design to go with it. The month of May was past the season for lined kimono and embroidered obi, but too early for the ro (open weave) of summer. When I arrived at Ichiriki at 6:30 P.M., the proprietress greeted me at the door. She was friendly and I felt more at ease.

This time I was a geisha rather than a guest. I accompanied the Gion geisha – there were only four – into the zashiki, where the fifteen guests were waiting. We distributed ourselves somewhat unevenly around the table and began to pour sake for toasts. There was nothing particularly memorable about this party. The geisha did not even dance. When the zashiki ended at 8:30, rather early as these things go, the Gion geisha all disappeared, running off to other engagements. This seemed a little rude, as the Tokyo customers were hardly ready to call it a night, yet they were at a loss about where to go here in Kyoto.

The host waved me over to his seat. "Give your okāsan a call and let's all go to the Mitsuba." I called home, but the auntie answered the phone and said okāsan was out. I had forgotten that this was the night of her Kyoto Cuisine Club party. I went back to consult with him. "Well, how about some other place in

Pontochō? I'll leave it up to you," he said. Again I went off to make some calls, but nowhere was there room for a sudden party of fifteen.

I felt responsible because this was one of my okāsan's customers. "I know a place," I said. "It's a bar, but a very interesting one. The man who runs it is like an old-time male geisha." I called and was told the zashiki-style room was open, and to come right over. This bar was the sort of place that turned away customers the master didn't know. Kyoto is full of bars that are more like private clubs, really. Someone from out of town with no local entrée has little chance of getting a foot in the door.

The okāsan of Ichiriki was half embarrassed, half relieved – relieved because the guests were not simply being turned out to wander the city, embarrassed that I took charge rather than the Gion geisha. I was curious why the man hosting this party, supposedly one of my okāsan's loyal customers, should have arranged a zashiki in Gion, especially since he obviously had no special pull here. He, too, seemed to feel that an explanation was in order because as soon as we were settled into the bar he took me aside. First he thanked me for helping him save face in front of his colleagues, who looked to him as the Kyoto connoisseur, and then, apologetically, he said he had felt obliged to hold the zashiki at Ichiriki in Gion to impress them. "It's the only teahouse that any of them had ever heard of," he concluded.

The bar I chose turned out to be perfect. The person who supervised it and provided entertainment was a man, called the "master," an English loan word used as the male counterpart of "mama." I had described him as an otoko geisha because, like the original male geisha, he sang, played shamisen, and could hold his own as a traditional comedian. The master had professional names in kouta, *hauta*, nagauta, and *kiyomoto*, and could also do *gidayū*, *tokiwazu*, and *itchū-bushi*. Most in demand, however, were his renderings of *dodoitsu*, a late eighteenth-century style of popular song that usually contains a funny twist and a ribald pun in the last line.[5] People listened to the first part with one ear, then put down their drinks waiting for the punch line. The master would pause, a sly grin on his face, and someone would call out, "*Sore de* (And then) . . ." I usually missed the point, but everyone else in the place broke up with laughter.

Japanese Humor

The group I had shepherded into the bar consisted of writers, editors, and publishers: all men involved with words, who seemed to relish the master's talents for word play. Japanese humor leans heavily toward punning, and with the great number of homophones in the language, puns are not as contrived as they usually are in English. To be clever with words is a tremendous asset for a geisha, and in the end such talent will probably take her further than a pretty face. The emphasis on conversation in the zashiki makes these parties doubly uninteresting to foreigners, translated Japanese humor being about as flat as day-old ginger ale. Boredom is not merely a matter of ignorance of the language, however. Japanese humor contains a large element of what appears to foreigners as opaque or just plain silly.

What tickles the funnybone of one culture may shock another and leave a third scratching its head.[6] A situation is thought humorous largely when it is incongruous, when it is somehow different from what is expected. What is comical depends on what is proper. Whenever the rules of any culture are bent (not broken: that's usually not funny at all) there is a good chance that people will laugh – if not at the time, then in the retelling. Japanese society is firmly corseted with strictures that define appropriate behavior for almost every social situation. They are not always followed, of course; it would be a mistake to think that Japanese behave with ritual punctiliousness all the time. But the awareness of the existence of the rules is apparent even as the Japanese depart from them. Just because these cultural rules are so fine-grained and pertain to such a detailed level of behavior, that much more possibility exists for them to be bent and for humor to be found. Of course one must know the rules to get the joke, which is why this faux pas category of Japanese humor will leave non-Japanese knitting their brows.[7]

Foreigners can accept the idea that humor is the last bastion of cultural inscrutability and not be disturbed when they don't understand. Many Americans appear more dismayed with what they *do* perceive and recognize, namely the more farcical, slapstick aspects of Japanese humor. Japanese undeniably demonstrate a schoolboy silliness and delight in gutter-level stories and jokes, regardless of social class. Given the appropriate place, Japanese can be silly and scatological in inverse proportion to their propriety in everyday life. One such appropriate place is of course the zashiki.

Geisha must be able to cater to the "naughty boy" mode that Japanese men often adopt when drunk, and they must endure a certain amount of giggly poking. If all this becomes too much, geisha can counter by adopting the scolding tone of a stern mother. Japanese men seem to enjoy this, too, and play the role of the spoiled *bōya* (little boy) with relish. American men are usually appalled if they see their Japanese colleagues indulging themselves in this totally "unmanly" fashion.

In fact, much of the laughter caused by the touching, the party games, and the slapstick that Japanese find so hilarious reminds Americans of nothing so much as their own childhood amusements. In adulthood we Americans are supposed to maintain an ironic distance from such foolery, but Japanese are constrained by no such scruples. For sheer exuberance, silly and fatuous as it may appear to Americans, this sort of humor has no parallel. It may be a kind of paradise in a playpen, but within the walls of a zashiki, Japanese men are permitted a freedom found nowhere else.

After the dodoitsu and more drinks, the master loaned me his shamisen and I sang several kouta. My covey of neophyte guests was surprised and impressed. By the time we left the bar, most of them were ready to return to their hotel. I led the four who were interested in a midnight snack across the river to Pontochō, to an old noodle shop that was a favorite among the geisha for their own late dinners. A Pontochō maiko was there with her okāsan. "Guests of yours, Kikuko?" inquired the okāsan as we took a table. "Yes," I replied. "Guests from Tokyo."

The host of the evening's gathering handed me an envelope before heading back to his hotel. "Okini," I thanked him, tucking it into the front fold of my kimono. When I opened it at breakfast the next morning, I found four 10,000-yen notes (about $120) as go-shūgi. I was a bit taken aback at the amount, but okāsan beamed from across the table. "You did fine last night, you deserve it," she said. "Popular these days, aren't you?" sniffed the old auntie as she cleared away the breakfast dishes.

DINNER DATES

Sometimes geisha go out to dinner with their customers. Except for the fact that here, too, their company is paid for, the occasion looks like an ordinary dinner date. Once when my okāsan was out of town I received an invitation through her friend Korika for dinner at a nearby steak house. Korika was making the arrangements for a customer who had also invited her, Satomi, Ichiume, and Ichiteru. My okāsan would have been included had she been at home. The host planned to take the two mothers, two geisha, and me to a dinner that would cost close to $50 per person, plus the wages of Ichiume and Ichiteru.

We ate our fill of meat that night, and ended the evening with our host singing military songs in Satomi's bar. Although he had fed us royally, I found him officious and rather unpleasant. "Here," he said to me at the end of the evening, "theater money. You like Kabuki? Go see some Kabuki." I had seen him confer with Korika and obtain an envelope from her earlier. I thanked him and put away the envelope he gave me. In Japan, one never opens any gift in the presence of the giver. I was tired by the time I got home, so I didn't open this go-shūgi envelope until the next morning.

I had expected around 5,000 yen ($15), the price of a Kabuki theater ticket. Instead, the envelope contained 50,000 yen. My immediate suspicion was that this was an advance "tip" for presumed future favors. I put the money back in the envelope, wishing my okāsan weren't out of town. It irked me to think that as long as the money was in my possession the man might be assuming that his broad hint was accepted. As soon as I was reasonably sure she would be awake, I walked down to Korika's teahouse for advice.

"Good morning, Kikuko," Korika called from the kitchen. She emerged into her sitting room, where I showed her the contents of the envelope. "Well, that's a generous go-shūgi," she remarked. "Did you want to talk to me about something?"

She didn't seem to understand, so I asked her straightforwardly. "What does he expect from me?" She raised her hands, exclaiming, "Oh, no. You've misinterpreted it. I see what you're thinking, but you needn't worry. He asked me before he gave you the money whether it was proper for you to get tips. I didn't know exactly how much it was going to be, but I'm not too surprised. Really he wasn't trying to pull something – he's got a lot of money to throw around, and it makes him feel big to do that. You impressed him, that's all, and you said thank you last night. That's the end of it."

"Is that really true, Okāsan?" I was still not convinced, but with her repeated assurances I decided to take her word. I never heard from the customer again. When my own okāsan returned from her trip several days after this incident, I told her the story over a cup of tea. "You shouldn't have gotten so upset in the first place," she said after I had finished. "The mothers who were along knew what was happening. You can trust them to watch out for you. At least you went and talked to Korika before doing something rash."

As I listened to her, it struck me afresh to what an extent the mothers are intermediaries between guests and geisha. The mothers have their own customers, whose interests they keep in mind, but they juggle those with the interests of the geisha. Striking a balance is the secret to their success; but they can be criticized by either side to the extent that they have a say in the activities of both. The mothers do watch out for the geisha – part of the meaning of "mother" is someone who protects those who are "daughters." From the customers' point of view, though, this can sometimes be regarded as interference.

Once in a while some of the familiar customers of Pontochō would take me out to dinner alone and confide their opinions, of geisha in general and geisha in particular. Perhaps they thought of me as someone in that society but not of it, who could understand their long and sometimes complicated relations to the flower and willow world. One man complained that he had given up on romance with geisha because the mothers always entered in. Yet this same customer preferred attending zashiki with geisha over bars with hostesses because, he said, he felt easier with geisha, knowing that they were taken care of by their houses. With hostesses he couldn't tell, and the idea that they might be lonely women with tragic stories unnerved him.

For him, the zashiki was a nicely circumscribed place of amusement that did not encroach on his orderly everyday life. "But you're such a popular guest with everybody," I said to him, "surely you would have no trouble choosing a geisha who would be happy to have you as a patron." "No, no. I don't want the bother of it," he said. The reason he liked going to zashiki was because he could flirt but not get too involved. Now that he was in his mid-forties, with his family secure and his job running along smoothly, he didn't need a torrid romance interrupting his life.

COCKTAILS VERSUS OSHAKU

A Japanese *enka*i, or party, is different from an American one. We usually think of parties as social functions for a mixed group. If it is a same-sex party, such as a bridal shower or a stag party, the occasion is usually qualified as a special variety of this larger notion of party. In contrast, a Japanese enkai is frequently a gathering of the same sex, for it is in groups of men with men, or women with other women, that Japanese can best relax and reveal their most exuberant selves. The main exception, if it *is* to be a mixed group, is a geisha party.

A group of geisha with guests is radically different from a Western-style gathering of couples. Consumption of liquor leading to a heightened degree of conviviality is an aim of both, but an American party and a Japanese enkai have separate styles for accomplishing this. These differences can be distilled into the differences between the American cocktail and the Japanese style of social drinking called *oshaku*.

Shaku means "to pour [sake, for someone else]." The word implies companionable drinking, an absolute prerequisite for a party atmosphere. The stereotype of desolation for a Japanese is the lone drinker pouring sake for himself or herself. To do oshaku is the geisha's most important function at a party and her performing it establishes the proper festive tone.[8] "To drink sake poured by one's wife" is not at all the same thing; and this proverb is a catch phrase for a henpecked husband, conveying its gentle irony in the clashing images of a wife doing oshaku. In Japan the form that drinking takes is as important as the actual alcoholic content for establishing the convivial atmosphere.

Japanese think that the cocktail, in contrast, shares many characteristics of its American imbibers.[9] Having a cocktail means having to assert individual preference in choosing a particular drink, receiving the whole thing at one time, impersonally poured and delivered, and, in the end, taking responsibility for getting one's own glass refilled. Everyone seems encapsulated, holding his individual drink. There is no quick way to break the ice by an easy gesture of exchanging cups. Japanese tend to find this way of socializing unsatisfying. One must wait until the actual alcohol takes effect before barriers really break down. The stand-up, mixed group cocktail party has yet to make any headway at all in Japan.

I had been attending zashiki in Kyoto as a geisha for half a year when I had occasion to spend a few days in Tokyo at the home of the parents of an American friend. After having been immersed in my life as Ichigiku, sitting on chairs and speaking English seemed a little odd. One evening I was included in a cocktail party given by my friend's parents for three other American couples, and to my Japanese-adjusted eyes the interactions were strange indeed.

Mr. H., the host, mixed drinks and took them around on a tray, fulfilling the man's responsibility as host. From the Japanese perspective, it seemed slightly ludicrous to see this dignified gentleman doing what geisha would have done for an equivalent group at an enkai. Mrs. H. was the perfect hostess, smiling and radiating sincerity to her guests. Because I had heard her speaking ill of the others before they arrived, the effect was spoiled somewhat for me.

The geisha, too, have one face before the guests arrive and a different one in front of them, but I had never been so struck in the geisha world as I was by these sour remarks followed by sweet social smiles. The cocktail party ended in a state of high inebriation as the women exchanged kisses on the cheeks and received lingering squeezes from the men, and the men exchanged hearty handshakes. Again, I felt like a stranger in my own culture, for in partying, Japanese do not touch one another in quite the same way. A great deal of physical touching occurs during the course of an enkai, but the farewell is the time to draw back. Perhaps the contrast stands out because Americans consider greeting and parting as the only times when physical contact is permissible – and so they make the most of it.

True Intentions and Social Facades

The ability to plow smoothly through social life often depends on masking one's real opinions, in Japan as in America. The wide gap between true intentions and social facades is recognized in both cultures, yet the reaction to this social reality is somewhat different in each.

The Japanese express this human dilemma by the concept of *honne* versus *tatemae*, the truly felt as against the socially required, and they see the dichotomy as a necessity of civilized life. In the example of a situation from a novel or a movie, everyone feels the pathos of the mother who sits stiffly correct, conversing with her son's teacher – even as we know that her heart is broken by the recent death of that son. In Japan she will be admired all the more for not breaking down and exhibiting her true feelings. The observer feels them all the more keenly because they are contained. Japanese know that certain kinds of social situations demand tatemae. There is nothing insincere about facades. They are a ready-made way of helping people through social occasions. One simply cannot get by wearing one's honne on one's sleeve.

The American version of this human predicament casts suspicion on the social facade and tends to view it as deception, in opposition to true intentions. We feel that bad faith has intervened if the gap between honne and tatemae becomes too wide. Mrs. H.'s guests would have been hurt if they had heard her remarks earlier in the day – or they would have had their necessarily cynical opinion of her confirmed. Although social realpolitik demands awareness of these two states, somehow we are uncomfortable recognizing the fact too openly. This is yet another reason why Americans are suspicious of geisha.

"How could you enjoy such insincere flattery?" an American wife exclaims to her husband, just back from an enkai hosted by a Japanese colleague. She imagines geisha flocking around him, and she sees their behavior as reprehensible. They could not possibly be acting on their real feelings, she thinks. It is hard for her to accept that the geishas' actions are the required facade for their work, and that there is nothing necessarily insincere at the root of it at all. Riding home from zashiki where foreign wives were present, puzzled geisha have queried me about the daggers they felt flying from the eyes of those women across the language barrier. It makes them uncomfortable because Japanese wives do not react that way. It is, I think, a silent accusation of bad faith that lies behind the blank hostility.

CASUAL ZASHIKI

Some customers are as comfortable as an old shoe. Mr. Sato, for example, has been coming to Pontochō teahouses for a decade. He takes kouta lessons from the same teacher the Pontochō crowd does, and the geisha are very fond of him. Mr. Sato is not the sort of guest for whom they feel they must put on airs, and they blithely carry on quite frank discussions in his presence. Sometimes geisha call a familiar guest *oniisan* (older brother), and if he is elderly perhaps they will call him *otōsan* (daddy), but these are flirtatious gestures. Sato-san is actually *treated* like an elder brother, and that is not coquettish at all.

I shared the same genial relationship with Mr. Sato as did the other Pontochō geisha. As a fellow kouta student, he had seen my early struggles in learning to sing. He had encouraged me with praise and hints on technique that he had discovered over the years. Unlike many middle-aged businessmen who take a few kouta lessons to embellish their images as connoisseurs, Sato has a genuine interest in the songs. He asked me out to dinner once, and we spent the entire time discussing our favorite kouta images.

The restaurant where Mr. Sato and I had dinner was owned by another member of the kouta group, a man who had inherited his mother's ochaya and, with his wife's help, had transformed it from a teahouse into a restaurant. Ten years earlier it had become plain to him that Pontochō could not continue to support the same number of ochaya, but that his riverside location would be superb for a less specialized establishment. His restaurant, Uzuki, retains much of the flavor of the previous teahouse. Not all former teahouses in Pontochō have been able to make such a graceful transition. Near the Uzuki is the old ochaya Yamatomi, which has become a noisy, family-style eatery. It is a cheerful place, but the tatami mats are frayed, and it takes some effort to imagine its former elegance. Other defunct teahouses have simply been torn down, and modern concrete structures housing bars have squeezed themselves into the spaces.

After our meal at the Uzuki, Mr. Sato suggested continuing the evening at Korika's teahouse, so we called her and ambled over. Korika welcomed us at the vestibule wearing a cotton blouse and skirt – this was certainly going to be a casual zashiki. She rummaged around her kitchen for a snack to serve along with the beer and could only come up with simple dried sardines to roast over the gas flame in the kitchen. She knew we had come mainly for her company, not for food and frills.

This zashiki was musical but extremely low-key. Korika's voice was primarily trained in the kiyomoto style, and people with a knowledgeable ear said they could hear the kiyomoto manner even in her kouta. Like hearing an operatic voice sing a folk song, there was a certain odd charm to it.

Korika called Kazue, an older, shamisen-playing geisha, to join us. Kazue's repertoire was tremendous. After I had played the shamisen for every kouta I knew, Kazue took over. There was not one she wasn't familiar with. During a break, Sato asked my age, and I said I had been born in the year of the tiger. "I'm a tiger, too," said Kazue. That would have made her sixty-one years old, I figured.[10] As a general rule, the older the geisha, the more outspoken, and Kazue was no exception.

Kazue put her shamisen down, and Mr. Sato poured her a glass of beer. Then she began talking about men, and Korika and I joined in as if the lone Mr. Sato were not a representative of the very Japanese men we were discussing. He listened with curiosity and perhaps a bit of surprise.

"I'm happier now than I've ever been before in my life," claimed Kazue. "You know why? Because I don't have any danna to cause me trouble. As long as I can make it on my own I can't see any benefit to being tied to a man – begging your pardon, Sato-san."

Korika agreed with Kazue. "The one who gets the worst deal of all is the wife," she added. "A wife has to put up with everything foolish her husband does because, in the end, she has no power, no economic base, of her own. Men can have a wife, a mistress, and girlfriends on the side, yet can a woman do that? Hardly. It's really an unfair situation – begging your pardon, Sato-san."

Mr. Sato was not saying a word. It was a mark of how much the women liked him that they would talk this frankly to his face, but even though none of their conversation was directed at him personally, Sato could not help squirming.

"My choice would be either to be born a man or be born a geisha," said Kazue. "That's where the freedom is." "You've got a point," nodded Korika. "It can be painful to be a wife in Japan. Michiko [okāsan of the Mitsuba] says that wives feel at ease knowing their husbands are at zashiki with geisha rather than fooling around with hostesses or secretaries, but I think if a man takes a mistress, a wife will be just as upset even if it is a geisha."

Kazue was really warming to the topic now. "Even in the world of art, people at the top level are always men. Take shamisen, for instance: no matter how good a woman might get to be, she could never be the top master." "What do you expect?" commented Korika. "The whole thing is just a mirror of Japanese society." I asked them about the karyūkai as a society of women. Surely in the geisha world women attain high positions? "That's true enough," Korika concurred, but then she added, "It doesn't seem to offset the other disadvantages of being female, though." Mr. Sato added what was meant as a compliment: Take

167

the okāsan of the Mitsuba – now if she were a man she would really be somebody to deal with. A politician, what a politician she would make." It did not even occur to him to question why, as a woman, she could never parlay her skills with people into such a position.

Later, Kazue, Sato, and I left Korika's place to wander toward Gion. It was a beautiful night in early June, and we took our time walking over the Shijo Bridge. Sato didn't know Gion very well, so I suggested Kayoko's bar. Kayoko had been a geisha in Gion but had retired at age twenty-nine to be the mama of her own tiny bar. She was very tall and slender and had been one of the sources for my hand-me-down kimono. Kayoko was not there, but her bartender urged us in anyway. It was 11:00 P.M. when we arrived, 2:00 A.M. when we left. Kazue was cheerfully nonchalant the whole time, except during certain lags in the conversation, when I noticed that her eyes looked tired.

PART TWO

VARIATIONS

NINE

THE ELUSIVE GEISHA

Geisha are not as crafty as the politicians who devise schemes to create disorder and then profit from the ensuing situation by fattening their own bellies. Geisha at least have more grace and dignity than members of parliament.

Nagai Kafū, Ude Kurabe *(1937)*

FLOWER WARDS

IN 1976 THERE WERE approximately seventeen thousand geisha in all of Japan. Where were they to be found? This was the first question I faced in my study. I knew, of course, that there are geisha in Kyoto, the old capital. Picture postcards of Kyoto, if not of a temple scene, will most likely display smiling maiko or geisha as emblems of the city. Some postcards even combine the two motifs – a maiko with bowed head at a temple – thus dispensing a double dose of quintessential Kyoto. But geisha are also found in Tokyo, even though that aggressively up-to-date city would hardly use pictures of geisha to project its image to the outside world.

The geisha of Tokyo are a slightly different breed from their Kyoto sisters. I composed a questionnaire to investigate regional differences among geisha in several parts of Japan, and there were many. Geisha may be beloved and respected symbols of Kyoto, but among the ten million people of Tokyo they play but a limited role in public consciousness.

Geisha everywhere work out of communities called hana-machi, yet some hanamachi have more community spirit than others. In Kyoto, the women are likely to live in the hanamachi where they work, in a small house or apartment a couple of doors down from the teahouses where they see customers. Their sister geisha and the mothers live there too, and everyone sees everyone else casually on the street.

In Tokyo, by contrast, although all geisha must be affiliated with a hanamachi, they commonly live somewhere else and com-mute to their evening's work. Tokyo contains some twenty com-munities (compared to Kyoto's five). The best known and most prestigious Tokyo hanamachi cater to politicians and business-men of national stature, the leaders of Japanese society.

Financial and political power is highly centralized in contem-porary Japan, and Tokyo is the heart of it all. The two most famous Tokyo hanamachi, located in the central business-politi-cal district, are Shimbashi and Akasaka, both playgrounds for the rich and the influential. Everyone knows that many of Japan's behind-the-scenes political maneuvers and big business transac-tions take place here in the dining rooms of elegant old establish-ments, often in the presence of geisha. For the most part, this is accepted as the way things are done in Japan, although the term *machiai seiji* (teahouse politics) carries the same shady overtones we associated with "back-room politics."[1] Some geisha commu-nities in Tokyo have a considerably less glossy image than Shim-bashi and Akasaka – but I did not discover this until I began meeting geisha themselves and customers familiar with the back streets of the other hanamachi.

Kyoto and Tokyo are the two Japanese cities with the largest and most varied geisha populations. Outside these cities there are the *chihō*, "provincial," geisha. Most large Japanese cities have something that passes for a hanamachi, but the number of geisha in these has substantially dwindled, as a few examples will show. The populous city of Fukuoka, on the island of Kyushu, was once famous for its many high-spirited and brash *bazoku* geisha (bazoku means horse-riding tribes), but now only about eighty geisha remain in the entire city, a number approximately equal to that of Pontochō alone in Kyoto.[2] In other cities, such as the mid-

Kyushu provincial capital of Saga, geisha have vanished completely. Even the once thriving geisha communities in Osaka, Japan's second largest city, have largely disappeared, perhaps because the still numerous cognoscenti there have only to make a forty-five-minute train trip to patronize the Kyoto teahouses – a journey that is next to nothing by commuters' standards in modern Japan.

The sophisticated urban geisha tradition thus is mainly preserved in Tokyo and Kyoto; the *largest* groups of geisha, however, do not inhabit the big cities or provincial towns at all but are found in countryside resort areas. Natural sulfurous baths have been used for centuries in Japan as spas and recreation spots. Atami, a town on the Izu peninsula just an hour's train ride out of Tokyo, is the largest of these *onsen machi*, or "hot springs resort towns." Atami had a thriving population of over seven hundred geisha when I visited there in 1976.

The women of such resorts generally go by the name onsen geisha, a term with a derogatory ring and with overtones of sex for hire as well as low standards of artistic skill. Of course, fine dancers and musicians are still found in the onsen towns, but as a group, these geisha suffer a tarnished image in the popular imagination. One hears terms like *korobi* (roll-over) geisha, *shomben* (toilet) geisha, or Daruma geisha, who, like the papier-maché Daruma doll, are supposed to tumble over at the slightest nudge.

The more I found out about the geisha world, literally the world of flowers and willows, the more diverse it appeared. But soon I understood one thing. The common misunderstandings and arguments about the connection between geisha and prostitution spring from an indiscriminate collapsing of a wide variety of categories of geisha. Whereas in one sense we may speak of a Kyoto apprentice and an onsen geisha in the same breath as part of Japan's living geisha tradition, in another sense combining them at all is ludicrous. When I began my detailed look into the various characteristics that differentiate geisha – the part of the country where they work, the prestige of their particular hanamachi, their ages and so on – it became clear that I was dealing with a very complicated phenomenon indeed, and that making an easy general statement about "the geisha" would inevitably be misleading.

GEISHA AND WIVES

The modern world of flowers and willows seems to be an exotic garden, surrounded by a fence of tradition and closed to outsiders. I began my study with no idea what my chances were of being allowed to step behind the fence, but I decided to begin my research in Tokyo. I lived in a tiny apartment sublet through a Japanese friend in the United States, relatives of whom lived nearby. I often had dinner with his cousin and her husband, an editor for one of the big daily newspapers. They had a small, respectable house on a quiet street, and in terms of family background and education they were both part of Japan's upper-middle-class intelligentsia.

Yuriko's father had been a doctor. An only child, she inherited the house when he died in 1970. Her husband had married into her family and taken her last name, rather than the other way around.[3] The two of them lived together with Yuriko's parents in the house for many years until the doctor's sudden death, which was followed by his wife's death within a matter of weeks.

Yuriko had been very close to her parents. She had, in effect, never left home – not even at her marriage. The sudden loss of both father and mother had left her incapacitated with grief just when she was called upon to take the major responsibility for arranging a funeral for her socially prominent father. During this extremely difficult period, she told me, several of the geisha whom her father had known for many years helped her immensely.

Because geisha are expected to know social etiquette, and because their clients tend to be older, they are especially well versed in the intricate rules pertaining to Japanese funerals. On those occasions, special notices must be sent out, condolence gifts of money must be carefully noted, and reciprocal gifts of a precisely specified value must be returned to those people who bring a cash gift to the service. Several geisha from the prestigious hanamachi of Shimbashi, which her father had patronized, had led Yuriko by the hand through these social obligations. Yuriko had met the geisha before, although this was certainly her most intimate contact with them.

Geisha had visited the respectable, quiet house where Yuriko grew up twice a year: once in the first few days of January for the New Year season and once at the mid-summer Obon, the Buddhist festival of the ancestral spirits. These two holidays, which divide the Japanese year more or less in half, provide occasions for elaborate social exchanges of gifts. The geisha came to Yuriko's house with presents, not for her father, their customer, but for her mother: handkerchiefs, scented soap, sugar, a length of cloth. Yuriko's mother received the geisha in the sitting room, and their brief but cordial exchange would have contained phrases something like this:

GEISHA: "Thank you for your [husband's] business throughout the year.

MRS. S.: "I am indebted to you for taking care of things [for me] so well."

After a brief chat, the geisha would excuse themselves and proceed to the homes of their other important customers with similar presents and holiday greetings.

On occasions of this sort, two types of Japanese women whom one is tempted to see as polar opposites – the wife and the geisha – come together in a totally appropriate social meeting. The geisha pays deference to the wife, and the wife's place is to respond graciously, just as she would to any professional person contributing to her husband's business or social success. Although the lines between the private sphere of the Japanese home and the social world outside it are not as sharp as they once were, they still exist. Geisha and wives view each other from opposite sides of these lines.

The role of wife in Japan places a woman in the center of the home. She is not expected to socialize with her husband's colleagues, and indeed, she leaves that vitally important activity completely to her spouse. In the social sphere, the geisha (or their modern counterparts, the bar hostesses) take over. Many Japanese women are quite conscious of their positions as wives vis-à-vis geisha. They see the distinction in terms of complementarity: as a feminine division of labor, where neither side need be jealous because one identity does not overlap with the other.

Complementarity without antagonism came up often in my conversations with the wives of men who routinely patronize geisha. An American or a European wife would feel threatened and angry in this situation, altogether rejecting the thought that another woman might accompany her husband to social affairs, perform small services on his behalf and perhaps even be involved with him sexually. Any of these activities is an integral aspect of the role of wife as defined in European and American culture, and their performance by another woman threatens a wife's position in a fundamental way. Why then are Japanese wives usually so blasé about such matters?

The answer, as one would expect, lies in the cultural definition of the wife in Japan, and in Japanese expectations of what marriage implies. Looking for a spouse is not so much a hunt for the ideal romantic partner, as we tend to view the process, but rather, it follows from the social conviction that marriage is the appropriate thing to do when one reaches a certain age. One hears of "love marriages" all the time in modern Japan, as opposed to arranged marriages; but in fact these categories are not all that clear-cut. Even the affianced couple in a love match is likely to have sought the services of a go-between at some point. Of course it is desirable that a husband and wife be mutually attracted to each other, but romance is not necessarily the main pillar of marriage.

Marriage is one of the most important steps into social adulthood in Japan. A person who fails to make this step is considered a bit odd and out of the mainstream. Because a woman's adult social life is shaped most definitively by the roles of wife and mother, remaining single makes her even more a social anomaly than it does a man, for whom the roles of husband and father do not carry corresponding weight. Marriage also inevitably implies the bearing and raising of children. A young wife will usually become pregnant early. When children are born, her attention shifts almost completely to them, and the mother aspect of her domestic role then comes to overshadow that of wife. The initial de-emphasis on romance in Japanese marriages is further decreased when even the husband starts calling his wife "mama."

WIVES VERSUS GEISHA

From the viewpoint of American women's liberation, a middle-class Japanese woman is seen as almost totally constrained by the bonds of domesticity. What this view does not take into account, however, is that as a wife and mother, a Japanese woman attains the highest possible social approbation. As is well known, a Japanese husband usually hands his paycheck over to his wife, who will be responsible for planning the family budget. She doles out a weekly allowance for his personal expenses. The domestic realm may be a limited one, but within it the Japanese wife is as sure of herself and as confident of her authority as any company president. The outside world of her husband's work only rarely impinges upon her world, and she is not expected to be competent in the arts of entertaining. More becoming to her, it is felt, is a retiring modesty.

Geisha embody precisely those aspects of femininity that are absent from, or only incidental to, the role of wife. Where a wife is modest, a geisha is risqué. A wife is socially reticent; a geisha is witty and talkative. If a wife lacks romantic or sensuous appeal, a geisha, whether she sleeps with a man or not, has a certain sexual allure and can be an object of fantasy. The wife is devoted to her home and family. A geisha has no such ties. With all the oppositions between these two roles, a married geisha would indeed be a contradiction in terms.

Both wives and geisha derive their livelihood from their relations with men: as husbands or customers, respectively. Men, on the other hand, freely cross over the lines separating the women's spheres. On the face of it, such an arrangement would seem to lead to jealousy between the two groups of women, but in fact this is rare. It would be unusual for a geisha, with her professional code, to try to insinuate herself into the position of wife by badgering a customer to obtain a divorce. A wife would have reason to feel uneasy if her husband were having an affair with a bar hostess or a secretary at the office, but she would probably not feel so threatened by a geisha mistress.

Of the Japanese men who entertain using the services of the karyūkai, in any case, only a small number are actually able to keep geisha mistresses. And though a geisha may have (indeed, often hopes to have) one customer with whom she is involved in an intimate, long-lasting relationship, she will take pains to maintain a clientele of other steady customers whom she can depend upon for engagements and for patronage of her dance and music recitals. She may have many customers, but she virtually never has more than one patron.

Yuriko laughed to think that her father might have had a mistress; he was much too busy even if he had wanted to, she said, but he had been a popular customer with many of the geisha. She regretted that he was not alive now to take me to Shimbashi to meet some of his favorites. I asked Yuriko's opinion of the notion that geisha had become ordinary working women, as some people had told me. She disagreed.

In one sense, she thought, geisha would stand low in a ranking of occupations by prestige. They are, after all, part of the service industry, and the sexual aspect of their profession is always a matter of prurient speculation. On the other hand, geisha are, literally, artists, and the arts they profess are valued highly in Japanese society. The same classical dance or traditional music that geisha practice are part of the repertoire of attainments of a well-bred middle-class girl, who often is expected to take lessons in such arts before marriage. So although in one sense geisha are something less than ordinary working women, in another they are something more.

Both less and more, geisha cannot be fitted easily into preconceived categories based on social function or occupational prestige. An organization exists that claims national representation of geisha, and it has tried to give the profession a whitewash of respectability by disguising the less flattering realities and portraying it ultimately as no different from a nine-to-five secretarial job.[4] The organization is having a hard time convincing people. I

*Typical Kyoto postcard, showing
a pair of maiko at a temple.*

have also heard speculation that, in the future, geisha might be stripped of any erotic nuance and given a government subsidy for their arts, so that they would become straightforward public performers. Some people think this is how geisha could preserve their heritage in a prim and proper way. It could indeed happen, but I can't help but feel that a government-subsidized flower and willow world would be a pale hybrid indeed.

Marked as she is by both high and low prestige, the geisha and her place in Japanese culture remain elusively ambiguous. These ambiguities never coalesce into a state of contradiction; they are inherent in the very nature of geisha. One can look at the spectrum of the geisha world in purely socioeconomic terms and say that, on the lower end of the scale, in the hanamachi of the hot springs resorts, the low outweighs the high; to the contrary, at the upper end, the geisha of hanamachi like Shimbashi or Pontochō can be characterized as demonstrating the most refined side of

179

geisha life. Yet an irreducible element of high *and* low, prestige and ill repute, persists at any level of the flower and willow world, whether onsen town or Kyoto teahouse. Would one boast of one's connections with geisha or proudly present an evening of their entertainment to the visiting Queen of England? Most certainly. Would one want one's daughter to become a geisha? Probably not.

SERVICE

One of the most striking things about geisha is the fact that they do not marry. At the same time that they are symbols of Japanese femininity, they do not tread the social path pointed out as the proper one for women in general and followed by a good 98 percent of Japanese women. Instead, geisha live in communities of other women, among ritual mothers and sisters. The terminology echoes that of a convent, and in contrast with the "normal" life of wife/mother, the affinity between geisha and nuns is not as far-fetched as it might first appear. Both groups are marginal, and both have somewhat larger-than-life images that spark the curiosity of ordinary society. In more than a few cases, geisha have retired to Buddhist convents in their old age.[5] This seems neither inappropriate nor strange to Japanese.

The image of femininity embodied in geisha is complicated. Their work is naturally characterized as being part of the service industry yet they are anything but servile. The notion of a geisha as simpering slave to male whim is an absurd stereotype formed outside Japan. Neither are geisha simply glorified waitresses. Maids of the establishment handle the actual serving of food at banquets. Pouring a cup of sake for a customer is about the extent of the physical "service" expected of a geisha, and that is clearly more a ceremonial action than a functional one. It is de rigueur, in fact, for customers to return the favor by pouring a cup for the geisha.

Face-to-face interaction in Japanese society takes place either with superiors (literally, those above one's eyes) or with inferiors, "those below one's eyes." Seldom does a person meet another as his precise social equal. Indeed, there is no Japanese phrase meaning "someone at just eye level." The differences between superior and inferior are far from absolute, however. They shade off into fine gradations of hierarchy.

These nuanced ideas of superiority and inferiority provide the framework for the ritual of host and guest. Japanese etiquette prescribes that a true host place the guest before himself in all respects. He will insist that the guest sit in the place of honor, he will yield to the guest in the order of serving food or drink, and he will use special forms of speech to do his guest honor.[6] Geisha, not surprisingly, behave in the manner expected of a host in treating their customers, who are never referred to as anything but *okyakusama*, honored guests.

A host's major obligation is to make his guest feel comfortable and relaxed, thus giving him the opportunity to enjoy himself. If a geisha were asked what it is, precisely, that she is supposed to *do* at banquet engagements, she would undoubtedly give some form of this answer. As an English-speaking geisha from Akasaka wrote, "Our function is to act as 'oil' so that banquets and dinner parties may proceed smoothly."[7]

Acting as hosts, and not as maids, geisha are called upon to exercise initiative, individuality, and ingenuity in dealing with customers. They should be able to draw out a shy guest, turn the conversation toward subjects they know their customers are interested in, and generally be sensitive to the mood of the gathering as it develops. No one could accomplish such goals by being servile. Geisha are remarkably self-possessed women, I have found; and this, among other characteristics, sets them apart from the common bar hostess, who *is* likely to be a cynical panderer to the worst excesses of the Japanese male ego. The interaction between guest and geisha depends on mutual respect, and it is much less one-sided than many male-female interactions in Japan. A geisha usually gives as good as she gets. The older ones, especially, will brook no nonsense from rude customers.

The geisha's style thus is purely feminine, yet it lacks the qualities of meekness and subservience so often thought basic to Japanese womanhood. Sweet, well-mannered Japanese ladies are called *Yamato nadeshiko* (native wild carnations). Such fragile blossoms are rare in the flower and willow world. Instead, the willow (the *ryū* of karyūkai) is a particularly appropriate symbol of the geisha. She must have resilience to bend gracefully in many different directions, depending on the winds of fortune and the personalities of customers. In addition to flexibility, however, geisha are well known for their strong sense of loyalty toward their valued patrons. These are the qualities that would naturally lead a Shimbashi geisha freely and substantially to help the adult daughter of a mourned customer smooth the last of his formal public obligations.

Any Japanese will have an opinion about geisha, whether he has actually met one or not. I discovered this on numerous occasions. For me, such impressions, opinions, and prejudices became the elements of a picture of the geisha's place in Japanese society. Through Yuriko, an upper-middle-class housewife, I saw an aspect of the geisha that would have been obscured from a purely inside view. The connection between geisha and wives, the opposition of their roles mediated by men, was made apparent as Yuriko related the personal experiences of her whole family with the geisha of Shimbashi. From this perspective and others, I began to sense the complexities of the modern geisha world in Japan.

TEN

THE RISE OF AKASAKA

The great metropolis of Edo is honeycombed
with canals and waterways, and wherever they
flow, the water laps and washes the city's many
geisha. In Yanagibashi, the geisha bloom in
rivalry like primroses in the grass. Those mad
for chess go to Tachibana-chō, where they find
geisha who make music so heavenly one thinks
of the goddess Benten, while their beauty calls
to mind tales of Lady Komachi.

Ryūtei Tanehiko, Geisha tora no maki

BLOOMING IN RIVALRY

DURING THE 1830s, when Tanehiko's romance was written, geisha could be found in eight separate areas of the city of
Edo, now Tokyo.[1] Among these hanamachi, Yanagibashi
(Willow bridge) was the most stylish. Shimbashi and Akasaka,
which today are at the summit of the Tokyo geisha world, did not
even exist as geisha communities.

During the half-century between 1830 and 1880, the geisha
population of Edo/Tokyo grew from fewer than two hundred

Tachibana-chō (present-day Nihonbashi Sanchōme) was one of the first areas in
Tokyo where *odoriko* (dancing girls) performed. The mention here of Benten,
patron goddess of music and dance, is an allusion to this connection. Lady
Komachi was a Heian period poet who now serves as a conventional figure for a
beautiful woman.

women to approximately twelve hundred. By 1880, upstart Shimbashi had rocketed in fame and prestige to stand in first-class rivalry alongside Yanagibashi; a magazine called *Tokyo gijō* (Tokyo geisha: true romance) sponsored a survey of popular opinion in 1882 that proclaimed this ranking as its result. Akasaka is also listed in the survey, but only as the second last entry in the fifth class: "Some women try to pass themselves off as geisha in Akasaka, but they are nothing but prostitutes – operating illegally at that."

Shimbashi was perhaps the most popular geisha area patronized by the leaders of the Meiji government as they settled themselves into their new capital of Tokyo. A few of their former geisha friends from pre-Restoration days in Kyoto were induced to make the 250-mile move as well. Most of them set up shop in Shimbashi, managing the Tokyo equivalent of teahouses.[2] The patronage of government officials, so important since the turn of the century to the creation of any first-class Tokyo hanamachi, has continued to sustain Shimbashi now for almost a hundred years. Given the close relation between geisha and politicians, it is no wonder that different political factions tend to patronize not only different individual geisha and teahouses, but entirely different hanamachi. The flower wards bloom or fade in response.

Shimbashi now is associated with the staid political old guard, but in the 1870s, when it got its start, it attracted the Young Turks of the new regime. For those men, Yanagibashi was too closely associated with the old style of Edo. Likewise, in post-occupation Japan, newer political factions and younger leaders, though they have not completely ignored Shimbashi, have built up Akasaka from its somewhat sordid origins into its present glamorous position. Alas for the formerly proud Yanagibashi, it has slowly sunk into oblivion, although a few geisha still remain.

Today Akasaka has a reputation among Tokyo-ites as the most modern, most expensive, and most flamboyant of all the hanamachi. It attracts many of the leading Liberal Democratic Party politicians and other public officials on expense accounts. A total of 267 geisha were registered in the Akasaka kenban in 1975. They tend to be somewhat younger than the geisha of other hanamachi. The average age of geisha in general is currently around forty, but Akasaka geisha are preponderantly in their late twenties or early thirties.

Every hanamachi has something its geisha consider a strong point; for Akasaka, this is precisely the youth and stylishness of its members. The geishas' style, however, must be considered in the context of the overall pattern of permissible variation in the flower and willow world. Only within this pattern do variations among geisha areas take on their real significance. For example, even the chic Akasaka geisha must wear kimono to engagements, so their modishness must lie inside the subtle limits of Japanese traditional women's dress.

The basic shape, length, and form of women's kimono is fixed. Today's adult version consists of one underkimono (of which only the white silk collar band shows) and the kimono itself. The sleeves should be long enough to touch the wristbone, and the sleeve depth extends approximately to the waist, or a bit below, when an arm is held outstretched. The outfit is basically a flat robe lacking darts, shaping, or fasteners of any kind. It is held together by tying long, supple belts at the hip bone and the waist, secured finally with a wide, heavy obi. One last cord, the *obijime*, is threaded through a loop made in back by the sash, and it holds the obi in place. One cannot tamper with these basic and necessary elements of the costume. A sleeveless kimono, for example, is an impossibility. Consequently, most of the experimentation with kimono fashion takes place in color combinations and design.

In the mid-1970s, there was a vogue for kimono in light pastels with little or no design on the sleeve or hem – a striking departure from the previously popular rich, deep colors and all-over floral motifs. Furthermore, contravening the longstanding rule that the obi should provide a contrast to the color of the kimono, women even began to choose obis in pastel shades similar to that of the kimono itself. I first saw this sort of ensemble effect worn by Akasaka geisha. Some two years passed before geisha of other areas picked up the pastel-on-pastel theme, and still more time was needed for the average Tokyo-ite to adopt this innovation. Whatever the latest word in kimono fashion may be, the Akasaka geisha are likely to pronounce it first, with conviction.

Not everyone shares the opinion that Akasaka is the most exclusive geisha area in Tokyo, however. "For all that they are young and stylish," an elderly Shimbashi geisha will sniff, "they can't dance to save their lives." Once when I attended a banquet in Akasaka as a guest with my okāsan and Ichiume, I was asked to perform on the shamisen. The mistress of the teahouse was embarrassed to admit that there wasn't a shamisen on the premises. A teahouse in Kyoto, or in Shimbashi or some of the other more conservative Tokyo hanamachi, would as a matter of course keep two or three shamisens strung and in reserve for such impromptu performances. The simple request for an instrument, so rare an occurrence in this Akasaka establishment, points directly to the tastes of the customers. The men who patronize an area play a great role in determining the atmosphere of the geisha engagements there. If the customers are not particularly interested in shamisen music or dance, the geisha have little incentive to develop facility in these arts.

Because politicians and businessmen often entertain foreign visitors in Akasaka, a group of mostly older geisha have remained adept at performing a few of the flashier music and dance pieces. But these numbers are performed in shortened form, and one feels they are trotted out simply to give the guests a taste (but not too heavy a dose) of "traditional" Japanese art and entertainment. Nothing impromptu marks such performances. The geisha bring their own shamisens.

AKASAKA, PREJUDICE AND PRESTIGE

Geisha Demographics

When I began my study in Tokyo, I knew only that Akasaka is a famous geisha area. On a muggy early August afternoon in 1975, I found my way to the tiny nondescript office of the Akasaka kenban to ask a number of questions of a Mr. Watanabe, the man hired by the Akasaka geisha association as chief administrator. I thought the room was surprisingly musty and cramped to be the registry office of an area as fancy as Akasaka. Much later, after many interviews with various kenban officials, I concluded that

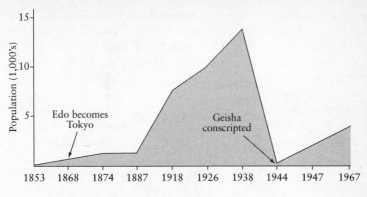

Geisha population of Tokyo, 1853–1967.

all such offices were rather dingy. The men who ran them, too, shared certain characteristics. Generally over fifty, with a faintly wistful aura of faded elegance, most of them seemed pleased to be sought out by someone interested in their esoteric knowledge, opinions, and reminiscences, which were often of a rowdy youth spent in gaining firsthand knowledge of the pleasure quarters.

As I learned in most kenban about most hanamachi, the number of geisha in Akasaka had been declining. In 1975, Akasaka's geisha population stood at 267 women, down from 300 geisha who worked there in the 1960s. Although the population of most geisha areas experienced a small surge in the 1960s – Japan's period of explosive economic growth – it had often dipped 20–30 percent by the mid-seventies.

Some people point to such figures as evidence that geisha are becoming an endangered social species. Knowing of this opinion even before I left for Japan, I thought perhaps I would be the Margaret Mead of the geisha world, recording for posterity the quaint customs of a subculture soon to vanish. My illusions were dispelled as soon as I examined the past fluctuations in the geisha population. See the figure above.

Although geisha will never again flourish in great multitudes (there were eighty thousand in the 1920s), they have nevertheless managed to reconstruct their professional corps from point zero in 1944, when all bars, restaurants, teahouses, and geisha

187

houses were shut down, and the remaining geisha conscripted as factory labor for the military. In October 1945, when the Allied occupation began, geisha were permitted to work again, but so many had either scattered to the countryside or found other work that several years passed before significant numbers of them began to regroup.

The entire organization that had supported the karyūkai was in pieces at the end of the war. The few places able to open their doors for business in 1945 usually employed "house geisha" (*uchi geisha*), women who lived and worked in one establishment rather than accepting calls through the kenban to make the rounds.

For the shriveled flower and willow world to reassert itself and spring up anew would have been a considerable recreation in any event. Yet it revived remarkably quickly, working to reestablish its customs. By 1948 the Shimbashi geisha had once again managed to perform their traditional yearly dance spectacle, the Azuma Odori. But there were only 1,695 geisha active in Tokyo and only 2,478 in all of Japan in 1947;[3] so the geisha world might not have revived at all after the war had it indeed been as outmoded or moribund as some people thought.

Discipline Without Punishment

The modern geisha world has done remarkably well in regenerating its numbers. Some people will say, however, that the standards of the profession are not what they used to be. The average length of the minarai period of new geisha in Akasaka is a mere six months. The brevity of this apprenticeship comes as a great surprise to foreigners, who have been assured by Japanese friends that geisha, contrary to what they may think, are actually artists who have undergone arduous training since childhood. In fact, modern child labor laws in Japan preclude the kind of harsh training that was not uncommon for geisha apprentices before the Second World War.

Geisha now in their late fifties or older had an adolescence very different from that of the young woman embarking upon a geisha career today. They may well have gone to live in a geisha house as early as age eleven or twelve, spending several years as household drudges and maids for the established geisha and their "mothers" even before being permitted to become apprentices at about age fourteen or fifteen. Attainment of full adult geisha status was yet another substantial step down the line. Most girls were eighteen before they became full geisha. During the eight to ten years of minarai, they studied shamisen, singing, and dance, so that by the time they appeared before customers, proudly bearing the Shimada hairstyle of a full-fledged geisha, they had become highly competent artists.

In the postwar karyūkai, however, geisha do not even begin their careers until age eighteen. The maiko of Kyoto are the only exception, but according to child labor laws, even they are supposed to be at least seventeen. Some young women may have a background in the arts, but usually only as a hobby. Those who aspire to become geisha because of amateur inclinations toward the traditional performing arts must undertake their training in earnest, in a more professional manner, if they are to gain the necessary proficiency and respect. A few who have already become geisha are obliged to start lessons from the very beginning, but whether or not they are far advanced into their artistic training, all will be plunged almost immediately into the midst of their new occupation at nightly banquets with customers. Only in that setting can they gain a real sense of a geisha's proper demeanor with guests. The context for a geisha's art, after all, is the zashiki.

During the first six months (or whatever the minarai period is for a particular area – it can range from one month to a year and a half), at the beginning of every engagement a new geisha will introduce herself to customers as a novice. Guests will then be more likely to view with an indulgent eye any small gaucheries she may commit; one of the most common occurs as a young geisha becomes so engrossed in conversation that she neglects to fill a guest's empty sake cup. An older sister, if she notices this, will frown and reproach her then and there. For a more experienced geisha, the act of filling an empty cup is automatic.

The modern foreshortened learning period is almost all that remains of apprenticeship in the Tokyo geisha areas. Only the maiko of Kyoto still preserve the ritual form of geisha apprenticeship with any authenticity. The Tokyo equivalent, called *han'*-

gyoku, has completely disappeared.[4] Today, though a young woman may acquire the basic patterns of banquet etiquette fairly easily (and so can begin that aspect of geisha work right away), she will have to practice for several years before her dancing or music becomes really presentable. If a young Tokyo woman is fascinated more by the glamor than the art of the geisha life, she may minimize her difficulties by choosing which hanamachi she will enter accordingly.

Free to Choose

Just as elite universities vie with one another to promote their own images, so the elite geisha communities cultivate their particular atmospheres and styles. This was illustrated strikingly at the shamisen-less Akasaka party I attended along with my Kyoto geisha "family." The okāsan of the Mitsuba had brought Ichiume and me to Tokyo to see her childhood friend, actress Yamada Isuzu, perform in a stage play. We also paid calls on some of okāsan's customers who, though they lived in Tokyo, always threw parties at the Mitsuba Inn on business visits to Kyoto or Osaka. One of them, a politician, was scheduled to entertain colleagues in Akasaka that evening and invited the three of us along, as guests, not as geisha.

Okāsan had a wonderful time, judging from her cheerful loquaciousness, but Ichiume was unusually shy and quiet under the scrutiny of the glamorous Akasaka geisha, who were naturally curious about a genuine former-maiko Kyoto geisha. Sophistication had never been Ichiume's strong point, and she appeared even more naïve than usual that evening. As a foreigner, I, of course, was another object of interest to the Akasaka geisha, but I was able to reciprocate the curiosity and to find out a little about their backgrounds. When we discovered that, of the twelve geisha at our party, four had actually been born and raised in the Gion district of Kyoto, the other conversations around the table stopped in amazement as everyone listened in.

It was indeed curious that these young women, so eligible to become maiko and then geisha in authentic traditional Gion, had instead chosen to live and work in Tokyo – and that they had chosen Akasaka. They let slip their opinion that tradition and authenticity are a drawback now, rather than an attraction. In closed, ingrown Gion, they said, everyone knows everyone else, a maiko is supervised and chaperoned almost every moment, and even for a full geisha there are few places where she can find real privacy. Moreover, every geisha is expected to spend a lot of time on music or dance lessons; any lallygagging would surely occasion malicious gossip. Like the big city itself, Akasaka, whatever it may lack in terms of a feeling of community, does allow for a much greater degree of personal freedom and privacy.

For all these reasons, the Kyoto girls had forsaken the genteel tempo of life in their home city and opted for the verve of fast-paced Tokyo instead. The maiko's life does not appeal to everyone, despite its picturesque charms. The long hours of practice came up again and again in my conversations with geisha. They appear to be a symbol of the less appealing side of a geisha's dedication to her profession. If a girl has any choice, my new Tokyo acquaintances concluded, she really ought to make her debut in a hanamachi like Akasaka rather than Gion.

Geisha Houses

Kyoto geisha are likely to live with their geisha sisters and mother in the same house. Most Tokyo geisha take apartments. Some even live in the suburbs and commute to their hanamachi, an idea that would have been inconceivable to their predecessors in nineteenth-century Japan.[5] Obviously the Gion-born Akasaka geisha saw this looser affiliation as one of the chief advantages of working in Tokyo. One should still report to work promptly in the evening, they said, but otherwise, when off-duty in Tokyo, one's time is one's own.

What then is the function of the okiya, the geisha house, in Tokyo? Usually run by elderly ex-geisha, the okiya are situated close to the restaurants of the hanamachi. Because of their atmosphere of shoptalk, gossip, workaday concerns, and genuine professionalism, the okiya help a novice geisha adjust to the geisha life. Even in Tokyo, it is to a new geisha's advantage to live in an okiya.[6]

After she has gained some experience and a steady clientele, a new geisha often moves to her own apartment. But even then she will keep her kimono at her okiya and begin her working evenings by dressing there. An okiya is, then, a combination of a home away from home and an "office" for commuting geisha. Finally, it is legally required that every geisha must belong to an okiya, whether she lives there or not.

The Tokyo geisha houses thus are strikingly different from the teahouses, the ochaya, of Kyoto. Men almost never have occasion to go inside a Tokyo okiya. These establishments are completely separate from the ryōtei, the restaurants where geisha actually entertain. Kyoto teahouses can serve a dual purpose – as drinking places for customers, but also as a home for geisha. The mistress of a Tokyo-style okiya does not stand in quite so exposed a public position as does the mistress of a Kyoto ochaya. She retains but little contact with customers except as she may have known them from her practicing geisha days, or as she hears about their current activities from the geisha in her charge.

There comes a time when an older geisha may feel it is appropriate to retire her party kimono. But she can continue to be part of the society she has come to know so intimately in the behind-the-scenes role of mistress of a geisha house. Such women often have no family except their geisha colleagues, anyway. The would-be okāsan applies to the registry office of the hanamachi for a license and pays a fee (quoted to me in one hanamachi as 100,000 yen, about $300 in 1975) for permission to go into business. The geisha affiliated with her okiya in turn pay her a fee for being associated with her house. If they live there, they also pay room and board.

At the time I questioned Mr. Watanabe, the administrator of the Akasaka kenban, 158 licensed okiya were doing business in that geisha area. The distribution of the 267 Akasaka geisha among them was uneven: some places had four or five geisha, some only one, and a few were holding on to their registration but currently had no geisha at all. By custom in Akasaka, only women are allowed to own and operate okiya. This appears to be true for most of the other hanamachi I investigated, too, although occasionally I heard of a male head of a geisha house. Generally these proprietors turn out to be a man and wife, with the man as nominal owner. Something faintly improper clings to the idea. Nine times out of ten, these okiya are in one of the less reputable urban geisha areas or the countryside resort towns.

SUCCESS, AKASAKA STYLE

Toward the end of my interview with Mr. Watanabe, I inquired about meeting a few Akasaka geisha. He was sorry, he said, but he couldn't help me there – geisha were busy ladies. I replied that I would be happy to give English conversation lessons to any who might be interested, and he in turn promised to mention my offer to them. I did not expect much to come of this, and ultimately nothing did.

The following day I paid a visit to a man "of broad face," as they say in Japan, who had many contacts at all levels of society. When I explained that I had been having problems in meeting geisha, he immediately told his secretary to make a phone call. After a minute I could tell that he was talking with a geisha, trying to get her to meet him that evening after her banquet commitments were fulfilled. Judging from his expression when he hung up, she had turned him down. Covering some irritation, he suggested we go out to dinner and afterward to a bar in Akasaka run by a geisha he knew. This, at last, seemed promising.

We ended up at Bar Simpatico, a tiny establishment about the size of a large American living room, and elegant as the inside of a jewel box. The mama-san was a slender woman with short, wavy hair, wearing a pale beige kimono. Her name was Komame, little bean; Japanese consider beans as cute as the French do cabbages. She greeted us at the door and sat at our table for a few minutes, then she smiled and bowed and disappeared out the back. Komame had a wealthy patron, I was told, who had provided the capital for this bar. She had not retired completely from her geisha work, and she still accepted engagements at Akasaka ryōtei when she felt so inclined. In between, she popped back to Bar Simpatico to make sure things were running smoothly. After her last banquet, usually around 10.00 P.M., she would return to the bar for the rest of the evening.

Komame was a real success story, Akasaka style. Apparently only in her early thirties when I was there, she had already taken the step dreamed of by many enterprising geisha: she had her own establishment. Many geisha remain geisha for their entire working lives, but the more entrepreneurial among them, given the opportunity, gladly retire to be independent businesswomen. Becoming the mama-san of one's own bar can be an ideal situation. A proprietress maintains contacts with her geisha sisters and with customers, as these are the very people whose patronage is essential for her enterprise to succeed. Once she is established, though, she can relax a bit. Her time is then her own. Above all, she will have the opportunity to make a great deal more money than she ever could as a geisha.

Being mama-san is a different proposition from being a bar hostess, and the two positions should not be confused. A *hosutesu* is the opposite of an independent businesswoman: she is hired help. She too can be very well paid, but only if she has a clientele of loyal customers who will follow her should she move to a different bar. The bars vie with one another to entice such women to work for them. Nevertheless, a hostess almost never enjoys a truly secure financial position. She is a commodity in the bar, like the liquor; but, alas, she will not age nearly so well.

Entrepreneurship is the only route to future security and success for a bar hostess. Unlike geisha, the hostess does not have the option of continuing her regular work into middle age. A mama-san finds aging to be less of a problem. As her title indicates, she can get away with being a bit more mature, even nurturant, in her behavior. Most hostesses plan, scheme, and dream of the time when they can become proprietresses of their own bars.

Japanese men, it is often remarked, like to be babied when they go out drinking, and an indulgent mama-san handles this perfectly. Once she has her own place, the mama-san chooses the decor, sets the tone, and in general is the focus of the particular ambience that attracts a certain group of customers. She presides over her bar like a court lady in her salon. A bar run by an ex-geisha is likely to be somewhat different from one where the proprietress is an ex-hostess.

No matter how different they feel themselves to be from one another, geisha, bar hostesses, and mama-sans are, viewed from the outside, all part of Japan's mizu shōbai. A certain studied familiarity prevails among women of the three categories. Geisha commonly accompany customers when they go on to drink in a bar after the conclusion of a formal geisha party. Naturally they get to know the hostesses and mama-sans. Sometimes a novice geisha decides her training is too arduous and drops out to become a bar hostess. Only rarely does the opposite occur. If a hostess decides to become a geisha, she probably lives in an onsen town – or, as an over-the-hill bar hostess from the city, she may have migrated there to try to hold out a few more years as a "geisha" in the sticks.

The three types of "water business" commingle in subtle ways. Komame, for instance, embodies a bit of each. As an Akasaka geisha, the nature of her work might be seen as intrinsically close to that of a hostess: a role high on glamor and glibness, lower on artistry. A Kyoto geisha would certainly volunteer such an opinion, anyway. Komame managed to keep one foot in her geisha work even as the other edged outward toward greater financial independence at the Bar Simpatico.

In an area like Akasaka, there is little to distinguish the young geisha from the bar hostesses at the very toniest clubs. Their actual work, the entertaining of well-heeled customers, may differ only in that the geisha entertain in Japanese-style rooms, whereas the hostesses do so in plush surroundings with elegant Western-style sofas, tables, and chairs. Precisely because of this ambiguity, real cognoscenti of geisha entertainment do not take Akasaka too seriously. When such customers are relatively well off – or, more and more these days, are on expense accounts – they may go to Shimbashi. If they know their way around but lack the money to frequent Shimbashi regularly, they will cultivate some of the less famous but often fascinating off-Ginza areas. Even in Tokyo, Akasaka's glamor isn't everything.

ELEVEN

DOWNTOWN GEISHA

Nanigoto mo	Whatever,
Gyoi no ma ni ma ni	As you like it,
Yanagi kana	The willow.

Haiku by Shimbashi geisha Kokichi (c. 1935)

THE GEISHA HOUSE YAMABUKI

THE FIRST GEISHA house that I actually set foot in belonged to the Tokyo hanamachi of Yoshichō. It was mid-August, four weeks after my arrival in Japan. The summer heat had just reached its climax with the celebration of *doyō no ushi*, a day when people are supposed to fortify their constitutions, enervated from weeks of eating little but cold noodles, with a hearty dish of broiled eel. Kineya Saki, my young shamisen teacher, had arranged this visit to an okiya, and he came along to provide the introduction I needed. Grumbling because of the heat, he thought he would waste his afternoon sitting in a geisha house.

Saki's interests were primarily two: music and his motorcycle. Geisha were pretty far down the list. As long ago as he could remember he had known geisha as his father's shamisen students and as visitors to the house for shamisen lessons, and although, professionally at least, he and the geisha had things in common, Saki was much more interested in "modern" women.

A young geisha from the Yamabuki house was waiting at the subway station to guide us through the twisting back streets of

Nihonbashi to her okiya. Sumi was a student of Saki's father. Her house was one that Saki had promised to show me as an example of an authentic geisha house where the women are serious about their art. He liked Sumi personally, despite his general lack of interest in geisha.

Yoshichō is a geisha community that has been in existence at least as long as Shimbashi and a good deal longer than Akasaka, yet many Japanese have never heard of it. It is located in an older part of Tokyo, away from the busy Ginza area and the big government and multinational business offices. Yoshichō may not be as prestigious as Shimbashi, but its special flavor appeals to the connoisseur.

The geisha here cultivate the flair and urbane manner said to be characteristic of the inhabitants of the "downtown" area of old Edo.[1] Nihonbashi, the section of Tokyo in which Yoshichō is located, is part of this traditional downtown, an area long a cultural stronghold of the "townspeople," as distinguished from the samurai elite of the eighteenth and early nineteenth centuries. Some merchant families here can trace their histories back several hundred years. A style – almost a cult – of spirited glamor enveloped the true "son of Edo," the Edokko, and his companion in sophistication, the geisha. Yoshichō geisha feel that they maintain this style.

This part of Tokyo escaped the worst of the firebomb raids in 1945, so the buildings are not uniformly of postwar ferroconcrete construction. The older wooden houses give a sense of what Tokyo must have been like in the 1920s and 1930s. Old-fashioned sweet bean and rice-cake pastry shops still have heavy wooden shutters that the owners batten down at closing time. Wandering through these narrow streets, one drifts back in time. Inside the vestibule of the Yamabuki, the sensation of having walked into another era is even stronger.

Saki had never been inside a geisha house. As a man, he would have had no occasion to step into the private, all-female world of an okiya. Despite his professed lack of interest in geisha, even he became intrigued by the atmosphere. The unassuming exterior of the Yamabuki, half hidden by a trellis of morning glory vines, opens to a surprisingly spacious interior. Because Japanese etiquette demands that a host apologize for cramped space, even in what is objectively a large house, Sumi modestly deflected our admiring comments with the proper phrases as she showed us to the informal sitting room on the first floor.

As we sat down, we were confronted by a wall-eyed black and white *chin*, or Japanese spaniel. No one but the women who lived at the Yamabuki could scratch his ears or pick him up. Nasty though he was, the spaniel did his part to add to the authentic atmosphere of his surroundings. Nineteenth-century woodblock prints often picture a geisha with a Japanese spaniel turning somersaults at her feet, or playfully nipping at a trailing gown. Only recently have exotic breeds like Maltese or Yorkshire terriers ousted these long-legged, pug-nosed spaniels from their privileged perch on the laps of geisha. Here in Yoshichō, in any case, one chin was not about to be budged.

The Yamabuki is licensed as an okiya, but at one time it held a license as a ryōtei. A ryōtei resembles a restaurant, as food is served and eaten there, but the dishes are not prepared on the premises. In the geisha world, the two functions of preparing and presenting food are normally carried out in different establishments. Because it was once open to guests as a ryōtei, the interior of the Yamabuki is more elegant than most geisha houses. The hallway floors are of beautiful glossy wood, and the upstairs rooms are extraordinarily large, with elegantly carved tokonoma alcoves.

The seventy-six-year-old proprietress lives in the Yamabuki with four geisha. Two more geisha are affiliated with the house and have apartments nearby. The Yamabuki is always lively, and the pace steps up after about 4:30 P.M., when six women in various stages of dress help each other into kimono for the evening's engagements. The spaniel is careful to scuttle off to the kitchen then, so as not to be accidentally trodden underfoot. The natural mother of two of the geisha lives nearby and often comes to assist with the flurry of dressing.

After this introduction to the Yamabuki, I returned often by myself to talk with whoever was at home. Even after I moved to Kyoto in the fall, I took the Tōkaidō super-express train back to Tokyo at least once a month. In this way, over the course of a year, I came to know the mother and the geisha of the Yamabuki. I did not realize until the end of my stay in Japan that they in turn were slowly finding me easier to understand as well. Seeing me at these one-month intervals, the women of the Yamabuki witnessed a transformation caused by my deepening involvement in the geisha world.

On my last visit to her house, the proprietress felt she had to say something. "When we first met, Kikuko, you were so studious – all those serious questions that we had to try to answer. You've really changed a lot. First of all, you don't look like a student any more; your hair and makeup are much more elegant, and you even move in a different way. I'd say your training in Pontochō has taken very well. What a waste to go back to your country now, when you could be such a wonderful geisha!"

A GEISHA LIFETIME

One day in early September, when no one but the spaniel and the old proprietress were at home, I sat on the upstairs veranda with her, sipping chilled barley tea and taking notes on the story of her girlhood as a geisha. She sat compactly on a cushion on the floor, occasionally scratching her head with the coral-tipped hairpin that decorated her gray chignon. She was outspoken in her opinions about the changes in the geisha world during the course of her lifetime.

"My mother had twelve children, but most of them didn't live past childhood. Three of us girls were geisha, me, an older sister, and a younger one. This will sound strange, but none of us knew that mother herself had once been a geisha. Even when the three of us entered the life, she never said anything. She didn't tell us till right before she died.

"Mother was sent away from her family when she was seven years old to be a maid in a rich man's house, and she lived there till she was thirteen. After that she went back home, but her people were farmers, you know, and by that time she had gotten used to a different sort of life, so she wasn't happy there any longer. She left home again, and this time she went to train as a geisha in Omori. She already knew about manners and proper speech from living at the rich man's house.

"When she was seventeen she became an apprentice geisha and then she married my father, who was one of her customers, a year later. Her professional name was Meiji."

The mistress of the Yamabuki had been born in 1900, the thirty-third year of the reign of the emperor whose official title, "enlightened rule," had been adopted as a geisha name by her mother. She herself has lived in three imperial eras: Meiji, Taishō (1912–25), and the present Shōwa period of Emperor Hirohito, which began in 1926. She talked about the character of the geisha profession over the years in terms of these periods.

"The Meiji geisha were really something special. I think that many geisha then came from upper-class families fallen on hard times. These girls had training in manners and deportment, but sometimes it was hard for their parents to find suitable husbands for them – they could hardly become farmers' wives, yet they were too poor to expect a fancy match. They had everything necessary to be geisha, though, so that's what a lot of them did. The standards for geisha were very high then, not like later.

"I went to school for six years, which was all that was expected back then, and when I finished, I entered a geisha house for training. I was thirteen. About five years later, by the time I had turned my collar, there were an awful lot of women around calling themselves geisha but lacking any training at all.[2] We called them Taishō geisha, and they really gave the profession a bad image in the public eye, I think."

The rise of the Taishō geisha, so scornfully described by the mother of this geisha house, paralleled the great increase in the geisha population that began in the first decade of this century. It is probably no accident that this sudden swelling of the ranks was accompanied by a lowering of standards.

"The Taishō geisha had their own registry office, separate from the kenban of other geisha, but people never noticed that. Many geisha lost pride in their profession. You can still find something like Taishō geisha now if you go to Mukōjima.[3]

"When I was working, we didn't boast that we were geisha – not that I myself was embarrassed, but there was no reason to make a thing about it. It was more proper to be discreet. Now, though, it's much easier for a woman to say 'I am a geisha' with pride. This is probably because nowadays you find only girls who decided to be geisha on their own, and they have a lot more freedom than geisha used to have.

"Under the old system, geisha could be all tied up in debt to their houses. Then you weren't working because you wanted to, you just had no choice. Now when a girl is ready for her debut, she has to pay her house for various expenses. She'll probably have to borrow for that, but after she pays off her debt she gets to keep what she earns. Also, the registry office has to approve any loan from the okiya and the rate of interest it can charge. Things are very different now."

This old lady noted the changing times with a fairly objective eye, remarkably free from the prejudice, so common among elderly geisha, that the arts are not maintained as they used to be. The senior geisha of the house is thirty-seven years old. Her name is Chizuru. The proprietress knows full well how dedicated Chizuru is to her dancing, and she knows how much of her time and her own money is poured into it. She also recognizes that customers today simply don't demand that a geisha have deep and far-ranging control over a number of styles of dance and music as part of her essential training. At present, a geisha ought to be trained in one of the traditional arts before she can claim to be a geisha, but one is usually enough. Can she sing, dance, or play the shamisen? It is a rare geisha who does all of these with equal proficiency.

"When I started my training, I went for lessons every day. Now, lessons are usually held only three or four days a month. It used to be that by the time you passed out of the apprentice stage you had to be able to sing from [the music styles of] kiyomoto, tokiwazu, and nagauta. Kouta weren't even taught; you could pick up those little songs by ear at the parties. You were expected to be able to dance in several different styles. Being an apprentice was hard because you really had to buckle down and learn all these things. Most girls spent a full five years as apprentices. Again, now it's very different. Sumi in the house here [age twenty-two] has had three years of training, which is considered a long time now.

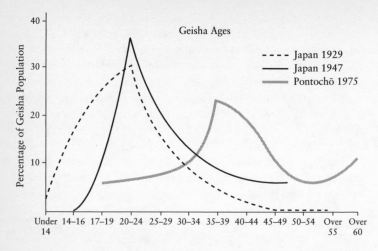

Distribution of geisha according to age. In the 1920s, more than half the geisha population retired from the profession at age twenty-four or twenty-five. This trend was still evident in 1947. The age profile of Pontochō bears out the oft-quoted statement that the average age of geisha today is fifty. Sources: Naimushō Keisatsu Torishimari Tōkei 6, "geigi nenrei" (1929); Keishicho Tōkeisho, "geigi nenrei" (1947); research of Liza Dalby (1975).

"Attitudes have changed, too. A lot of the young women you see have simply decided to go into business as geisha for a while. When they get tired of it, they think they'll get married. In my day, the geisha house used its authority to pretty much dictate whom a geisha could associate with. A geisha was supposed to follow the wishes of the proprietress in getting a patron, even if her own feelings for the man were not so warm. Conflict between *giri* and *ninjō* [duty versus human feeling] was built into a geisha's life. Now, I wouldn't dream of telling the girls in my house whom to associate with, or who their boyfriends should be. They make these choices themselves. Sometimes they come to me for advice and I give them my opinion, of course, but they don't necessarily follow it.

"It's possible to make a living as a geisha using just the income from engagements, but you wouldn't really be able to splurge much, and you might have to cut corners. I think geisha are not very good at pinching pennies. Most try to find a patron to give them a little extra income so they can live more stylishly – what's the point of being a geisha, after all, if you have to watch your budget like a housewife?"

I showed the mother of the Yamabuki some statistics on the age distribution of the geisha population in the 1920s. She remarked on the big dip in the figures when the women reached age twenty-five.

"In those days, when you found yourself a patron you could stop working. If you were lucky you would be set up in your own apartment and have a life of leisure, taking lessons when you wanted to for your own enjoyment. Of course, if something happened to your patron then you were in a fix, but you could always come back to the geisha life. I think it's pretty unusual nowadays for a geisha to stop working when she gets a patron.

"In the first place, it's much more expensive for a man to support two households – very few men could do that, the way the economy is today. From the geisha's side, I think most of them actually prefer to keep working. That's the difference now with women becoming geisha because they're attracted to the life. They find a patron or a boyfriend they like, and he buys them presents and takes them on trips, or maybe even gives them an allowance if he has money. But that's not enough to live on without working, too."

THE ART OF HAVING FUN WITH GEISHA

As we were talking upstairs, the spaniel sounded the alert that someone had come in through the front door. Chizuru and Sumi had just returned from lunch with one of their customers. They had come back to the house to get their bathing suits, as they had been invited to the pool at one of the big downtown hotels. This "date" was reported to the registry office as a regular engagement for which the geisha would be paid. They would not be back in time for the start of the banquets that day so they told the office that they would not be available for calls in the evening either. In effect, they would work during the day and take the night off.

A geisha's company, whether at the teahouse, the swimming pool, or the golf course, is paid for by the customer. All engagements not held at the licensed restaurants or teahouses of a geisha's own hanamachi fall under the category of *tōde*, distant outings. A geisha from Yoshichō, for example, can be called by a customer to attend a banquet at a ryōtei in Akasaka. This is tōde, but so is an afternoon at the pool. That the geisha should be paid for a swimming date, where they are being entertained as much as the customer, strikes some people as odd. In fact, though, taking a geisha to swim or play a round of golf is really not substantially different from the old custom of hiring a geisha's company for cherry blossom viewing.

The form of entertainment in which a man shows a geisha a good time has, if anything, been somewhat scaled down recently, according to Chizuru. Treating a whole bevy of geisha to an outing of some kind used to be one way for a man to show his magnanimous character. Although this sort of thing has become prohibitively expensive, the idea behind it lingers when a man engages a small group – or even a pair of geisha – for an afternoon date, or "o-deito" as the geisha refer to it.

The clientele for geisha services has changed as well. Chizuru has noticed differences since she began her career eighteen years ago. The man who owned a small or medium-sized company as a family business used to be the typical big spender in the geisha areas. The cash he spent was company money, although he had personal control over it. He was not on an expense account, nor did he have to worry much about misusing company funds because there were no definite lines between personal, family, and company monies. Naturally a profligate son could ruin the family business by squandering everything on his own amusement in the gei quarters, but spendthrifts were the exception. Most lavish spenders managed to keep the cost of their entertainment well within the bounds of financial prudence.

Still, there is a big difference between engaging geisha with personal money or ordering banquets for one's own amusement, and arranging a geisha party as a business dinner at company expense. Prestigious and impressive though these business-related dinner parties may be, as far as Chizuru is concerned they lack the personal flavor that used to characterize *geisha asobi*, the art of having fun with geisha.

To know one's way around the teahouses and to have connections with the top geisha are valuable assets for an ambitious executive. Such connections and the social skill to use them become part of the repertoire of men who are being groomed for the highest positions in their firms. Young men singled out for future responsibility are often brought to geisha banquets expressly so that they can develop such savoir faire. When these men reach early middle age, about the time they will be promoted to positions of real responsibility, they often decide to take singing lessons. They learn to sing a few kouta so that they can summon a geisha to accompany them on her shamisen at a party. This will impress their colleagues and evoke flattering cries of admiration from the geisha.

Through their business associations, then, many men who might otherwise never meet a geisha at all develop a real taste for geisha asobi. Their indulgence of this taste and even their connoisseurship is, however, linked to their company's expense account system. When they retire from the positions that warranted such expenditures, their geisha friends may very well have seen the last of them. But the geisha of a particular house do sometimes have a longstanding connection to a certain business firm. Its president will expect that whenever he calls geisha from that house, he and his firm will receive preferential treatment. His expectations are usually fulfilled, but often not so much because he is dear Mr. Tanaka, but because he is the current president of Akefusa Ltd. Two years down the line, the same loyalty will be transferred to the new president, and the Akefusa Company will continue as a special client of the geisha house.

The autonomous family-run business at the middle level of the Japanese economic system has gradually become incorporated into the overarching structure of the big conglomerates. As an employee rather than an owner, the fringe benefits and job security may be better for the contemporary son of Edo, but his opportunities to relax for an afternoon in the company of geisha have definitely been curtailed. The expense account guest has created other changes for the geisha as well. Although a company will view entertainment as a necessary and legitimate area for indulging its employees, it would be highly unlikely to approve a man's setting up a geisha mistress on his expense account. This is certainly part of the reason why geisha don't stop working even if they do acquire a patron. Most customers simply do not have the economic wherewithal to support a mistress in the grand style of old.

Opportunities for a geisha to enjoy a life of leisure are just not what they used to be. When the mothers sit drinking tea and reminiscing, comparing their days as geisha to the life now, they say it's better to keep on working. The main problem for a kept woman is that she usually won't keep all that long. She may fall from grace with her patron, or he may die leaving no provision for her future. Even in less ultimate terms, a kept geisha still has the day-to-day psychological problem of living as the second woman in a man's life. If a woman is really in love with her patron, then eventually the fact that he is married to someone else will gnaw away at her. When asked about their greatest occupational hazard, this is what most geisha mention. A geisha will, at some point, probably have her heart broken or at least sorely tried in such a situation. Much better, say the mothers, for a woman to be working, pursuing her lessons, and seeing her friends than to be moping and morbidly concentrating on the fact that she can't have her patron all to herself.

Some of the new clientele are attracted to geisha entertainment because of the snob appeal attaching to any activity that is expensive, exclusive, and stamped with the cultural seal of authenticity. Such men may not even particularly enjoy the banquets they arrange with attending geisha, but they are well satisfied if their colleagues or clients are suitably impressed. Paradoxically, there are probably more of these customers in the most prestigious hanamachi, like Shimbashi in Tokyo or Gion in Kyoto, just because these areas are the unquestioned epitome of geisha tradition in their respective cities. Chizuru recognizes such guests immediately, although she says that they are not likely to patronize Yoshichō. The Yoshichō geisha appeal more to customers who frequent a teahouse in preference to a bar because they truly enjoy the atmosphere that only a geisha party can create.

NO ILLUSIONS

Sumi, aged twenty-two, is small and slightly plump with a sweetly pretty moon face. Her teeth are like a string of matched pearls. She smiles often and gives an impression of softness and equanimity that customers must find charming in the extreme. She and Chizuru came upstairs to the veranda where the proprietress and I were sitting and poured themselves tall glasses of the icy barley tea. They had about an hour to rest before their swimming date, so we continued to talk about the geisha life.

Sumi is one of the modern young geisha who are interested in marriage. She had always wanted to be a geisha, she said, even from the time she was a little girl. By her own account she is quite happy with her life. Still, even though she has no one special in mind, Sumi likes the idea of becoming a wife and having children someday. "She'll get over it," Chizuru remarked dryly, and Sumi gave her soft laugh.

Chizuru entertains no thoughts of marriage. Her view of Japanese married life is a dim one, untouched by the rosy glow effusing from the mass media about the joys of respectable wife-and-motherhood. Yet, despite a decided touch of cynicism in her voice when she talks about the place of wives in modern Japan, neither is Chizuru a bluestocking. She has made her peace with the way women are treated in Japan, and she gives the impression of being very much her own person, secure and proud in her art and her profession, with no illusions about what she may have missed by following the path of the geisha rather than the more conventional one. She has clear ideas about the advantages of her work.

"One of the things I enjoy most is the chance to meet a lot of different people. Is there any other job, especially for women, that will bring you into contact with so many people? In Japan, anyway, I can't think of anything. I've met businessmen, government officials, actors, singers, sumo wrestlers. When you talk with so many kinds of people, you gain a real social education, I think. I've learned a lot about the world this way. A wife stuck at home with children doesn't have these opportunities. If you work hard you can reach a high position in the geisha world. The main thing is to respect yourself – then other people naturally respect you."

Chizuru has seen all sorts of women attempt the geisha life, with varying degrees of success. She told me about an acquaintance who had worked in an export company but was unhappy with the dull, repetitive nature of her job. At Chizuru's suggestion, she quit and began training as a geisha. She is now working full-time in the flower and willow world, wondering, according to Chizuru, why she didn't discover her true métier much sooner. Chizuru has also known women who were unable to stand the required discipline. Some of them dropped their geisha aspirations for the more immediate monetary rewards of bar hostessing.

"It's not so unusual for someone who starts out as a geisha to give up and become a bar hostess. Once in a while, the opposite happens – a hostess decides she wants to be a geisha. But I'll tell you, once they are used to the hostess life, it's pretty difficult for them to switch over and accept the strictness of geisha training. Hostesses really lead relaxed lives, in my opinion.

"For the first few years a geisha usually doesn't make much money at all. She is still training, she doesn't have steady customers yet, and she has to make a great investment in the kimono she needs. In fact, most geisha are probably in debt at the start. The ones who aren't really serious drop out early. I would say that if a girl can stick it out for the first three years, then the chances are she'll remain another ten at least. The first three years are really the hardest. If you don't find something personally rewarding in this sort of life, there's no way you could continue with it."

When Chizuru made her formal debut as a geisha in Yoshichō in the early 1960s, the obligatory practice of paying courtesy calls on all the ryōtei in the area took up the better part of a day. She was dressed in a formal black kimono with the design of her family crest dyed into the silk in the center of the back and the two sleeves. Her face powdered to a dead white, a glistening oiled wig on her head, she traipsed through the narrow streets of Yoshichō with a small retinue of officials from the kenban to announce her at each restaurant doorway. Eyes lowered demurely, almost like a bride, she was paraded around in her new role of geisha, leaving a small cotton towel with her new name artfully written on it at each of the establishments.

That evening she received calls from many of these places and skipped from one to another, perhaps spending no more than ten minutes at each, to meet guests and be admired as the newest geisha in town. She probably made a fair amount of money, both from tips given by guests wishing her good luck and through the fact that even a fraction of an hour is counted for a full hour's pay in the geisha wage system. She could easily have made four or five hours' wages in one hour that night.

Although no one comes right out and says so, it is understood that a new geisha has put up a lot of money for her debut. Consequently, the teahouses, restaurants, and customers are inclined to be generous on her first night. The ryōtei owners usually give a small cash present to the woman on either her afternoon visit or her evening appearance. This custom echoes a common practice in Japanese communities: friends and neighbors give small gifts of cash to a local child who has made an important transition in life, such as entering high school or college. Through such gestures, the recipient of the favors is enmeshed in a larger social whole and is made to feel that actions in his or her new role will be more than just an individual matter. As a student feels his larger family and community have made an investment in his success, so too a new geisha comes to feel a responsibility toward the community in which she works.

Tomiko, one of the younger geisha living at the Yamabuki, had made her formal debut the previous winter. As Chizuru had done she donned her wig, put on a brand-new black kimono, and, holding up the trailing skirt in her left hand, went out to pay her respects to the Yoshichō entertainment establishments.[4] Yet Tomiko finished her rounds in a few hours – an indication of the shrinking number of traditional establishments now operating in Yoshichō.

The geisha population is very sensitive to the fluctuations of the larger economy. The 1960s were boom years for Japan, and the hanamachi flourished at that time. By the 1970s, however, a much slower rate of economic growth had necessitated a pruning of the flower and willow world. The proprietress of the Yamabuki said that the older geisha would feel the pressure first when times grew hard, and that she knew at least four geisha in their fifties who had retired the year before; there just was not enough work to keep them going. Younger geisha are quite aware of the extent to which their jobs depend on the health of the economy in general. They are also sufficiently well educated now to handle their own finances, often with considerable aplomb. Chizuru mentioned this as one of the major changes, in her opinion, in the modern geisha world.

"A great part of a geisha's appeal used to be her innocence – or perhaps ignorance – of practical matters. The image was of a charming creature who could hardly manage to find her way to the banquet hall by herself. Men come to the teahouses and engage geisha in order to get away from the worries of everyday life, and they like to think that the geisha are totally removed from such concerns as well. I find this a problem that I have to think consciously about now: creating an atmosphere that, to some extent at least, keeps reality at bay. For example, I'm not likely to get into a discussion of the stock market with a guest – unless I know him very well."

The Flavor of an Atmosphere

Creating an atmosphere that guests will find appealing is the major part of a geisha's job. When geisha talk about each other in terms of the profession as a whole, they are not particularly concerned with the ranking of one hanamachi vis-à-vis the others, as I had expected. Again and again, geisha discussed their own and other communities in terms of the *aji*, the flavor, created by each area. A real connoisseur of geisha entertainment, Chizuru explained to me, could appreciate these ineffable flavors by experiencing evenings in the company of the best geisha in several hanamachi. As a geisha, Chizuru felt that there are hard-working and lazy geisha in any community, and she was loath to say that one area was "better" than any other.

Because Japanese are usually so conscious of status differences, I was surprised to find that Chizuru and other geisha I questioned were not very concerned with how they stood in some hierarchical ranking system. Of course some broad distinctions exist between the urban hanamachi and the lower-class country geisha areas, but geisha themselves, it seems, contemplate their world according to criteria different from those used by people on the outside. Whereas the Japanese man on the street would say that Akasaka is one of the top Tokyo hanamachi, a geisha from a different area, thinking of the middling level of artistic skills found in Akasaka, would probably not share that opinion. But, Chizuru admitted, it all really depends on a customer's taste.

COLD CASH

Chizuru and Sumi had to leave for their swimming date, but before they left Sumi politely wheedled the loan of a 10,000-yen note (about $30 in 1975) from the proprietress to hold her until payday, two days off. Payday, depending on the community, comes either once or twice a month. The registry office collects the receipts from the places where geisha were engaged, cashes them, and makes sure each geisha is properly reimbursed for the amount of time spent in each place. It is because of this monthly wage reckoning that the kenban must be kept informed of when and where a geisha works. The geisha gets her actual cash wages in these monthly or semimonthly lump sums several steps removed from the time and place where she earned them.

Cold cash rarely appears in this system of transactions. Customers of the geisha restaurants are either well known to the owners or come on the recommendation of an established client. All their expenses are recorded and sent to them later by the ryōtei, for presenting a bill at the end of an enjoyable evening

211

seems rather crass. Customers thus are extended a floating credit line at the places they patronize.

Obviously this system can work only on a personal level, maintained by trust. The ryōtei are ultimately responsible for turning over that portion of a customer's bill itemized as geisha entertainment to the kenban in time for its wage reckoning; so if they have not yet managed to collect from the customer, ryōtei owners must pay the fees themselves. No wonder they adhere to the credo "ichigen-san kotowari" (no first-time guests).

Handing over the 10,000 yen, the mother of the Yamabuki gave Sumi a mock scolding about being a spendthrift. She cares deeply for the geisha in her house, and the tone of affectionate banter between them shows that the regard is mutual. Only within the past five years has this proprietress taken young geisha who have no previous familiarity with karyūkai life into her house. She admitted that it had been a real education for her to see that much of what she took for granted as the natural and proper way of doing things was in fact completely new and unfamiliar to the recruits.

I thought this seventy-six-year-old lady, familiar with but one milieu in her entire life, had made a remarkable attempt to understand the problems newcomers now face. Some of her cronies drive prospective geisha away with their unyielding attitudes and strict demeanor. By contrast, should one of the young geisha of the Yamabuki commit a faux pas, the proprietress will calmly and kindly explain the matter to her. Perhaps this does not sound remarkable, but explicit explanations are rare in the geisha world. Her willingness to lay out the whys and wherefores of geisha custom is quite enlightened.

I happened to visit the Yamabuki one afternoon when just such an occasion arose. Tsuzumi, the newest geisha of the house, had had no contact with the geisha world prior to her acceptance at the Yamabuki. She casually mentioned to the proprietress that a Mr. Nakano had given her a nice tip the night before. Mr. Nakano was an old customer of the other geisha of the Yamabuki, and the proprietress knew him as well. The tip was given directly to Tsuzumi – a crisp 10,000-yen note tucked into a specially made fancy paper envelope.[5] The problem was not that the

A woodblock print of two geisha by Kitao Shigemasa (1739–1820).

money wasn't meant for Tsuzumi. It was – but for Tsuzumi as a member of Yamabuki, as opposed to Tsuzumi the new geisha whom Mr. Nakano had just met.

And the problem was that Tsuzumi had mentioned the matter casually, almost by chance, when she should have made a point to report the favor to the other members of the house. The next time one of the geisha from Yamabuki happened to meet Mr. Nakano, she would be obliged to thank him for his generosity toward her younger sister. Mr. Nakano would assume that all the Yamabuki geisha knew about the tip and would feel slighted if they did not mention it, even out of ignorance. The perceived lack of manners would reflect badly on the house as a whole. The proprietress later said to me that she never would have thought a geisha would need to be told about this sort of thing. Certainly a girl who grew up in a mizu shōbai household would naturally know these rules of etiquette toward a customer.

But the mother of this house finds the way modern geisha use money more shocking than these gaps in etiquette. For someone who has lived through the depression, wartime deprivation, and postwar inflation, the level of luxury taken for granted by young geisha can be difficult to comprehend. The old lady estimated that the geisha at Yamabuki earned about 150,000 yen a month then (around $450 in 1975) but that the money invariably was all spent on clothes, taxi fares (geisha would not be caught dead on public transportation, she said), the hairdresser, travel, and food delicacies.[6] "You develop expensive tastes as a geisha," she said. "Once you become accustomed to this way of life it is pretty difficult to give it up and enter regular society. In a way, geisha get spoiled and can never become good, thrifty housewives."

Before I left the Yamabuki that afternoon, I passed out copies of the questionnaire I had just had printed. I asked these geisha to fill it out and tell me whether they thought the questions made sense. There was much laughter and comment as they went through the items, and I remember that the question regarding future plans drew particular attention. The women all agreed that someday it would be nice to become the mistress of one's own place. I think the old proprietress was secretly pleased to hear all these voices affirming the value of a position like hers.

She thrives on the comings and goings of the young women in her house, vicariously sharing their triumphs and their troubles. Her life is hardly a quiet one, but that has been her choice.

"You only live once," she said, "and if it isn't at least a little bit lively then it's really a waste. I'd rather be here than be an old lady whose children have gone off and married, and be stuck at home now with a crochety old husband." Chizuru glanced up and gave a little snort of a laugh.

TWELVE

ART AND LIFE

Sakura sakura to	Sakura, sakura,
Hitobito ga	When is it that people
Ukaretamau wa	Gad about under the cherry?
Itsu no koto?	From the end of March
Sangatsu sue	To the middle of April,
Kara shigatsu	it's nothing but
No nakaba kana	Bloomin' blooms of
Hanazakari	Sakura.

A kouta

LADY OF THE CHERRY BLOSSOMS

GEISHA ARE THE only Japanese who ride in rickshas now. Yet at the turn of the century these vehicles were the most common mode of intra-urban transportation in Japan. Over a hundred thousand men made a livelihood by pulling rickshas. With the advent of the streetcar and the growing popularity of bicycles in the 1920s, however, rickshas disappeared like fireflies in the fall. No more than twenty-five or thirty rickshas are left in Tokyo now, and most of them cluster in an alley behind the dance theater of the Shimbashi geisha. They sit idle during the day, the two poles by which they are drawn resting on the ground. In the evening, the ricksha pullers, about two dozen wiry old men, appear in the alley. They transport geisha from their houses to the restaurants where they have been called to entertain wealthy clients.

The men of the ricksha association will carry no one but a geisha. At dusk, their black carriages quietly glide through the tiny side streets of Shimbashi and Akasaka. Because of the frailty of vehicle, passenger, and puller, they don't venture far from this limited area of central Tokyo. A Shimbashi geisha called to a restaurant in a different part of town will not ride in a ricksha, but in a black limousine. One wonders how long these quaint two-wheeled anachronisms will continue to trot through the alleys of Shimbashi. The men who pull them are as tough and lean as old chickens, but there are no young men anxious to follow in their footsteps. To be a ricksha puller is to be obsolete in modern Japan.

Sakurako is a young Shimbashi geisha who, at five feet five inches, is a good deal taller than the average Japanese woman. She is pretty, though not what anyone would call "willow hipped." She feels sorry for the ricksha man when she goes out, for she is taller and heavier than most of them. Sakurako entered the profession in spring 1975, just when I went to Japan to research the subject of geisha. When I met her at a party in a Shimbashi restaurant, she had been on the job for only two months. Before her formal debut into Shimbashi geisha society, she had had a mere two months of minarai. Her training period had been short because she was already an accomplished dancer. For Sakurako, dance was the prime reason for becoming a geisha.

Sakura, of course, means cherry blossom(s). With the feminine suffix -*ko*, it becomes a woman's name, albeit a somewhat unusual one. Sakura are rich in meaning for Japanese. They are without question the foremost flower of Japan. To go flower viewing means to admire the sakura, not some other tree. In classical poetry the very word *hana*, flower, when used alone, is understood to mean precisely *sakura no hana*. The cherry represents springtime brilliance and nature's opulence, clouds of petals in a floral jubilee. Yet sakura are by no means frivolous flowers. The samurai picked the cherry as a metaphor for the ideal death of a warrior because sakura scatter in the breeze while still in their prime, not waiting to fade on the bough.

Flowers and personalities can intertwine. The cherry blossom is pure and noble, yet also gorgeous and extravagant. A vivacious

Sakurako is quite the opposite of a Yamato nadeshiko, the demure, phlox-like carnation used as a symbol of a prim and rather shy young lady in Japan.

Sakurako does not have a special older sister. She would be a rarity in Tokyo if she did, for the formalized older sister/younger sister relationships of the Kyoto geisha world are not often seen in Japan's modern capital city. Sakurako chose her professional name herself, thinking that it was a bit different, and that it somehow fit her personality. Only afterward did she discover that she actually had become the fourth "generation" of that name in Shimbashi. She found that there was a Sakurako III, retired from geisha life, who was passing her days quietly in a small apartment outside Tokyo. And so, as Sakurako IV, she had a box of cakes wrapped and went to pay the old geisha a courtesy visit.

In these days, elderly and retired geisha complain that the traditional values of *on*, a humble acknowledgment of indebtedness to another, and giri (a sense of proper social duty) are as unfamiliar to young geisha as the feudal custom of blackening women's teeth with iron filings. The elderly Sakurako III must have been very touched by this spontaneous gesture on the part of her accidental namesake.

THE WARP OF MORALITY

Even though the older generation likes to compare the present unfavorably with the past, especially in terms of the behavior of juniors, the geisha world is in fact one of the great remaining strongholds of traditional notions of duty and obligation in Japan. Here, actions and attitudes are often discussed using the vocabulary of on and giri. Many young geisha, especially those not from a geisha background, find it old-fashioned and confining to have expectations of their behavior couched in these terms.

The older generation, on the other hand, sees the very fabric of society and proper human relations as woven from exactly these moral threads. Nevertheless, despite differing opinions on the importance of conduct according to the virtues of duty and obli-

Two maiko in a ricksha at the turn of the century.

gation, the terms themselves are not anachronistic in geisha society. A novice or apprentice who ignores them imperils her acceptance into the community she has chosen. But there are some
young women, and Sakurako is one, who actually consider the
old-fashioned notions about human relations to be a positive
aspect of geisha life.

Sakurako has good reason to appreciate the different quality
of life as a geisha, as she had previously been a more conventional career woman. Before she became a geisha at age twenty-
six, she had attended junior college, majoring in psychology.
After graduation, she had worked as a secretary – the kind of job
that coeds in Japan often obtain when they finish their formal
schooling.

Like many daughters of the bourgeoisie, Sakurako had practiced classical Japanese dance since childhood. But rather than
give it up, as so many women do when they become busy with

schoolwork, social life, and preparation for marriage, Sakurako had continued dance lessons along with her job. Copying memos and serving tea during weekdays, she postponed her real interest, dance, to evenings and weekends. Her life was thoroughly divided by her interest in dance and the constraints of making a living. Sakurako's growing dissatisfaction with her job did not worry her parents because they assumed she would quit in short order to choose a husband and settle down. They were shocked when, instead, she announced her intention to become a geisha.

If there is a new breed of geisha, Sakurako is a woman who exemplifies it. Unlike so many geisha of earlier periods – women who had some connection with the flower and willow world through a relative, Sakurako is from a shirōto (nonprofessional, that is, not from the mizu shōbai) middle-class background. She admits to having been fascinated with the romance of geisha life since childhood, but she had no natural entree into it, as a geisha's daughter would have had. All the options of study, jobs, and marriage presumed to be available to young middle-class Japanese girls were indeed available to Sakurako, yet she deliberately chose the occupation of geisha in preference to a secretary's job, or, more profoundly, to marriage.

For Sakurako, becoming a geisha was the solution to contradictions of life and livelihood; it allowed her to accommodate her passion for dance within her professional work. It was no accident, furthermore, that she chose the highly touted Shimbashi as her hanamachi; or, within Shimbashi, that she sought out an okiya run by one of the premier geisha dancers in all of Tokyo.

The prescribed length of Sakurako's term of minarai may have been only two months, but in practice her probation extended far beyond that, especially in the eyes of the older, established geisha. When I asked her what she had found to be initially most difficult in her new career, she mentioned the sharp eyes of the older geisha always upon her. She was self-conscious, as she had never before been in her life, about keeping her back straight, her feet tucked under her, as she sat on the tatami mat next to a customer. As anyone not accustomed to sitting properly on the floor knows, the temptation to ease one's weight toward one side or another, surreptitiously resting each foot in turn, is nearly overwhelming.

Most Japanese born after the war are uncomfortable in the correct sitting posture, and this is mainly due to the encroachment of the chair into Japanese living space. Legs that have dangled from chairs since childhood don't take easily to being folded under hips on the floor. Men are permitted to adopt a more relaxed half-lotus sitting posture and yet remain within the bounds of propriety, but women dressed in kimono have only the option of shifting their feet slightly from under their posteriors. A geisha doesn't even have this alternative, as Sakurako was constantly reminded.

Even when she felt she was chided unfairly by an older geisha, Sakurako knew that the proper response in this hierarchical world was to bow her head meekly and accept criticism. Everyone was in a position of seniority, and thus to some extent authority, over her as a new member of the profession and also the community. She often had to bite her tongue to refrain from making excuses or justifying herself. Silent acquiescence was the lesson to be learned.

Rather than chafing or complaining, however, Sakurako seemed to regard this as part of a process of "polishing" her character, as a spiritual discipline that would make her a stronger and better person, not simply a better geisha. Of course this was difficult, but so too was the ideal of dance she pursued. If she continues to practice as a geisha, Sakurako will someday be one of the elders in the hierarchy and no one will tell her to sit up straight. Even at that point, though, she will probably still be taking dance lessons from a master teacher, for discipline is interwoven into a geisha's life.

ART AS LIFE

The generation of Japanese who came of age just before and during the war years thinks that it alone truly understands the idea of discipline. Those now in their fifties say that young people are soft and have no appreciation for rigorous training – seemingly unaware that a passionate yet highly disciplined dedication to an ideal is rare in any generation. Yet for Sakurako and many other geisha whom I came to know, the discipline of the various arts, the gei, literally infuses the name of their profession, gei-sha, with meaning.

The arts that geisha practice are, specifically, those of traditional music and dance. The way these arts are taught and learned is also traditional, based on the unquestioning subordination of pupil to teacher. In effect, the discipline involved is as much discipline of the self as it is technical mastery of the art form. Because the two are not separable, one can pursue the arts throughout a lifetime and still not attain mastery in any final sense.

Sakurako was accustomed to the discipline of dance. She slowly came to accept the idea that the same subordination of will was necessary to master the professional conduct of the geisha. The art of the geisha transcends the particular and specific sorts of gei they practice. What attracts a woman like Sakurako to this profession is, above all, the conscious and deliberate choice to make art her life.

This choice engenders its converse: if, for a geisha, art is life, then it is also true that her life must become art. A geisha strives to become so permeated with her art that everything she does is informed by it, including the way she walks, sits, and speaks. For this ideal to become real, constant watchfulness is necessary until the required deportment and professional manner become second nature. To polish one's life into a work of art, however high flown it may sound to non-Japanese, is the idea behind the discipline of a geisha.

Geisha are more than simply traditional female entertainers. They do not merely change into kimono at six o'clock in the evening so as to rush off to work; their lives are far more integrated. The actual time for which they are paid, the banquet hours when they are in the presence of customers, constitutes only the most obvious aspect of their professional lives. Ideally, what a geisha brings to the banquet room is an elegance that has been cultivated, like a rare orchid, in the special environment of the flower and willow world. Whatever is special about geisha and imbues them with a certain mystique arises because their lives are set apart from everyday society. Today the walls of their world are art and discipline.

This is the geisha ideal. Different communities and individual geisha may emphasize the essential elements of the profession differently, however. The stronger the emphasis on the rigorous pursuit of one's gei, and the more coherent and bounded the community, then the more likely the geisha will think of their work as a calling that completely absorbs their time, energy, and sense of self.

When the gei of geisha is downplayed in favor of the glamor, and the actual community is scattered because many geisha commute from their own apartments rather than a geisha house, then the tendency to think of one's work as a job is much more pronounced. It is not surprising that geisha in the more conservative old capital city of Kyoto are much more likely to be conscious of themselves as geisha at all times, and that they make this the defining principle of their lives. In modern Tokyo, a Shimbashi geisha is more likely to feel this way than a geisha who works in Akasaka.

WOMEN WHO BECOME GEISHA

Women choose the geisha life for different reasons. A sixteen-year-old who decides to try out the life of a maiko has thoughts and priorities different from those of a twenty-six-year-old woman, who knows that by becoming a geisha she may preclude her chances for ordinary married life. The late twenties are called *tekirei* in Japanese – literally, the appropriate age – meaning the prime period of marriageability that, once past, especially for women, means a significant lowering of marriage prospects. Naturally a geisha's daughter will have a perspective on the profession different from that of an ordinary high school graduate. Yet, one thing unites all these women in their career choice: an inclination toward the arts. When I talked to geisha from many areas, art was the one topic mentioned over and over again.

A woman entering the geisha life today makes her choice of career freely, unaffected by the social conditions that in prewar days sometimes forced families to sell daughters to geisha houses.

Unless she has some interest in the arts, therefore, a girl has no reason at all to become a geisha. She could easily save more money and be less restricted in some other line of work.

Recruiting young geisha has become a serious problem for the profession. Only an unusual woman is attracted to the geisha life nowadays, often someone with a romantic or nostalgic frame of mind to whom the image of the kimono-clad geisha appeals. Yet a girl who simply longs to see herself outfitted in a geisha's wig and black, nape-revealing kimono will soon have had her fill. Such trappings must be laid on a solid basis of gei in order for a woman to make this a true career. A young geisha is in a situation that many of her friends are apt to deride as feudalistic. The rules of propriety, the stress on obligation, duty, and discipline that are deeply ingrained in most areas of the flower and willow world, are not likely to attract a great number of modern young women. A few like Sakurako nevertheless persevere because they find something valuable and fulfilling there.

Finally, it takes an independent-minded young Japanese woman indeed to be able to resist the pressure of the idea that a woman's main goal in life is to marry and have children. The middle-class notion of a nuclear family couple with a small child or two, striving as their life goal to establish themselves in their own house, no matter how small, is practically universal in modern Japan. The media have even coined a term for this national state of mind: my-home-ism. The image of the wife as lady of the house (rendered in Japanese as *okusan*, literally, lady of the interior) is constantly developed and recreated in film, television, and magazines. After the glorious wedding ceremony, advertised as the crowning moment of a girl's life, comes the transformation to okusan. Society still looks askance at almost any other career or life plan for a woman.

It is thus a momentous decision for a young woman to enter a career that she knows is socially and culturally the opposite of the one followed by 98 percent of Japanese women. A geisha can (and often does) have children, but motherhood without wifehood is not at all the same. When a girl of "good background," like Sakurako, decides she wants to be a geisha, disapproval and opposition from parents is to be expected.

Part of the parents' apprehension, understandably, comes from the fact that however much one may praise the traditional arts and enjoy the company of geisha, if the question comes down to "Would you want your daughter to be one?" the answer is likely to be "No." To be a professional nonwife, dressing and acting in ways antithetical to the style of the proper okusan, may be fine for other people's daughters, but not for one's own. That a geisha often becomes a man's mistress is naturally on parents' minds; but even if that were not the case – and some geisha manage perfectly well without a patron – the more diffuse aspect of geishas' interaction with customers remains troublesome. Geisha become experienced in dealing with men socially, and in developing this social sangfroid they lose the modesty, innocence, and purity that are deemed desirable qualities in wifely Japanese women.

GEISHA DAUGHTERS

Born a Geisha

One woman I know had two daughters, one of whom never married and became a university professor. The other became a geisha. This mother felt she had failed in raising both her daughters because neither had followed the matrimonial path. When parents resist the idea that their daughter wants to be a geisha, they seem to be rejecting the negative corollary – that she would not marry – at least as much as the profession of geisha per se.

But not all parents frown on this career choice. From my questionnaire I found that if a woman had a geisha mother, she was likely to have been encouraged to become a geisha herself.[1] Kyoto geisha, whether their mothers had been geisha or not, were less likely to suffer parental opposition than Tokyo geisha. The reason for this may be that Kyoto geisha have a somewhat more respectable image in their city than Tokyo geisha have in theirs. Because Kyoto claims to have the oldest and most authentic traditions, of course including those of the geisha world, the geisha there are more in evidence as part of the ongoing cultural life of the city.

In premodern Japan, a geisha's daughter probably had little choice but to follow in her mother's footsteps. A geisha's baby son might have been adopted by his father, the geisha's patron, to be brought up by the man's legitimate wife, but illegitimate daughters were more often left to be raised by the geisha mother within the predominantly female environment of her society. It no doubt seemed very natural to these little girls that they would become geisha later on.

If geisha daughters married at all, they were more likely to take up with men connected in some way with the entertainment world. There was always the chance, however, that a wealthy patron might pluck the odd geisha out of flower and willow society and ensconce her in the respectable role of wife. Aside from that unusual case, though, a life within the boundaries of the gei quarters was the usual one for a girl born to a geisha. I suspect that, during the late 1800s and the early part of this century, most geisha were in fact "born into" their profession.

Recruited

The geisha population of Japan soared in the first two decades of this century. Geisha would have had to have been as prolific as rabbits to supply the burgeoning demand; so new members were recruited from other sources. One such source was impoverished rural areas, via the notorious practice of selling female children into a period of indenture, for which the father was given a lump sum against his daughter's prospective wages as a geisha.

Early in this century, a geisha might have lived in a variety of circumstances ranging from complete independence (*jimae*) to a state of virtual captivity (*kakae*). Young girls shepherded in from the countryside usually found themselves in the latter situation. They would live in the okiya, first as maids and then, if the mistress of the house thought they showed promise, as apprentices. At last, they would earn their keep as full geisha. After this, everything they had, from the food that went into their mouths to the kimono on their backs, was sold or leased to them by the okiya.

The owners of the geisha houses were then in a position to reap some profit from their investment in the once scared and unpolished rustic child; therefore the house felt entitled to receive all the woman's wages as a geisha. The geisha houses that routinely recruited members in this way were often managed by unscrupulous owners who charged the inmates exorbitant rates for room and board, intentionally keeping them in a state of dependence.

If a woman were diligent and lucky, she might be able to work herself out of this system of bondage, pay all her debts, and become independent. Some geisha even formed cooperative houses with their peers, with each member contributing half her earnings toward household expenses but remaining independent in all other respects. Many women, though, were unable to free themselves and no doubt led quite miserable lives. If a girl decided to run away from the okiya that had indentured her, she had to do so with the knowledge that she would bring shame on her family back in the countryside, and that her father would be legally responsible for reimbursing the geisha house. Having made the difficult decision to send a daughter away so that the rest of the family could eat, a father could only be honor-bound to hand her back if she turned up on his doorstep again. A run-away girl would be doubly punished, first by her father, then by the mistress of the okiya after she was forced to return. If she did not retrace her steps, but instead tried to melt into the hubbub of urban life, she would soon have the authorities on her trail as a piece of missing property rightfully belonging to the geisha house. A captive recruit truly had nowhere to turn.

Sacrificed

An elderly retired geisha with whom I stayed for a few days in her small house in the country described how she and her sister had been chosen by their father to be "sacrificed" for the benefit of the rest of the children in the family. They had been sent to an okiya in a seedy section of Tokyo, where they were two among six young girls acquired around the same time. In the beginning they were treated as menials and were not even allowed to sleep in rooms with tatami mat floors; at night they spread blankets on wooden planks. High in the wall of the room they all shared were sliding windows that the mistress of the house could open to spy down on them. This woman's memories of her younger days were concentrated in the image of the bitter tears that fell into her bowl of *ozōni* soup on New Year's Day, a day that most people, even servants, were allowed to spend with their families.

She and a friend had once tried to escape. She remembers darting through the city streets, running until they came to fields at the outskirts of Tokyo. But then, realizing the utter hopelessness of going further, they calmly sat down and made necklaces out of purple clover while waiting to be caught.

Dreadful as life was for these girls, abruptly torn from their families at age ten or eleven and thrust into what was often a harsh existence, they were yet better off than the girls who were sent not to geisha houses but to brothels. This was more likely to be the fate of an unattractive or dull farmer's daughter who showed little indication of future ability as an accomplished geisha. A geisha house usually would not waste time and money on such unpromising candidates.

During recruitment forays into impoverished areas, procurers would assess the qualities of the children before any contracts were signed. Once a girl had worked for a while as a servant in the okiya, the mistress would have a still better sense of her aptitude and could decide whether she would be worth training in music and dance to prepare for geisha apprenticeship. Some girls would not be given lessons, but would be kept on as servants. At this point, their contracts of indenture might also be renegotiated with a brothel.*

All such girls were to be pitied, of course. The one consolation they had was knowing that by gracefully submitting to their fates they were fulfilling a moral ideal of filial piety. This may not sound like much, but in their situation it meant a great deal. To be pushed out of one's family into an unknown life in an unfamiliar place was undoubtedly traumatic. Promises of good food to eat and pretty clothes to wear may have eased their anxiety in the beginning, but whether reality corresponded with the honeyed words of the recruiters was another matter. The shock of realization when young girls destined to be prostitutes found out what was expected of them was another cruel blow. To be able to

Family background of geisha, 1975:
Professional (or white-collar), includes businessman, doctor,
newspaper editor, writer, government employee.
Labor (means skilled labor), includes machine engineer,
construction worker, mechanic, paper maker, plumber, weaver.
Mizu shōbai *includes teashop owner, chef, inn owner, okiya owner.*
Merchant includes grocer, fishmonger, candy store owner,
traditional pharmacist.
Source: Questionnaire responses of geisha (37 from Tokyo,
43 from Kyoto, 5 from Atami, 4 from Nagoya, 5 from Fukuoka,
and 4 from Matsue).

believe that because of one's noble sacrifice parents and brothers and sisters were not starving was of no little importance in salvaging a remnant of pride and honor.

The lives of those who began to receive training in the arts did not necessarily become any easier, for the discipline here too was rigorous and harsh. Suffering was thought a necessary component of mastery. One of the most common learning techniques was called *kangeiko* (lessons in the cold). The girls would be sent outside in winter to practice playing the shamisen until their fingers bled and their voices cracked. There was no musical notation for them to study, so in order to avoid a rap on the head or hand from the teacher's shamisen plectrum, they had to absorb the music perfectly and entirely by ear. Dancing lessons were equally strict. A lapse of memory or a clumsy turn was punished by a smart blow from the teacher's closed fan. Still, lessons were a break from the drudgery of household labor, and even though many more tears fell in the course of learning to play the shamisen, there was the satisfaction of making the musical skill one's own.

Here lay the clearest reason why girls indentured to okiya were luckier than the prostitutes-to-be. With some initial talent and cleverness, they could take advantage of the training they received and parlay it into a successful career as an independent geisha. The practicality of such skills is expressed in a phrase that geisha are fond of: "sanbon ga areba, taberareru (if you have three strings [can play the shamisen], you can eat). By contrast, a girl who had been indentured into a life of prostitution had only the slim hope that she would find favor in the eyes of a customer who would rescue her by paying off her debts to the brothel. But here, too, the geisha was much more likely to be "redeemed" by one of her customers.

The Dark Image Lightened

Heartrending stories of forcible recruitment contribute heavily to the dark side of the geisha's image. Some people still think that girls become geisha this way. In present-day Japan, however, any such notion is economically absurd. If a girl must support parents in dire need of financial assistance, it would be easier and more lucrative for her to become a bar hostess. Women are no longer caught unwillingly in a system of debt to geisha houses, either. A law prohibiting such arrangements was passed in 1948. Finally, apart from the legal prohibitions and economic unfeasibility of the old system, there is no longer a supply of female children from families so impoverished as to have to sell a daughter's flesh and labor. A farm family in Japan today is more likely than not to have a color television and a car or truck, and to send its daughters to finishing schools.

I doubt that geisha of the more prestigious areas in the big cities ever had great numbers of rural recruits in their midst.

Rather, the girls who gravitated toward hanamachi like Gion and Pontochō in Kyoto, or Yanagibashi and Shimbashi in Tokyo, were more likely to have been city girls, from the ranks of the artisan or merchant classes. They may have been indentured, but their families could be more discriminating about the okiya they entered and could also watch over them to some extent. Sometimes a girl would be sent deliberately to a geisha house so that she would be self-sufficient later in life, much as a boy would be apprenticed in a particular trade. I suspect, too, that by far the preponderance of cases of trafficking in little girls involved brothel keepers rather than the owners of geisha houses. The distinction between these two sorts of places is often blurred when people talk about the practice of forcible recruitment.

I met a few older geisha who told pitiful stories of a childhood of near-slavery. The ones who had had such bitter experiences were not from the better geisha areas. In the higher-class communities, I heard no such tales from the elderly and retired geisha. Most of them had been daughters of geisha, of teahouse owners, or of other urban mizu shōbai, artisan, or petty merchant families. I encountered no cases of girls being forced into the geisha life at present.

Today, girls of varied backgrounds enter the flower and willow world. Sakurako, though not exactly typical, is nevertheless not a complete anomaly either. Of the geisha who answered my questionnaire, a tally of family background revealed that one-third of them were second-, or in some cases third-generation geisha, and the rest were fairly equally distributed among family categories that can be loosely described as white-collar or professional, merchant, skilled labor or blue-collar, and mizu shōbai.

A fair number of geisha are still born into the profession, but that is hardly a prerequisite. Now, too, there is no compulsion to become a geisha even if you are born there. Some geisha mothers are delighted when a daughter follows them, others would rather see her settle into a respectable marriage. When I inquired about their feelings, should a daughter become a geisha, almost every geisha emphasized that the choice was the girl's own and would depend primarily on her wishes.

GEISHA BRIDES

What are the marriage prospects for a geisha's daughter? Much depends on what the girl herself has done in the way of obtaining education and other sorts of work. The fact that her mother is a geisha will limit her range of prospective marriage partners, but only slightly. Although she will probably not marry into an upper-class family or one that stiffly cherishes its samurai heritage, a girl whose mother was a respectable geisha in a prestigious hanamachi will not suffer much restriction from that fact alone.

Geishas' children attend regular public schools along with other children, and they are not noticeably set apart from their peers. Geishas' daughters used to attend a special "geisha school" under the assumption that they would grow up to become geisha. Their separation and differentness from the rest of society was emphasized, and the boundaries of the narrow quarters of their birth were more or less the boundaries of their lives. Nowadays, although girls with geisha mothers may realize that their home environment is unusual compared to that of their classmates, they still share the common high standard of Japanese public education and the homogenizing influence of television, which penetrates every Japanese home. They have not been systematically set apart from mainstream society, but have participated in it right along. To the extent that they also absorb its norms, especially concerning the proper life course for women, they are more likely to reject the career of their geisha mothers.

Often by the time a geisha's daughter reaches early adulthood, however, her mother is no longer a practicing geisha but has become the proprietress of a bar, teahouse, or restaurant. She may well be supporting her daughter's college education in order to increase her marriage prospects or help her obtain a better job. The mother is also then a businesswoman and the respectable owner of an exclusive establishment, which a daughter is likely to inherit. This throws a somewhat different light on the phrase "so-and-so is the daughter of a geisha."

A few women enter the profession with the idea that they will find a husband among their customers, but most geisha I talked with seemed to think this a bad reason to choose that life. Occasionally a geisha will drop out to marry, but not so frequently that any woman should expect the same to happen to her. In any case, a geisha with glimmers of marriage in her eye is the last thing that would appeal to most guests.

When a geisha does marry a customer, often her new husband will be a widower with grown children, a house to be kept up, and a need for companionship. He thus may formally make his geisha mistress (once his "number two wife") into his second wife. Geisha can make prestigious matches in this way. Not a few wives of politicians and other prominent individuals have some roots in the flower and willow world.

At the turn of the century, Oyuki of Gion married American millionnaire George Morgan. Morgan was on a world tour when he visited Kyoto in 1902, and he happened to see a performance of the Miyako Odori, the geisha dances of Gion. Twenty-two-year-old Oyuki caught his eye. He extended his Kyoto stay for months, engaging her at teahouses, where he went with an interpreter every evening. Finally he proposed marriage, and even Oyuki's demurral didn't stop him from staying on to persist in his suit. Oyuki, it seemed, was in love with a university student close to her own age who had promised to marry her once he was graduated. In the meantime, the student accepted presents from her and money to continue his studies. He encouraged Oyuki not to dismiss the rich barbarian completely, so long as he seemed willing to ply her with the gifts that eventually made their way into his pocket.

The odd triangle continued until he graduated. But the day Oyuki had longed for turned out to be one of great bitterness: the student disappeared, and the young geisha was left heartbroken. Oyuki perhaps felt guilty when she thought of George Morgan's patience and devotion, compared to the fickle student with whom she had been infatuated. Finally, she was ready to accept his offer of marriage.

The couple returned to Morgan's home in New York after the wedding, but living there was impossible because of Morgan's family's prejudice against the marriage. The two returned to Japan; but by then Japan was engaged in hostilities with Russia, and anti-foreign sentiment in the country was high. Many insults were directed toward Oyuki for giving herself to a foreigner. The couple moved on, this time to Paris, where they were finally able to live in relative peace. Oyuki studied piano; and, although doubly expatriated, the couple enjoyed all the comforts that Morgan's wealth could provide in their urbane Paris setting. After Morgan had died in 1916, Oyuki went back to New York, where, as George's widow, she was treated more kindly than she had been as his wife. In 1948 she decided to return to Japan, and she settled in Kyoto for the remaining years of her life.

Oyuki Morgan: her story is famous. A Madame Butterfly without the bathos, she began and ended her life in the old capital, with an incredible sojourn in between. She cannot even be called a geisha "success story," for her life could never be emulated. Geisha are in a position to associate with the rich and the famous, and occasionally this leads to marriage; such things happen. But it is doubtful that any man goes to the geisha quarters expressly looking for a wife.

By the time geisha reach their thirties, they have usually given up the idea (or the secret thought of) marriage altogether. Many view the role of the typical Japanese wife as dull and constricting. They say they could never give up their independence for married respectability. Sakurako is one who feels this way. She must experience at least some small thrill every time the ricksha calls for her at her okiya, and she sits back under the lacquered hood knowing that all eyes will turn to catch a glimpse of her as she glides past.

THIRTEEN

COUNTRY GEISHA

Hana ga chōchō	Is it a tender blossom
Chōchō ga hana ka	Or a butterfly?
Kite wa chira chira	Whatever – I am led astray
Mayowaseru	By what I glimpse flash by.
	[Refrain]
Asaikawa nara	If it's a shallow river
Hiza made makure	Lift your skirts up to your knees
Fukaku naru hodo	But as the water deepens
Obi o toku	Untie your sashes please.
Shintai happu o fubo ni uke	My body flesh and hair is
Oya nimo misenai	Received from Mom and Dad,
Kono shina o	
Omahan bakari wa	But the one thing I don't show them
Tanto tanto	I'll show to you my lad.
	[Refrain]
Asaikawa nara	If it's a shallow river
Hiza made makure	Lift your skirts up to your knees
Fukaku naru hodo	But as the water deepens
Obi o toku	Untie your sashes please.

Asaikawa *"Shallow River" (shamisen ditty)*

ATAMI HOT SPRINGS

THERE ARE MORE geisha in the seaside resort town of
Atami than in any other single hanamachi in Japan. Over seven

hundred geisha belong to the town's three hundred geisha houses. One of the stops on the limited express bullet train, Atami is just a one-hour trip from Tokyo Station, making it Tokyo's Coney Island. A huge new amusement park complex sprawls over the flat land by the beach, and hotels ranging in capacity from three guests to over three hundred nestle in the hills. The smell of sulphur permeates the air, for Atami is an onsen, bubbling over with mineral hot springs. Steam issues from cracks in the earth, and the mountain streams run hot. Every house and hotel taps the springs for a never-ending supply of scalding bath water.

Atami was a favorite stopping place for travelers on the old Tōkaidō Road, the route from the city of Edo to the former capital of Kyoto. For centuries female attendants in teahouses and bathhouses lured customers with whichever liquid their shop sold. Atami has thus always functioned as a tourist town, much as it does today. Almost everyone who lives and works in Atami caters to visitors' needs in one way or another.

I went to Atami on the first of July. By that time I had become well known in Kyoto as Ichigiku, the American geisha. I was engaged almost every night, and okāsan joked about what an urekko (popular) geisha I had become. But July is a slow month, and many geisha use this opportunity to take short vacations. So that's what I did: I left the connoisseur's world of the Kyoto geisha for a few days to investigate the much more earthy sulphur springs hanamachi of Atami.

My destination was the Koyomi, a small geisha house and the home of Kikugorō, a fifty-six-year-old musician. Kikugorō knew my okāsan in Kyoto through a customer they had in common. Once off the train, I was to meet her at a large hotel called the Dream Island, which all the taxi drivers in Atami were sure to know. Her house was just a few steps away. I was standing in the hotel lobby at noon when a stocky, smiling woman dressed in a blue and white *yukata* (informal cotton kimono) came striding in. Her hearty manner was very different from the coyness and reserve of the Kyoto geisha. I liked her immediately.

Visitors to Atami are offered a hot bath as they are offered a cup of tea anywhere else in Japan. Any time of day is appropriate

"*Female teahouse attendants lure travelers dressed in the yukata of their inns.*"

for taking a quick soak in Atami's abundant natural resource. Almost one-third of the first floor of Kikugorō's small house was taken up by the bath, which I was invited to enter as soon as we arrived.

Accepting her hospitality, I stepped in and saw that the roomy tub overflowed in a steady stream originating from a spout on the wall. "There's a faucet for cold if it's too hot for you," called Kikugorō. Cold water had to be piped in from a tank for drinking, cooking, and diluting the ever-full tub. My bar of soap produced only a thin scum of lather, so laden with minerals was this spring water.

When I emerged, Kikugorō loaned me one of her dozens of cotton yukata to wear. Like 99 percent of the yukatas one sees, it was dark blue and white. A foreigner would probably describe a yukata just as a cotton kimono, but to Japanese there is a world of difference between the two. A yukata is not even considered a kimono. It is summer wear, the most informal category of native dress – comparable to a bathrobe, which is a literal translation of the word. Generally, one should not wear a yukata in the company of one's superiors. An exception to this rule can be made when a person stays in an onsen town like Atami, where the yukata is perfectly proper almost anywhere. Guests wander through the shopping arcades dressed in the yukata provided by the inns. It is easy to spot who goes with which group: everyone's robe has the emblem of the hotel on it.

Japanese come to Atami to unbend and have a good time. The tone of relaxed informality is set immediately after arrival, as they step out of their first bath and don yukata. The transformation from harried clerk to expansive playboy is instantaneous. Here clothes don't just match the mood, they create it. Tanaka-san in yukata is a different person from Tanaka-san in shirt and trousers. One of the reasons parties here often get rowdy is that the yukata signals a loosening of the tight jacket of etiquette; it is impossible to stand on ceremony while wearing a yukata.

For the same reason, geisha never wear yukata when they work. They are not supposed to relax with customers. Even in Atami, no matter what one may say about the vulgarity of some of the banquets, geisha always appear in proper silk kimono.

When they are off duty, however, like other people who live there year round, they may wear yukata outside during the day as they shop, visit friends, or do errands.

It was three in the afternoon when I finally got out of the bath. I stood in Kikugorō's small garden admiring a large leopard plant with great spatulate cream-spotted leaves. There were no flowers in the heat of July, but she had planted some azaleas that still retained a few withered brackets from their May bloom. Cicadas droned everywhere, so much a part of the air that their occasional silences were startling.

Kikugorō was preparing to go to her nagauta shamisen lesson. She asked if I would care to accompany her to the Atami geisha lesson hall, a fantastic building with pillars and gables modeled on the Kabuki-za theater in Tokyo. The stage is tremendous, accommodating over a hundred dancers at a time. Atami geisha most often perform en masse, doing choreographed versions of Japanese folk dances rather than pas seul or pas de deux classical pieces. Dance classes are mass drills, done to records.

The room for shamisen lessons is much smaller than the auditorium. Music is taught on an individual basis. Although all the Atami geisha can dance, at least in the simple folk song group numbers, relatively few are accomplished musicians. Unlike Kyoto, where dancers have more prestige than musicians, in Atami a shamisen player gets one-third more pay for her ability. The nagauta teacher comes from Tokyo once a month for five days to teach the Atami geisha musicians. Kikugorō has become more a colleague than a pupil, but the teacher was coaching her for an upcoming recital.

Her lesson lasted thirty minutes, though we spent another half hour with the teacher, drinking tea and talking about nagauta. Curious, they asked me to play, so I suggested we do the interlude called *gaku* from the piece "Ren Jishi" (Lion's Dance). Two shamisens take different parts in this stately instrumental duet – which the teacher and I played, to Kikugorō's great amusement. "You could be an Atami geisha right now," she remarked. "We need more shamisen players."

On our way down the slope back to her house, we passed numerous gift shops. I wanted to take some dried fish back to

Kyoto for presents, but Kikugorō said that if I waited until the day after next she would take me to the best place to buy them. Dried fish is a specialty item in Atami. No proper tourist goes home without smelling up his luggage with a parcel of it.

The late afternoon had turned surprisingly cool from a sharp sea breeze. On our return, Kikugorō had just twenty minutes to change to kimono and rush to the Dream Island by six. While we were out, her sister had come to the house and started dinner. But we had stayed too long at the lesson hall, and Kikugorō had no time to eat. "It's all right. I have built-in reserves," said Kikugorō, patting her obi-wrapped stomach. "Don't wait up for me." She grabbed her shamisen box and hurried out the door.

SHALLOW RIVER

Kikugorō goes to work at the Dream Island at 6:00 P.M. every day except Sunday. She scribbles her name in a ledger that is the equivalent of a time clock. Most of the geisha in Atami are affiliated with one or another of the hotels, showing up each evening as if they were its employees. Atami operates very differently from the smaller urban geisha areas.

Atami's registry office keeps the roster of legitimate, dues-paying geisha, and its employees arrange lesson schedules and group performances.[1] It is not, however, the central exchange between the customers, the okiya, and the geisha. Given the size of operations in Atami – parties of four hundred guests are possible, and seventy geisha often attend a single banquet – the kenban is just not staffed to handle these logistics. Instead, the hotels and inns have evolved their own system of assuring a sufficient supply of geisha for their guests.

Only rarely does a customer know which geisha to call. Guests in Atami are tourists who have had little experience of geisha and who prefer to leave all the arrangements to the inns. The geisha show up every evening not knowing who their clients will be, but assured of a banquet to attend upon.

The women's fees are not itemized separately. The guest pays a flat sum for dinner-with-geisha. This system is very matter-of-fact compared with the way geisha are paid in the cities. A city geisha usually nets as much in tips as she does from her actual wage. In onsen towns like Atami, customers hardly know the geisha. They treat them more like waitresses, and tipping waitresses is rare in Japan.

Atami has tailored its geisha operation to meet the needs of its particular clientele: the lower-level white-collar or even blue-collar worker on an overnight binge. Most of the parties in Atami are huge: a class reunion; a division manager of a company taking all his employees on a spree; an amateur sports club on an outing. There are few intimate gatherings with just a couple of friends, a couple of geisha.

An Atami geisha party reeks with prurience. The managers of the inns have erected a standard that proclaims "our geisha are artists, please," while simultaneously encouraging the guests' wildest imagination as to what they can get away with. One establishment has even published a small booklet, *Primer in Geisha-ology*, ostensibly to instruct tourists not yet savvy in the art of having fun with geisha. In it a customer will be interested to read the following "conversation":

GEISHA E: When we were young apprentices, sometimes we'd have to play "Shallow River" at a party. We were made to lift our skirts up all the way then.

GEISHA A: I cried because of "Shallow River" when I was young too.

GEISHA D: The shamisen player wouldn't stop until we lifted our skirts all the way up. She started out slowly, playing "Shallow River," then got faster and faster, playing higher and higher.

GEISHA B: The guests watched with big grins, saying "Where's the hair? Where's the hair?"

GEISHA A: They wanted to see some pussy, and until they did they made us go on, drinking sake and leering all the while.

INTERVIEWER: But weren't you wearing panties?

GEISHA D: Oh no, we were dancers. A line from panties showing through the kimono was disgraceful.

GEISHA B: When I was made to do "Shallow River," I was so ashamed I ran away crying and locked myself in the bathroom.

INTERVIEWER: Did you show it?

GEISHA B: I had to. The shamisen kept going on and on.

GEISHA D: The poor young girls – some of them didn't even have any grass grown in yet.

INTERVIEWER: So what did they do?

GEISHA D: Before a party, they took a brush and black ink and drew grass all over their mounds.

When I asked one of the geisha whether "Shallow River" was still popular entertainment, she said she had never seen the number since she'd been working in Atami. Even Kikugorō claimed not to know the shamisen tune for it. Yet after reading the booklet, a customer would certainly hope that "Shallow River" would be included as part of the evening's entertainment. But then, in a quick reversion to propriety, the last page of the booklet contains a message warning guests to make sure their geisha are wearing badges proving that they are proper members of Atami's geisha association. Heaven forbid that someone less than a real geisha should appear at a party!

Geisha of Easy Virtue

Onsen geisha is usually taken as a euphemism for a prostitute. There is reason for this, although the identification of the two is by no means absolute. Lewd joking, pawing, and braggadocio regularly take place at an onsen geisha party. The guests can get as drunk as they please because they have only to crawl up to their rooms later, and they are already in yukata, which serve as nightclothes. The fact that the geisha entertain at the inns and hotels where customers stay the night also adds to the atmosphere of titillation.

Yet some of the same factors make it more difficult to sleep with a geisha, assuming she were willing. Many men drink so much at these raucous parties that sex is beyond their capabilities, if not their entreaties. Privacy is another problem. When large groups come to Atami everyone usually sleeps together in one or several big rooms. (If there are a few women along – for example, if the secretaries have come along on the outing too – they get quarters to themselves.) So a man could not very well take a geisha to his room because of his ten or fifteen roommates. He would have to entice her to another hotel and sneak out, avoiding the eyes of all his friends.

Most geisha disapprove of taking all-night customers. They make a definite distinction between a danna, or patron, and one-night stands. Everyone knows that it happens, but women who are too flagrant about sleeping with customers are shunned by the other geisha and snubbed in subtle and not so subtle ways. Atami has separate registration systems for the longtime, proven geisha like Kikugorō and the ones who have worked for under a year. There is tremendous turnover in the latter group. Some were bar hostesses or waitresses yesterday and will tire of being geisha tomorrow.

I was told that men are one of the main reasons why Atami geisha drop out. Seldom does one of them get a marriage proposal per se, but not infrequently she may set up housekeeping with a man. If such an arrangement doesn't last, the woman may come back, disillusioned, to rejoin the geisha ranks.

Compared to city geisha, the geisha in Atami are less likely to find patrons among their customers. They do not enjoy the protection of women in the roles of mother or older sister, who carefully introduce them to suitable men. They rarely see the same tourist twice in one year. The customers in Atami are like the wind, blowing roughly one moment but gone the next.

An Evil Fate

I sat down with Kikugorō's sister to a dinner of fish fillets sautéed in butter, pickled eggplant, and rice. She was also a shamisen player, and she had been a geisha in Atami under the name of Tamafune. Several years before I met her, she had had a stroke, leaving her vulnerable to sudden faints and spells of uncontrolled twitching. One seizure occurred at a banquet, and the manager of the inn strongly encouraged her to retire. She has little money, and though she and Kikugorō have two brothers and two other sisters, they feel closest to each other. Tamafune comes and stays with Kikugorō for long periods in Atami. The house, the Koyomi, has a license as an okiya, but no other geisha besides Kikugorō live there now. The two sisters are good company.

We cleared away the dinner dishes and sat smoking cigarettes and drinking tea, waiting up for Kikugorō. Tamafune said that at times like this, when she sits alone waiting for her sister, she wishes she had children. Before she suffered the stroke, she had taken a young girl into her house, treating her like a daughter and hoping to adopt her formally. The girl was an orphan of sixteen when she went to live with Tamafune. If things had worked out, she would have been the comfort and support of Tamafune's old age. But as she related what happened, the older woman concluded that the girl must have had an evil fate.

The girl had lived in Atami, so she naturally wanted to work as a geisha. She took group dance instruction for three months and joined the ranks simply by appearing at a banquet one night along with everybody else. New geisha in Atami do not have coming-out ceremonies. Tamafune would sometimes attend the same banquets and try to keep her from drinking too much, but her "daughter" did not take kindly to interference. Soon she began stumbling home late at night, blind drunk, leaving her kimono crumpled all over her room. She was a common whore, friends informed Tamafune. Then she took up with a man, a gangster by all accounts, and became pregnant. Tamafune supported her through all this trouble – the daughter couldn't work when her pregnancy began to show – and paid the medical bills for the birth.

After the baby was born, the girl ran away with the child's father. "Good riddance," said Tamafune's friends, unable to understand why the older woman was so melancholy. "I'm too old to raise a baby properly. It needs its mother," she said, though she kept the infant all day, leaving the child with friends when she worked in the evening. She didn't know the whereabouts of her "daughter" until the phone rang one day and the police informed her that the young woman was dead. Things had not worked out with her lover, and, in a fit of depression, she had thrown herself in front of a train. Later, the man's family came to take the child away.

"I probably spoiled her," said Tamafune, getting up to refill the teapot. "When I remembered how rough things were for me as a child, I wanted to make life better for her. I was scolded so many times when I was her age, I couldn't bring myself to get angry with her. Maybe it wouldn't have made any difference anyway. Somebody told me she was manic-depressive and that I should have taken her for counseling. I guess I should have, but I didn't understand at the time." She opened a new pack of cigarettes and lit one. "It was probably her destiny to turn out as she did, and I guess I shouldn't blame myself for what happened."

"Did you ever think about marriage yourself?" I asked her. "I suppose now it would be nice to have someone around for company," she said, "but I never felt inclined to marry when I was young enough. I enjoyed my life as a geisha once I was able to support myself – I'd say my thirties were the best time of my life. When I was older, I think I appreciated the gei aspect of the geisha life more and more. I spent a lot of time with the shamisen and played in recitals several times a year, not only nagauta, but kiyomoto and tokiwazu too. I began to get bored with parties, yet that was the necessary part of making a living as a geisha."

Because of her stroke, Tamafune cannot play the shamisen any more. During the last rainy season, when the cat-skin belly of the instrument split because of the humidity, she did not even take it to be repaired. Kikugorō presses her to sell it because she doesn't play, but Tamafune can't yet bring herself to do that. "I'll probably die soon anyway, so I might as well keep it. The doctors explained a stroke to me, but I think of it as a person's brain just suddenly ripping, like a torn shamisen."

A SOCIALLY RECOGNIZED PROFESSION

Kikugorō had not returned by midnight, so I went to bed. The guests at Dream Island had decided to prolong their party, and she did not return until 1:00 A.M. We all slept till ten the next morning. I was awakened by the sound of the heavy wooden "rain doors" being shoved open on the first floor. They are pushed along a track to their storage compartment at the end of the wall, where they fall in with a crash that shakes the house. It had rained early in the morning, and the air was clear with a hint of salt and seaweed.

To start the day, Tamafune swept the front stoop and splashed some water on it, and we all washed our faces in the never-ending supply of hot water. Kikugorō took the first of her four or five daily baths. We had some of Atami's famous dried fish for breakfast with rice and raw egg (I was offered toast with jam if I preferred), then Kikugorō took me to the kenban. I was to observe a dance lesson and meet both the head of the registry office and the director of Atami's geisha association, two elderly ex-geisha.

Kikugorō once served as director of the performances department of the kenban. The office is always held by a currently active geisha who takes charge of planning the dance and music presented at the large banquets. It is a prestigious post, but pay is nominal, and it takes up a great deal of time. Kikugorō finally decided it was too much bother. "Ho," she called to a cluster of women drinking tea around a low table, "here's an unusual person who wants to talk to you." She introduced me to the group, and I felt, as I had the previous day when I met Kikugorō, an easy congeniality much different from the notoriously hard to penetrate "Kyoto facade."

In Kyoto it had taken many months before some of the geisha felt comfortable enough to talk about themselves with me. In Atami, I was amazed at the immediate candor displayed by the geisha. Perhaps the Atami geisha don't put on airs like their Kyoto counterparts, or perhaps I felt at ease because I had been introduced by the well-known and well-liked Kikugorō. In any case, the women made room for us at the table, poured two more cups of tea, and talked openly about geisha life in Atami.

The head of the geisha association said that, large as Atami's geisha population is (around eight hundred, she estimated), like all the other hanamachi in the country it had suffered a decline in recent years. During the 1960s, over a thousand geisha had been registered in Atami! I asked whether she thought of geisha now as ordinary working women. She answered:

"For better or worse, I suppose they are. Better in the sense that there is much more personal freedom in the profession, but worse from the standpoint of standards of art. The women who own the geisha houses don't have control over the girls as they did in the past.

"I used to run an okiya myself, for example, and there was one girl who decided she was going to manage her own mizu-age. So she went out, offered the opportunity to the highest bidder and then pocketed the money herself. Can you imagine? I'll tell you, you sure don't get any girls coming here these days selling themselves for filial piety.

"We have women here who come from all over the country, but I suppose the biggest group comes from Kyushu. It's always been that way, actually."

Another woman remarked how strange this is, as Kyushu is so far from Atami.

"Well, there's been a tradition in Kyushu for women to leave their families to find work. Think of the bazoku geisha from Hakata, going off to Manchuria, or the karayuki-san who went to Southeast Asia.[2] Kyushu has always been poor and its women self-reliant. As long as they have to leave home, most want to go as far as possible.

"I should know, I'm from Kyushu myself. I started out here in Atami when I was thirty. Nobody in my family had ever been a geisha – you hardly ever see daughters of geisha here – so I came with nothing but the strength of ignorance."

She laughed, and I could tell from her manner that she enjoyed her life in Atami. Another ex-geisha, the director of the kenban, had a story about her own daughter's becoming a geisha here:

"One day, when my daughter was about the right age, I brought up the matter with her and said, 'Why don't you try it out?' She asked what was involved, and I told her dancing, pouring sake for guests, and talking. My daughter had danced on stage before, and she always enjoyed her lessons, so I figured she would like being a geisha.

"So at the end of her first engagement, they gave her an envelope with her wages. 'What's this?' she says, and hands it back. 'That's not necessary.' The manager of the inn nearly fell over.

'Why not?' he asks. So my daughter says, 'Whenever I dance on stage my mother has to pay out a lot of money, but here I get to do it for free.'"[3]

"How long did that last?" one of the other women asked. "Not long," said the director of the kenban. "Now she's just like any other geisha, greedy for money. She'll leave a party early and still claim full wages for it." Kikugorō agreed that such practices had become typical these days. "Young geisha are getting too smart for their own good," she said. "Geisha used to have a certain charm precisely because they were different from the wife a man left at home. Geisha weren't so grasping and penny-pinching. The difference between a woman in the home and a professional is disappearing – and that's not good."

"It's true," said the director. "When a geisha knew nothing about money and finances, that wasn't good either, but it's really gone too far now. It's as if they come to the banquets and turn their taxi meters on."

The women agreed that geisha life had become much easier for younger women, mostly because a girl can choose to work as a geisha. Despite what they said about the profession's becoming "brighter," however, they still felt that many people view it, unfairly, as disreputable.

One geisha recounted an incident from the time her son went off to college. On the entrance form was a space marked "mother's occupation," which he was embarrassed to fill in. He said, "Mother, your profession is not socially recognized." Indignant, she replied, "Well, they certainly recognize my income for taxes."

At breakfast I had asked Kikugorō if I might put on a kimono and accompany her to work. I wanted to see what a banquet in Atami was like from the geisha's perspective. She said she'd be happy to have me come along if I thought I could handle it, but she would have to make sure it was all right with the office. She brought the matter up before we left the kenban. The women in charge consulted with each other briefly. "There's no precedent for it, so we won't be able to pay you," they said. "It's okay," I said. "That's not necessary."

ICHIGUKO IN ATAMI

I spent the afternoon in the local beauty parlor, having my hair washed and done up, then wandered through the arcades and souvenir shops along the winding street back up the slope to Kikugorō's house. She was just getting out of the bath. "I'm afraid my kimonos will be a bit dark for someone your age," she remarked, opening a drawer and riffling through her summer robes. "I prefer the darker colors, actually," I said, and chose a navy blue narrow-striped silk kimono with a pattern of thistles on the hem. Tamafune helped us both tie our obis and stood back to approve the effect. "It's been a long time since two geisha went out from the Koyomi," she said.

We walked over to the Dream Island, where Kikugorō checked in and received her first assignment: a banquet for one hundred guests in the Pine Room. I watched with a group of geisha standing in the hall while other geisha in folk costume danced on a stage at one end of the huge room. Their program of song and dance lasted about twenty minutes, during which the guests talked noisily and ate dinner. When the set program ended, those of us waiting in the hall entered with bottles of beer and sake. Kikugorō and two other older geisha with shamisens stayed on stage to play requests from customers.

Inside nearly every Japanese man is a hidden performer who needs only a few cups of sake and a word of encouragement to pop out. Folk songs, nostalgic military songs, chansons, and Stephen Foster melodies are among the tunes one is likely to hear at such banquets. The stage in the Pine Room had a microphone, which encouraged guests to imitate their favorite singing idols, tremolo and all.

During a break, Kikugorō came down from the stage and was drawn aside by the hotel manager. The man hosting this party apparently thought I was a reporter or something of the sort, and my presence was making him nervous. Rather than try to explain, Kikugorō put me in the charge of two younger geisha who were headed for an even bigger party of nearly two hundred guests. I was to stay with them until the first engagement ended, then meet Kikugorō back in the lobby.

An entire office from one of the Sumitomo industries in Tokyo was having its annual summer bash in the Peony Room upstairs. Many younger people, women as well as men, were in this group, although none of the young women (a bit nervous at how relaxed their male colleagues had become) had had quite enough nerve to change to yukata themselves. The party was in full swing by the time we walked in. Guests as well as geisha were circulating around the low tables pouring drinks. Early formalities having been dispensed with, yukata-clad figures gallivanted here and there, toasting one another.

The bacchanalia in the Peony Room was not at all the sort of gathering I had become accustomed to in the teahouses of Ponto-chō. The difference in scale was staggering. A soiree with geisha in Kyoto rarely involves more than fifty guests, and usually they are much smaller: four or five men call as many geisha. I was used to classical pieces performed by one or two dancers on the tatami at the lower end of the room in a teahouse, not to a chorus line of sixty-five geisha in costume on a stage. A Kyoto geisha would have been horrified at the wild scene in the Peony Room. At precisely 7:30, however, all the geisha got up and left.

A group of tourists at a hotel like the Dream Island is given the choice of having its banquet with or without geisha. Most opt for geisha. The parties all begin at 6:00, and the geisha are engaged until 7:30. This hour and a half is the "first set" of the evening and the minimum period for which they can be hired. After 7:30, the customers decide whether they want some of the geisha to stay on, and their time is paid for in half-hour stints thereafter. Unlike the urban hanamachi, where the economic aspect of engaging geisha is veiled, Atami customers know exactly how much a certain number of geisha for a certain number of hours will cost them. They prefer it that way.[4]

The difference in the way money is treated makes a great difference in the atmosphere of a geisha party. In the more prestigious flower wards, efforts are made to sustain a feeling of mutuality in these gatherings. The geisha are supposed to be pleased to see the guests, and vice versa. The best parties are those where the people on both sides seem to be enjoying themselves; the economic fact that the geisha's company is hired is therefore carefully set aside to be dealt with at another time.

Setting a taxi meter really is an apt image for Atami geisha services. This is not so much because the geisha here are especially cold and calculating as because the customers treat them in such an impersonal way. In fact, the *Primer in Geisha-ology* advises tourists to think of a geisha as a running meter from whom they should wring as much enjoyment as they can before time is up. Besides the innuendo clinging to this "advice," the phrase highlights the economic aspect of engaging a geisha in a way that women in Pontochō or Shimbashi would consider extremely offensive.

After leaving the party in the Peony Room, the geisha returned to the lobby to find out the location of their next assignment from the manager. I rejoined Kikugorō. We set out to a small party in the Plover Room, whose members had decided to have geisha on the second round. It seemed a bit odd when we got there, however – that it was only Kikugorō and me, and that the guests were mostly women, very drunk. Some were doing parodies of classical dance using the clumsy hotel dinner trays and round fans for props. A few wanted to sing, so Kikugorō obliged them by playing accompaniment on her shamisen, while I went around pouring sake.

After about half an hour, a messenger sent by the manager poked her head in and summoned us from the room. Kikugorō had made a mistake. The host of the party that had requested a shamisen player was complaining that nobody had showed up. "I thought that group of ladies back there was a strange one to be calling geisha," Kikugorō said, laughing it off and heading to the Deer Room. She would not be paid for the time just spent.

Kikugorō went straight up to the small stage of this room and started to play. I joined the dozen or so geisha already with the guests. By Atami standards this was a small party, about twenty men, but they were giving the geisha a hard time. The women tried to stay close to one another so as not to be cornered by one of the greasy-fingered guests. I soon began edging my way closer to the other geisha, too. Unfortunately, I was singled out for the attentions of a particularly crude customer, who leaped over the low table and grabbed me from behind. The other geisha froze, and Kikugorō, still on stage, fumed. The man was very drunk and, unable to fend him off with words, I finally pulled a small fan from my obi and rapped him twice on the head. He pulled back, greatly surprised, and the geisha all laughed nervously.

This broke the tension, though. Muttering, he staggered toward the stage and shouted at Kikugorō: "Oi, old lady! Play 'Kuroda Bushi,' I'm going to sing." She played the opening bars of this dirge-like drinking song, but he missed his cue. "You're not following me," he accused her. Kikugorō put down her shamisen. "That's because you're tone deaf, Mister," she said in a level voice. The guest became livid. "Call me a geisha who can play the shamisen," he roared.

By this time the manager had arrived, having been notified that a scene was brewing in the Deer Room. Kikugorō approached him and said for all to hear, "You call a geisha in Atami who can play the shamisen better than I can. I'd like to meet her." She was clearly ready to walk out.

The manager took her aside and calmed her down. If Kikugorō is insulted she will simply leave a party, saying to the guest, "Keep your money, I'm not taking this." The man was sulking at his seat, though he seemed to realize he had gone too far. Some of his cronies were trying to josh him into a better humor. Kikugorō stayed another few minutes for appearances, but I slipped out of the room to wait for her in the corridor.

I leaned up against the wooden pillar of the doorjamb, listening to the howls of laughter and snatches of drunken song issuing from each of the rooms down the hallway. A maid came by with a tray of beer bottles. She glanced at me. "How do you like it?" she asked. "It's really something," I said, "I don't think I could last a week here." "You get used to it," she said, deftly balancing the tray with one hand and sliding the door open with the other. I glanced in and saw that the obnoxious customer had fallen asleep on the floor and the party had quieted down. Kikugorō was preparing to leave.

We went back to the lobby where there was one more request for her to play the shamisen. To her amusement, I decided that I had seen enough. Instead of accompanying her, I joined a group of geisha who were finished for the evening, sitting with cups of tea in a secluded corner of the lobby. One of them had been at the party in the Deer Room, and she recounted the incident with the fan. "I can't stand customers like that," one geisha exclaimed. "Good for you, maybe that will teach him." She held out her arm, brushing at a grease mark left on her kimono by the fingers of a careless guest who had tugged on her sleeve.

"You really have to put up with a lot," I said, "it's exhausting." "It's not always so bad," said one younger woman brightly. "I like it a lot better than being a secretary. I can put up with anything so long as I know that I can be out of here by ten o'clock. I can also take off any days I don't want to work without a boss yelling at me to keep to a schedule. There are a lot of advantages to working here, I think. Any job has inconveniences, and you just have to learn to deal with them." "Yes, like dry-cleaning bills," said the other geisha glumly.

They asked me how I liked living in Kyoto, and I invited them to visit me if they had a chance to take a trip to the old capital. Two of them had never been to Kyoto and felt that their education as Japanese would be incomplete until they had. A few minutes after ten o'clock Kikugorō marched in, her shamisen packed up, ready to go home for dinner. Tarō, one of the geisha in the group I had been talking with, came along.

Tarō is a masculine name, and so is Kikugorō (the name of a famous Kabuki actor). The geisha names that many of the women in Atami choose seemed odd, flamboyant, and humorous to me: Kujaku (peacock), Donguri (acorn), Kacha and Chacha (flower-tea and tea-tea), Tamago (egg), Konabe (little pot). There were many more flowery-sounding names too, but I found myself preoccupied wondering what a geisha calling herself Chacha would be like. Undoubtedly she knew that customers would be just as intrigued.

Tamafune had a dinner ready for us that included a Western-style green salad in my honor. Tarō, who was short and fat, shunned the lettuce. "Never did like fruits or vegetables," she said, sprinkling black sesame seeds on her rice and filling up the bowl with hot tea. She was good-humored and coarse, with tiny pearly teeth that she seemed to realize were her most attractive feature. I had not seen her at any of the banquets but could imagine how she titillated guests with her figure spilling over the top of her obi and her lewd jokes. "My kimono always gets stains here," she complained, holding her bosom as if it were a small cuddly animal. "I guess my boobs are just too big." "Oh no, Tarō-chan," said Tamafune, not catching the air of self-satisfaction in her remark, "they're a good size. Better too much than not enough."

Kikugorō excused herself early and went to take her last bath and go to bed. Pleading exhaustion, I did the same soon afterward, and was mildly ribbed by Tarō, who thought it was funny that I had had to defend my virtue with a fan. I hung the kimono Kikugorō had loaned me on a pole in the room and examined it for grease stains before I went to bed. I was relieved to find it unspotted in spite of its rough handling earlier.

The following day, I took the train back to Kyoto. The old auntie who worked at the Mitsuba gleefully made off with the dried fish I brought back for her, and okāsan gave me a list of people who had called while I was away. "I hope you had a nice rest in Atami," she said.

FOURTEEN

THREE STRINGS

Sanbon ga areba, taberareru   If you've got three strings, you can eat.

A geisha saying

THE SHAMISEN

TSUYU BEGAN WITH a crash of thunder and a sudden downpour. I woke up at 5:45 the morning of June 9 with rain dripping through my roof. June is the rainy season, tsuyu, written as "plum rain" or, alternatively, "mold rain": the rains that come when the plums are mottled yellow with ripeness, when mold has ideal conditions to grow. The air is warm and so damp that things never completely dry out. Mildew creeps into closets, bathrooms, and kitchens. If a kimono is not allowed to air after being worn, mildew will stain the sleeves and creases where perspiration has soaked in.

Later in the morning after the skies had cleared, I noticed a single blue hydrangea in the cool, steamy garden of the Mitsuba. Flowerets had opened only at the edges of a head of tightly closed buds. By afternoon, torrents of rain were falling again. People said the rainy season that year had a rough, masculine temperament. A feminine tsuyu, I supposed, would have been one where soft rain drizzled without break, day after gray day.

Tsuyu is hard on clothing, crisp foods, and nerves. It is also hard on shamisens. The body of the instrument is a hollow wooden frame, covered back and front with a tautly stretched skin – cat skin for the finer instruments, dog skin for the cheaper practice models. The high humidity during the rainy season will often cause the skin to split open along the line of some small imperfection, rendering the shamisen completely unplayable until it is re-covered.

I owned an old nagauta shamisen that I had brought back to Japan. This kind of instrument has a relatively slender neck compared with the thicker shamisens used for other types of music, so when I began studying kouta, I borrowed a larger shamisen fitted with stouter strings for practicing. My own shamisen, wrapped in a green satin dustcover, sat idle on the cabinet in my room.

One day in mid-June, shut up in the grayness of yet another dank, misty day, I heard something snap. I wondered vaguely what had made the noise and went back to my reading. Several days passed, and I decided to take out my shamisen. I slipped off its dustcover and there it was – completely split down the middle. I was taken by surprise and felt a pang of guilt. Even though I knew full well about tsuyu, it seemed to me that my shamisen had burst with jealousy as it sat there in the same room while I carried on with another instrument.

O-shami is the affectionate term geisha use for their shamisens, and, though I was shamelessly anthropomorphizing, I realized how much I had absorbed of the geisha's attitude toward the instrument. Traditionally the shamisen was the badge of the geisha profession, the "three strings" upon which the women made their living. Until the postwar period, every young girl who entered geisha apprenticeship perforce learned to play it. Even now, despite the usual division of artistic labor between geisha who are primarily dancers and those who are musicians, a serious dancer also learns enough shamisen and singing to increase her understanding of the dance, even if she never plays music publicly for customers.

In spite of such aberrations as guitar-playing geisha (an ephemeral idea aimed at attracting younger customers to geisha entertainment in the 1960s), the shamisen is, and has always been, the instrument of the geisha world. The prototype of the shamisen was introduced into Japan from China via Korea in the

1560s. Within the space of a hundred years it had attained its present form and had become the mainstay of the newly developed profession of female artistes called geisha. Wherever there were geisha there were shamisens.

Whenever one heard a shamisen, one heard the music of the city-dwelling merchant class that provided the main support for the entertainment districts. The upper classes – the samurai and the small coterie of the nobility – did not play (and were not supposed to listen to) the plaintive and sentimental lyrics that went with shamisen tunes. The thirteen-stringed harp-like *koto* was (and largely still is) considered a much more genteel instrument than the twanging, vibrant shamisen. Inevitably, then, the status of the shamisen partook of that of its practitioners. But, like many of the other officially despised art forms of the Edo period, shamisen music had vitality and originality. It was played everywhere, despite occasional government bans.

Even in Japan of the late twentieth century, the shamisen still enjoys general popularity alongside the piano, violin, and guitar and traditional Japanese instruments like the koto and the breathy, haunting bamboo *shakuhachi*. There is no danger that the shamisen might disappear, as its predecessor the *biwa* is in danger of doing. Neither does the shamisen rely solely on the geisha for its public preservation; it is even enjoying a small boom in popularity among younger Japanese. Still, some of the older styles of shamisen music (schools like itchū-bushi, *bungobushi*, *sonehachi*, and *shinnai*) barely survive, nurtured by a few aging geisha musicians.

The most frequently heard schools of shamisen music today are tokiwazu, kiyomoto, and nagauta.[1] Of these, nagauta (long songs) is by far the largest in terms of its following, and it tends to be considered the most basic for amateur students. In this respect, a young geisha just learning to play the shamisen is just as likely as a businessman's daughter to start out with nagauta.

While living in Kyoto, I studied nagauta with Kineya Kimihatsu. She gave lessons in an upstairs room of her small house in the center of Pontochō. Ichiteru's lesson was scheduled right before mine, and if I arrived a little early I could listen to her fumble through a simple piece against the background of

Kimihatsu's patient corrections. Ichiteru was one of the younger geisha, newly graduated from maiko status, and was not much interested in nagauta. Already a fairly talented dancer, she would never be a musician, although eventually some of the musical training might seep in.

GEISHA MUSICIANS

Learning music in Japan is not an intellectual process; it involves listening, mimicking, and repetition. Although several styles of notation have been developed and published for the shamisen, most geisha learn to play the old-fashioned way by ear. To learn something means to memorize it, and the composition becomes part of a geisha's musical sensibilities as a piece of music simply played off the page cannot.

I had previously studied nagauta using notation and could sight-read almost anything. This was a somewhat useless talent, though, because in following the shamisen score I could not concentrate on the singing. It is pointless to recreate the nagauta shamisen line by itself because it is accompaniment for the voice, and except for some of the melodic instrumental interludes, it makes no musical sense without the vocal line. I still practiced with the books in front of me, but when I went for my lesson with Kimihatsu, I left them at home.

I found that playing the shamisen as a geisha was very different from playing it for fun. Geisha musicians display the fullest range of their virtuosity when they play for the dance performances and music recitals that are rehearsed and presented to the public. When they play together with their colleagues they can concentrate fully on the expression of the music. But a geisha must develop another sort of skill with the shamisen when she is asked to play at a banquet. A guest who has been taking lessons in kouta, for example, asks the geisha to provide accompaniment, and she – while in fact structuring the piece – must appear to be following his lead.

I learned the difficulty of this with great chagrin the first time I was asked to play. Another geisha and I were to do a section of a nagauta piece that I was fully confident I knew backward and forward, while the customer sang. He was no professional, however, and his voice began to wander in ways I had never heard. I was completely thrown off and unable to recover until almost the end. My face burned as the other guests clapped politely. One customer afterward said to me, "You're only pretending to play, aren't you?" Of course it was impossible to reply that it was the guest's fault because his singing was irregular.

A geisha has to know the music so thoroughly that no matter how much a customer may stretch it out of its intended form, she can structure it with her strategically placed calls and judicious playing.[2] I had had experience only in playing while a teacher or another accomplished pupil sang, which was nothing, I came to realize, compared to the difficulty of making an amateur singer sound good through skillful timing with the shamisen.

My respect deepened for geisha musicians and the unsung difficulties of their art. I was able to perform at banquets by singing kouta while accompanying myself, and a few times I single-handedly provided the music and song for Ichiume and Ichiteru to dance, but I was not steeped in the music as the older geisha were. Coaxing a guest's wavering voice along was for me the most difficult part of the geisha's gei that I strove to make my own.

Paradoxically, customers often feel that the zashiki gei, or banquet arts, that geisha present are inferior to their elaborate rehearsed stage performances. The former look simple, spontaneous, tossed off with casual virtuosity, and a guest with an untutored eye and ear may not think much of these short presentations. Many geisha feel just the opposite. With enough rehearsal, anyone can put on a fabulous stage show, but in the intimate setting of a teahouse, even small faults become conspicuous. If a performance is to be absorbing at all, it will be due not to costuming, props, or makeup, but to the unadorned skill of the dancer and her fan, or to "three strings" and a single voice.

A geisha who brings a shamisen to a party is expected to be able to accompany anything a customer might want to sing; she, after all, is the professional. But strangely enough, in the hierarchy of the performing arts, although the dancer is always applauded (and, if the event is a concert, so is the singer), the shamisen player is considered more or less as background.[3] Young girls are not often attracted to the geisha life because of the shamisen. The instrument requires years of work, and little evident glamor is attached to being the background accompaniment.

Geisha themselves have explanations for why some women become *jikata* (the "seated ones") rather than *odoriko* (dancers). They say that a girl who is strikingly tall is not encouraged to go on stage as a dancer. A glaring height discrepancy violates the sense of proportion on stage. Some women do not have the streak of exhibitionism necessary to enjoy the limelight and prefer the sidelines of the orchestra section. Kazue, for example, a short and rather plain elderly Pontochō geisha, just did not have the requisite grace for dancing. Also in keeping with the less flamboyant pose of the musician, the dancers tend to be younger, the musicians older. But some have always been attracted to the music for its own sake, and, had I been a Japanese geisha instead of an American anthropologist, this would have been my reason for choosing the profession.

When Pontochō's Kamo River Dance was held in May 1976, I saw the program six times. The main piece, "For Love of a Serpent," was a Kabukiesque ghost story with "new traditional music" (*shin hōgaku*) by Tokiwazu Mojibei. Dramatic rhythms and mysterious harmonies sent shudders up viewers' spines at the appropriate moments. The dancers punctuated the continuous musical accompaniment with bits of spoken dialogue, but the geisha musicians seated along the side of the theater provided the main narrative continuity. By the end of the month they all had dark crescents under tired eyes and had become hoarse from the strain of performing every other day for a month.

The Kamo River Dance that year played to a full house every performance and was extended three days because of its popularity. The dancers, of course, received most of the attention, but I admired the shamisen players and singers even more. I had seen the Gion Dances, the better known Miyako Odori, at the end of April. The music there was much more conventional, the dances done in the slow-moving *kyōmai* style choreographed by Gion's venerable Inoue Yachiyo.

The Gion Theater is bigger than Pontochō's, and it draws more tourists. One of the show's main attractions is a flamboyant massed dance of all the maiko, dressed alike in gaudy blue, red, and pink floral kimono. What the tourists do not realize is that the ranks of real maiko are padded with imposters: high school girls with wigs, hired to help create the lavish effect.

I saw the performance of the Miyako Odori with my friend Tokizō, a musician and teacher of the tokiwazu school of shamisen music. He had several Gion geisha among his pupils, so he always received tickets for the dances. Every year the same thing, he said, but still, every year he went. A note of unintentional humor was provided during a dance with an autumnal motif, when one of the "maiko" mistakenly flashed her cherry blossom fan as everyone else was showing maple leaves.

During intermission, Tokizō and I turned in our ticket stubs for a bowl of whisked green tea and a sweet bean cake in another room, where one geisha and one maiko were presenting a special form of the tea ceremony.[4] The small cake plates were decorated with Gion's trademark, and we were supposed to keep these as souvenirs. Some of the tourists seemed awed at receiving a bowl of ceremonial tea from the hands of a real live maiko, but Tokizō slurped his down matter-of factly and jumped up, leaving his cake plate behind. It was eagerly snatched up by the next person in line. Going outside to be away from the crush of tourists, we leaned up against a large stone artfully placed in the mossy garden. Tokizō said he had a strange request to make.

DIVERTIMENTI

Tokizō and his father, the premier master of their particular branch of tokiwazu, were planning a student recital for the end of June. He asked if I would play shamisen on that occasion. I was puzzled; I had never played tokiwazu, as he knew. That didn't matter, he said. His idea was to put together a medley of instrumental interludes that the tokiwazu and nagauta repertoires had in common. It would be unusual, certainly, yet it was the sort of thing that would pique everyone's interest.

I agreed to give it a try. We had six weeks to choose the pieces, string them together, and rehearse our creation. Tokizō held lessons every other day during this time to help his students with their recital numbers, and I visited him whenever I could spare a few hours. He used the second-floor sitting room of an old teahouse in Gion to give these morning and afternoon lessons. When he was busy with another pupil, I would wait downstairs and have tea with the elderly proprietress. No geisha were affiliated with the house, and its quietness was rarely disturbed by parties. There was not a speck of dust to be found, but somehow the place was slightly faded, its solitude not quite suitable for a teahouse. I liked it immensely.

Tokizō can sit for hours on folded legs, playing accompaniment for his pupils who sing, and singing for his pupils who are learning shamisen. He holds almost the entire tokiwazu repertoire in his head, having begun formal training with his father at age three. Tall and gangly, he is not anyone's idea of what a traditional musician should look like – until one notices the deformity on his right hand, the dead giveaway of a professional shamisen player. On the inside bottom joint of his little finger there is a huge, knobby callous, caused by the bite of the edge of the plectrum, held to strike the strings. My own finger had a dent at that spot, but how many years had it taken, I wondered, to grow that mushroom of flesh on Tokizō's finger.

At our first meeting we sorted through a selection of our favorite shamisen pieces, all of which are known by specific names. The instrumental interludes, called *ai no te*, have symbolic associations similar to but more involved than Wagnerian leitmotifs. Anyone acquainted with traditional music who listened to our potpourri would surely experience a series of extra-musical impressions; so we wanted to arrange them in order to produce a poetical as well as a musical effect.

Our starting piece was an easy choice: the beginning of a *sambasō*, a category of shamisen music with ancient roots, originally connected to Shinto votive dance, from the tokiwazu repertory. A program commonly starts with a sambasō, and we felt it would be propitious to begin our endeavor with a few bars from one. Then, still in the same tuning, we proceeded to the stately interlude called gaku without missing a beat. Echoing a trope from music of the No theater, gaku occurs in both nagauta and toki-wazu pieces, lending a tone of solemnity when it appears.

I was then to play a repeat of gaku while Tokizd played the famous koto classic *rokudan* along with it. This was the first hint of the musical quirks and odd combinations to come. On the day of the recital we would be joined by a young girl playing the *taiko* drum, which would give additional zest to the already rhythmical shamisens. The character of each musical motif we used became more theatrical as we continued. A melody called *chidori* (plovers) had an unusual obbligato part that I played, and then a drum solo led us into the fast-paced bars of the festive *yatai* interlude.

At this point both shamisens changed tuning for the haunting melody called *tsukuda*, associated with the skiffs that once ferried geisha and guests across the Sumida River. Tsukuda led right into *sugagaki*, a musical motif used in Kabuki to herald the approach of an *oiran*, a resplendent lady of pleasure, with her retinue. Our medley had worked up to a feverish rhythm by this time. Then, abruptly, we changed pace with our central piece: the slow, mysterious interlude called "snow" (*yuki*). I played the melody while Tokizō kept up a monotonous single-note background.

This proved to be spectacular timing. On the day of the recital itself, we had so thoroughly captured the attention of the audience by this point that the room fell completely still. As I played I was conscious of the chirping of a bird outside. The recital took place in an old mansion-turned-restaurant whose sliding doors had been removed to make the large reception room contiguous with the azalea-clad garden. People could move easily from room to garden, and so they did. Recitals are usually played to a squirming audience. Listeners pop in and out, listen to a friend's or relative's number, then move away to chat. But everyone was spellbound for the brief, quiet interlude of snow.

Of course, such an effect was only possible because of its brevity, and we snapped it with another drum solo and a retuning for the frivolous *sawagi*, a melody intended to represent a riotous geisha party in Asakusa. The next three parts, leading to the close of our combination, were *sarashi*, *kakesu*, and *kurui*, each exhibiting more brilliant rhythms than the one before, accompanied by the drum, which had been quiet during snow. We finished off with a musical joke: the introduction to *Nōzaki*, a gidayū piece that calls to mind the half-lilting, half-jerky movements of Bunraku puppets. It was funny because it was so incongruous.

My okāsan had come to this recital with her friend Korika, and when our piece ended I found them sitting outside on a stone bench fanning themselves. Korika kept slapping my knee with her closed fan to punctuate her amazement at the performance. My friend Motoko was sitting with the two okāsans, and she went into another round of applause as I came outside. Motoko had more than a casual interest in the shamisen.

THE PULL OF THREE STRINGS

A few weeks before this recital, I had received a telephone call from a young woman who had seen an article about me in a Kyoto newspaper. She wondered if she could visit to talk about Japanese music, as she, too, played the shamisen. I met Motoko the following day. She climbed the narrow stairs to my small apartment adjoining the Mitsuba, carrying a box of expensive sweets. She was tall, with shoulder-length blue-black hair unsullied by either permanent waving or the then popular henna rinse treatment. I had been practicing sections of Tokizō's and my medley before she came, so my shamisen, tape recorder, and texts lay scattered on the tatami floor. She glanced at these things and we began talking as if we had known each other for years.

After about ten minutes, she blushed and placed her palms on the floor, "Excuse my rudeness, I forgot to introduce myself. My name is Toribe Motoko." She slid the box of cakes toward me. I bowed in return, but already such formalities seemed unnecessary. Like me, Motoko had been attracted to the shamisen the first time she had heard it. Her parents, though, preferred that she take koto lessons, so she played that long rectangular harp for many years before beginning shamisen on her own. Unlike my geisha friends, or even my nagauta teachers, Motoko had studied music theory, so she was able to point out aspects of the musical structure of the pieces.

Finally, our conversation drifted toward geisha, and the underlying purpose of Motoko's seeking me out became evident. She thought she might like to be a geisha herself but had no idea how to go about it: could I please give her some advice? The irony of the situation made me laugh – that a Japanese should come to me for counsel about such matters!

Motoko was then living in a boarding house where the middle-aged woman in charge had once been a shikomi in Gion. This woman told Motoko stories of how roughly she had been treated, the strict lessons she had had to endure, and the fussy and never satisfied mistress of the house. Motoko had also once taken a summer job selling tickets at Kyoto's tourist attraction called Gion Corner, where a pastiche of traditional performing arts is presented to tourists. The dance of the maiko is one of the attractions, and both Pontochō and Gion maiko have done stints there.

Motoko had already formed definite impressions of the characters of these two rival geisha communities. She thought the famous Gion cold and snobbish, whereas the slightly less-well-known Pontochō seemed friendlier, more like a family. The geisha life, what she had seen of it, appealed to her sense of drama; on the other hand, she was afraid because of various things she had heard about geisha. This was the dilemma she had come to discuss with me.

As Motoko was about to leave, I received a call from one of the teahouses, so she waited while I put on kimono and walked with me down through Pontochō. We said goodbye in front of the teahouse where I was expected, and I promised to see what I could find out for her. Two other geisha, a maiko, and the okāsan of the house were sitting with two guests in the room that opened onto the Kamo River. The windows were slid completely back, revealing a summer dusk and mountains darkening on the opposite bank. From below, the river cobbled noisily, swelled by the June rains.

Motoko and her unusual request were on my mind, so I mentioned her visit during a lull in conversation. To my surprise, the mother of the house said, "Why didn't you bring her along?" The other geisha concurred, saying I should have introduced her to these two debonair customers. The gathering that evening was quietly elegant, and Motoko would undoubtedly have been impressed by the conversation, the music, and the atmosphere. Had there been a contract for employment, in fact she probably would have signed it on the spot.

The party ended around ten o'clock. I walked back to the Mitsuba, where I found my okāsan and her former younger sister from geisha days merrily drinking beer in her private quarters. They waved me in to join them, asking how the party had been. I told them about Motoko. "The next time she visits, bring her over," said okāsan. She mentioned several teahouses she thought would be happy to sponsor a new geisha, especially one who could already play the shamisen. Motoko would have no trouble whatever joining the Pontochō ranks. "Bring her along to the dance at the Gion Theater next week," called okāsan as I was leaving.[5] "We can introduce her to Korika and some of the other mothers of Pontochō."

Position Wanted: Geisha

The highest-class geisha communities do not advertise; neither do the teahouses solicit customers in this way, nor does the geisha association advertise for personnel. Geisha nowadays come from various backgrounds, but they find their way into the more prestigious hanamachi through personal or family connections, not through the "help wanted" columns.[6]

The kenban and the mothers in these areas realize that there are would-be geisha like Motoko who will never approach them, simply because the hanamachi seems so closed to outsiders. Nonetheless, to reach such women by advertising is a step they are as yet unwilling to take.

But the demand for young geisha is so great that when a plausible connection does exist, the mothers will take pains to encourage the prospective geisha to join the ranks. An attractive young woman with dedication and artistic ambitions makes the mothers' eyes gleam. From what I had told them about Motoko, they were most anxious to meet her. They were favorably impressed when they did, the following week, at the all-Kyoto geisha recital. Motoko, in turn, seemed to enjoy their company, the program, and sitting in an audience composed mainly of geisha.

Still, she was of two minds. Her priorities were clear, in that traditional music was her main interest; but she wavered about whether to follow the shamisen to its original milieu as a geisha or take it up as an object of advanced study in school. She had a notion of doing both – being a music student moonlighting as a geisha – but this would have been impossible in Kyoto. In any case, the academy of traditional music that she wanted to attend was in Tokyo. She held back from a decision, and, to their credit, the mothers remained very gracious, never attempting to push her.

Several weeks passed. One Sunday morning, I had a telephone call from Sakurako, my Shimbashi geisha friend, who was in Kyoto for the day. I had not seen Sakurako in some time, and I was wondering how she was getting along now that a year had passed since she had started work as a geisha. We arranged to meet that afternoon at the art museum. Sakurako was talkative and self-assured; and we now had much to compare in our experiences.

Sakurako's background was similar to Motoko's. They were both independent young women from middle-class families that did not approve of geisha, and both were fascinated by traditional art: dance for Sakurako, music for Motoko. No one could give Motoko a better idea of what geisha life was like than Sakurako. I called Motoko and asked her to join us for dinner.

One can enjoy the atmosphere of Pontochō even without going to an exclusive teahouse. Several establishments on the riverbank side of the street have been turned into restaurants. The Uzuki, with its neon sign of the rabbit in the moon, maintains the elegance (and expense) of its original teahouse form, but the defunct ochaya called Yamatomi has been turned into a Japanese pancake and fried noodle restaurant, well within a student or family budget. The three of us went to the Yamatomi, taking a table outside on the wide veranda, high above the river bank.

In Shimbashi, Sakurako was still one of the new faces, a youngster who had to defer quietly to the more eminent and older geisha. But with us she was the older sister, full of tales of customers she liked and loathed, opinions on the status of geisha, and advice to Motoko. Motoko felt more at ease with her than with the mothers of Pontochō because she saw herself in Sakurako, and the stories of her difficulties rang truer than the glowing assurances of the older women. The mothers, for whom geisha life was as natural and taken for granted as rice for dinner, were probably unable fully to understand Motoko's ambivalence.

Geisha are not interested in theory as opposed to practice. When a geisha knows her gei, she is imbued with it. Geisha are suspicious of study that does not proceed along the traditional path of a master's instruction and a pupil's deference. Sakurako could appreciate Motoko's desire to be a music student while working as a geisha, but she thought the Shimbashi establishment would not be likely to approve such an arrangement. The two modes of learning are entirely different, and a *gakusei* (student) geisha somehow would not strike the right tone.

Yet geisha had great opportunity in Shimbashi, Sakurako felt. All lessons are given by eminent masters, and the overall attitude of Shimbashi is to encourage younger geisha to spend time on their gei. The one thing Motoko should take the greatest care about would be the geisha house she joined, for once accepted into one okiya it was impossible to switch. A proprietress who felt strongly about music or dance was essential; at times, lessons and banquets would conflict, and an okāsan who insisted that every engagement be accepted could run a young geisha ragged.

Things had worked out well for Sakurako. She liked her house and the older geisha who ran it, and she felt she had made progress with her art. "It's not easy, though," she warned Motoko, who was drinking in everything she said. "Sometime you should come talk to Oyumi, who runs my okiya in Shimbashi."

Sisterly Counsel

A month before I left Japan, Motoko telephoned to say she had decided definitely to become a geisha, but in Tokyo rather than

*Watercolor of a geisha playing the shamisen
with her fingertips (tsumabiki), by Itō Shinsui, 1932.
The geisha slips her thumb along the neck of the instrument
using the sleeve of her silk under-robe.*

Kyoto. So it was that on my last visit to Shimbashi she came with me to visit Sakurako's okiya. All seven of the geisha affiliated with the okiya called Oyumi, the owner, "older sister" rather than "mother" because she was still a practicing geisha. Oyumi was then in her late sixties at least, short and wiry, her constant movement like that of an energetic sparrow. She was hardly ever still, but she consented to sit down for an hour with Motoko, Sakurako, and me.

Oyumi is too busy with the chores of the Shimbashi Geisha Association (of which she is the vice president), coaching advanced pupils in dance technique, and with her own geisha work to be concerned with coddling along recalcitrant members of her house. Consequently there are none. Sakurako is the youngest geisha there, and she had had to convince Oyumi of her seriousness before she could join that house. Oyumi is not in the business of recruiting, but if she is sincerely petitioned by a young woman who appears to have promise, she may open her doors. She told Motoko flat out what to expect.

Sakurako poured tea, answered the telephone, and took care of tradesmen at the door; Motoko sat attentively, listening to Oyumi; I took notes. There were two ways a girl could make financial arrangements to enter the geisha profession, said Oyumi. She could put herself completely in the hands of the okiya from the start, using a wardrobe of kimono owned by the house, and obtaining room, board, and an allowance from the mistress. Under this system, all her wages and tips would be taken directly by the okiya until she had earned enough to clear these first expenses. This process usually took about three years.

Oyumi did not take girls under this arrangement because it was too much bother. She was too busy to keep track of all the necessary calculations. The old system of forced debt and servitude is illegal, but geisha houses are very sensitive to charges of that kind; they must therefore keep careful, detailed records of the terms of agreement with a new geisha and of the week-to-week monetary transactions. For its own protection, the okiya will usually require a girl to have an outside guarantor before it will accept her on these terms.

The other arrangement was to be an independent (jimae) geisha from the beginning. In this case, a woman handles her own finances. She buys her own kimono and pays a fee to the okiya only for the privilege of affiliation. To live in the geisha house or not is a separate decision, and she can simply pay room and board there if she does. All wages and tips are her own, and she has to pay her own bills. A geisha could expect to make about 200,000 yen a month (a little over $600), Oyumi said, although for the first few years not much would be left over after expenses were met, even for an independent geisha.

Oyumi strongly implied that if a young woman could not bring herself to make an initial commitment for at least three years, it would hardly be worth the effort. It would take that long before she fully absorbed the professional attitude necessary for a geisha. Sakurako seemed a bit less sophisticated here in front of Oyumi than she had at dinner in Kyoto. I waited for Oyumi to offer some word of praise about her – surely Sakurako was a prize example of a young Shimbashi geisha, I thought – but Oyumi did not scatter her praise lightly.

Motoko was sober on our way back to Kyoto. For the first time she seemed to appreciate the seriousness of a geisha like Oyumi. She could not simply try out the geisha life for a couple of months. Her first idea of blithely giving the geisha life a whirl would not be fair to women like Sakurako, Oyumi, or my okāsan, who had given her counsel.

I was preparing to leave Japan in a few weeks, but Motoko promised to write to keep me apprised of her progress. That autumn I received a postcard announcing her engagement to a young man in the city where her parents lived. But she would still play the shamisen, she added in a postscript.

FIFTEEN

GEISHA CHIC

Chireba koso	Even more wonderful
Itodo sakura wa	As they fall,
Medetakere	The cherry blossoms.
Ukiyo ni nani ka	Does anything last
Hisashikarubeki	In this grievous world?

Tales of Ise, *chap. 82 (ninth century)*

THE FLOATING WORLD

THE WORLD WE see is painful, sad, and wretched, according to Buddhist thought. This being the case, it is fortunate that the world is also illusion, and that true reality lies elsewhere. The *ukiyo*, or "grievous world," in this poem is as transitory as cherry blossoms, and we would do well to recognize the fact.

The idea of the ukiyo appears again six hundred years later in Japanese history, but with a twist. It is still pronounced ukiyo, but it is written with a different character for *uki-*, a character that means "floating" rather than "sad." The idea behind this *ukiyo*, the floating world, is that life may be disagreeable and impermanent, but as we have to live it anyway, we might as well enjoy it and indulge in what worldly pleasures there are.

Ukiyo tsuma	This ukiyo wife!
Tsumasaki karushi	Mincing lightly
Koromogae	Changes her garment.

Kongōsha (*a collection of haiku from the 1670s*)

By the time this haiku was dashed off, *ukiyo* had come to mean modern, worldly, and stylish. The original metaphysical meaning had metamorphosed into a catchy description of an all-too-physical sector of society. The floating world of the Edo period was the world of the theater and the pleasure quarters.

Westerners know of this floating world primarily through woodblock prints, (*ukiyo-e:* pictures, *e*, of the ukiyo). The denizens of this demimonde and the subjects of the pictures were actors, courtesans, geisha, and common prostitutes. The floating world was a sophisticated café society except that its euphemism was tea, not coffee. Much of the nostalgia that modern Japanese feel for their premodern culture is evoked by the ukiyo.

The literature, the music, and especially the graphic arts that are most memorable from Japan's two and a half centuries of shogunal rule are those art forms nourished by the primarily merchant-class city-dweller's culture, which supported the ukiyo. Some Japanese today regard geisha as curious relics of this old floating world, a bit of flotsam left by its last receding wave.

Modern geisha society still contains water imagery, though the ukiyo is a thing of the past. Women, water, and sexual emotions are concepts that have tended to cluster throughout Japanese history.[1] In modern times they have come together yet again in the term for the after-hours world of bars and nightclubs, of singers, actors, and entertainers, called the mizu shōbai, the water businesses.[2]

The mizu shōbai of today is not quite as romantic as the old floating world. But though it has its sordid undercurrents and its backwashes of dishonesty and despair, it also holds undeniable glamor and attractiveness. Today, the geisha world is just one of the smaller pools within the water business, and, for the most part, geisha manage to float near the top of mizu shōbai society. Unlike more modern entertainers, geisha retain something of the aesthetics of the old ukiyo, which provided the very definition of chic in the seventeenth and eighteenth centuries.

In the floating world, style was everything. For the fashionable man or lady about town, a faux pas of taste was as mortifying as a breach of honor would have been to a samurai. Who dictated these styles? For the most part, the professional women of the licensed quarters and the actors of the Kabuki stage, people supposedly beneath contempt in the official social hierarchy, but in fact adulated, mimicked, and celebrated almost everywhere.

During that time the pleasure quarters were perhaps the only area in society, generally so stratified by fiat, where money spoke louder than class background. The quarters are often described in Japanese history books as a "safety valve" – not for repressed sex, but for class. They were an outlet for resolving the daily contradictions between status and wealth in this society where merchants were officially placed on the lowest rung of the class ladder, although in practice they had control over the country's economy.

Rich as they may have become, though, merchants were still vulnerable to the dictates of a government anxious to preserve the prerogatives of the samurai class. Officials vainly attempted to subordinate townsmen via edicts specifying in minute detail what people in each class could eat, wear, build, own, or decorate their homes with. By too flagrant a display of his affluence, a townsman ran the risk of having his wealth confiscated. A merchant's home therefore was likely to have had an unassuming exterior, yet to have been full of treasures. He might have worn a sober, plain wool kimono – with an exquisite silk lining. Opulence was channeled into subtle details.

IKI

An important development from out of this urban merchant-artisan mélange was an aesthetic of understatement: a certain type of chic that, of all people, geisha came to exemplify best. In a word, their manner was *iki*, a bold yet alluring sense of style that implied a whole philosophy of life. Iki fused human emotion with aesthetic ideals, touching all the arts of the period profoundly and, indeed, refashioning life itself into an artifact of taste. Geisha were the heroines of this cultural ideal.

In the early 1800s, a geisha's highest accolade was to be gossiped about as being iki. By this time a yūjo, or courtesan, was the antithesis of this style. Her gaudy and cumbersome wadded kimono, her heavy makeup and stilted, stereotyped phrases, were snickered at by the fashionable set. Neither was a shirōto, a "nonprofessional" woman, iki: the diffidence of a maiden or the modesty of a hausfrau were proper, but not very interesting. The style that geisha epitomized was one of a delicate balance between opposing aesthetic categories, and geisha spent innumerable hours perfecting the details of their dress, manner, and artistic pursuits so as to maintain this balance.

Belying the time spent to achieve the effect, iki was the opposite of contrived. Simple elegance was the aim. Geisha who were iki applied their makeup artfully and lightly, whereas wives wore none and prostitutes were heavily painted. A geisha might wear a kimono with a tasteful overall pattern in the *komon* style, or perhaps bold stripes or a solid color, her obi tied in a simple loose bow or square fold. Not for her were ranks of golden dragons in silver-stitched clouds, or butterflies sporting among embroidered peonies, such as came from the yūjo's closet. The eroticism of a geisha's dress was only hinted at, not flaunted.

Besides avoiding the obvious excesses of tawdry gorgeousness, a truly iki style had an element of daring and unconventionality. The geisha of the Tokyo hanamachi of Fukagawa became synonymous with iki because of their dress. They wore a kind of loose jacket, a haori, over their kimono, which had a somewhat masculine effect, akin to the chic of an attractive woman wearing a tailored suit. They became celebrated for this style to the extent that the term *haori geisha* came to refer to geisha with their proud, *raffiné* manner, women who lived by art alone.[3]

Fukagawa geisha were also renowned because they never wore tabi socks. The image of the geisha's cold white foot outlined by her black lacquered clog as she stepped out in the snow was the height of iki. Although here the erotic element was pronounced, it was the strength of character implied by this act that made it truly iki.

Eroticism still does, however, underlie whatever else one might say about iki and doubtless contributes to its fascination. The suggestiveness of one stray hair in an otherwise perfect coiffure, the glimpse of red at the collar of a black kimono, a shamisen picked up in an idle moment and strummed with the fingertips:

such are the classic images of iki, and they all, not surprisingly, pertain to geisha.

Iki also implied sincerity, but a sophisticated sincerity, not the blind devotion of the young or the eagerness of the inexperienced. Novelists of the mid-nineteenth century warned their readers that a yūjo would sell her sympathy along with her body, but that a geisha's loyalties, once won, were true. To be iki was to be sophisticated but not jaded, innocent but not naïve. For a woman to be iki she needed to have been around a bit and to have savored the bitterness as well as the sweetness of love. Young girls seldom had this quality. It was the woman approaching middle age who could be iki.

Iki was not an abstract ideal to which geisha struggled to conform. Geisha were instrumental in developing the mode, and it still remains an important part of a geisha's self-image. In her memoirs, the mistress of a famous Shimbashi teahouse, the Kikumura, recalled an elderly geisha whom she and her friends regarded as a model of iki:

That onēsan called Kiyoji always said a geisha should never forget iki. So she would never let her patron see her on the day she dyed her gray hair. Once when he wanted to see her, she made some lame excuse and said she couldn't, and he got jealous, thinking she was meeting someone else. Finally she had to tell him the real reason – we all got a laugh out of it . . . When Kiyoji died, it was discovered that she had hardly a penny left to her name; yet she had just had a new kimono made.

The maid who works here [in the Kikumura] says that if you work for a geisha who isn't iki, when she comes home she scolds you about the least little thing. But a geisha who is iki comes home and, even if you've been catching a few winks, thinks, "Ah, the poor maid, she has no pleasures in life," and she doesn't scold. So for me, I'll only work for a lady who is iki and enjoys herself.[4]

Shinohara Haru's reminiscences make it clear that a geisha should keep up her image at all costs. Through sheer force of will, appearance can create reality. Geisha always used to take a change of clothing when engaged at a banquet. About halfway through the party, a manservant (hakoya) would call out, "Time

Woodblock print
by Torii Kiyonaga (1752–1815)
depicting a geisha leaving the Heiroku Apothecary.
The subtle, subdued colors and the long, clean lines are
the epitome of the aesthetic of iki.

to change, ladies," and the geisha would all troop out to put on the other kimono.[5] Once, when Kiyoji didn't have a kimono to change into, she had the servant wrap up an old jacket instead. When the time came to change, she said nonchalantly, "Oh, today I don't think I'll bother." Kiyoji's act was the geisha version of the proverb about the pride of the impoverished samurai who uses a toothpick even though he has not eaten.

A Lesson in Iki

A woman who becomes a geisha today may have a predilection for an iki manner to start with, but that does not mean she can't learn a few things along the way. Mostly she absorbs style by being around other geisha, not by explicit directions on how to behave. When I was Ichigiku, however, I once received an instructive lesson in iki by a master: the Kabuki actor Tamasaburō.

Bandō Tamasaburō V is an *onnagata*, a specialist in female roles. He is exactly my age, precisely my height, and of a similar build. When I dressed in the formal geisha costume, people often complimented me by saying I looked just like him. Of all the modern Kabuki actors, Tamasaburō probably has the most avid coterie of fans all over Japan. We first met, in fact, at a banquet sponsored by the Kyoto chapter of the Tamasaburō Fan Club, where I was attending as one of the geisha. My okāsan had warned me beforehand not to talk about dance because he would be weary of the subject, so when I had a chance to sit next to him I asked him instead about the unusual silk suit he was wearing. It was made out of bolts of kimono silk in a subdued gray and white repeating arrow pattern. He had designed it himself, he said, as a fashion experiment. Dance was his business, but style was his passion. I mentioned the Paris designer Kenzo, and it turned out that he and Tamasaburō are friends.

It was early in the summer, and already warm in the banquet room of the Mitsuba where this party was being held. I took a small fan out of my obi and snapped it open as we continued to talk. After a few minutes Tamasaburō touched my hand. "Let me show you something. Give me your fan," he said. The people across the room glanced over with curiosity. "You're holding your fan strangely," said Tamasaburō. He sat up straight, grasped the open fan with his thumb on the outside, and moved it by rotating his wrist. "This is what you were doing. It's how a man holds a fan." Then he slid his legs to the side, arched his neck slightly, and picked up the fan with his thumb on the inside, moving hand and wrist as a unit, gently almost languorously. "This is how a woman should fan. It's much more iki, don't you agree?" I did, and so did his admirers attending the banquet. The other geisha took out their fans, anxious to see which way they held them. They were relieved to confirm that they all held them the right way. It was something they had never been conscious of before and something I had not even noticed.

After all the guests had left, Tamasaburō asked whether he might use one of the Mitsuba's small rooms to change clothes. I showed him to one, and a few minutes later he reappeared in an ochre-colored one-piece jumpsuit, a scarf tied around his neck. A maiko-to-be who had been allowed to help serve at this banquet let out a small squeal, then blushed crimson. Tamasaburō tactfully ignored her. "This is a Kenzo," he informed me. "You'll probably see them everywhere this fall." I told him I was looking forward to tomorrow's performance of Macbeth. Tamasaburō was to play the role of Lady Macbeth.

THE GRAND PERFORMANCES

Keeping up a certain image means not begrudging money spent on style. A stingy geisha is a contradiction in terms. Liberality is a large part of being iki, and it makes the profession expensive. A geisha rides in the first-class car of the train not because she craves the luxury of the slightly wider seats, but because she would be embarrassed to be seen in economy class. She tosses her slightly worn tabi when a frugal woman would bleach and starch these white cloth socks to wear them months longer. She pours her wages into a new obi when she already has a drawer-full that are perfectly suitable. But a geisha really throws money into her performances. Far from being paid for the programs they put on at such grand places as Tokyo's Kabuki-za and the National Theater, geisha may go into debt to finance them.

For the dancers especially, these showcases are the high points of their lives as geisha. A perfectly polished performance is the dramatic culmination of years of training, and it will establish a geisha's reputation among the small coterie that counts: mostly other geisha. The younger geisha don't dance publicly on this scale. Those who participate in the extravaganzas are usually geisha in their late twenties, or older, who have attained a professional dance name. Geisha are not required to put on a public performance, which after all is sure to take infinite amounts of work, time, and money. Some women simply don't bother. It is, however, terribly iki to do so.

Most of the geisha from Pontochō in Kyoto study Japanese dance of the Onoue school, taking lessons from the *iemoto*, the grand master, himself.[6] Though he lives in Tokyo, Onoue Kikunojō II, still a young man, travels to Pontochō once a month to give lessons. On his visits there his elderly mother, once a dancer herself, often comes along. The older geisha were his father's pupils, and some of them were dancing before he was even born. This makes it difficult for him as the teacher to command the proper level of respect. Watching rehearsals, I felt sorry for him whenever his mother would interrupt with her comments. He was a very sweet young man, and the geisha used to flirt with him to make him feel better.

The year I was in Kyoto was the thirteenth anniversary of his father's death. A memorial dance recital featuring the most outstanding pupils of the Onoue name was held in Tokyo at the end of January. Among the performers were several dance masters from other schools who had some connection to Kikunojō in their professional lineages. Fourteen geisha from Tokyo's prestigious Shimbashi hanamachi danced, and four geisha from Pontochō – Miyofuku, Hisayuki, Mameyuki, and Ichisono – appeared on the program under their dance names of Onoue Kikuryō, Onoue Kikukō, Onoue Kikuri, and Onoue Kikukōko.

Miyofuku and Hisayuki, then both in their late sixties, have performed together throughout their long careers as geisha. Ichisono, however, was then twenty-eight and Mameyuki thirty-two, and this occasion was only their third performance in such distinguished company.

The teahouses in Pontochō were almost deserted on the evening of January 28 because over a third of Pontochō's geisha population had gone to Tokyo to cheer on their two young colleagues at the Kabuki-za theater. I was there too, sitting in a box seat with my "mother" and one of her customers with his family.

My okāsan watches dance with a loving and critical eye, having been a dancer herself in her geisha days. After a well-executed performance, she is exhilarated and talks about taking dance up again as a hobby. She never does, though, because she had a mild heart attack a few years ago, and her doctor says dancing would be too strenuous. She is also rather plump. The excitement of watching the performances may be just about the right amount of exercise for her.

For this recital, Mameyuki and Ichisono danced a dramatic gidayū number, *Journey of the Butterflies*, the story of two lovers reincarnated as butterflies after their love suicide. As they struck the final pose and the audience began its applause, cheers of "Ichisono!" "Mameyuki!" erupted here and there in the theater from the places where other Pontochō geisha were sitting. My okāsan, right next to me, had shouted first, making me drop the box of chocolate balanced on my knee. Kabuki is routinely punctuated by such cries of appreciation from the audience, but I had not expected them here.

At intermission, the Pontochō group clustered in the lobby to evaluate the performance. It had come off nicely, they agreed, and had stood out especially well because it had followed a series of slow-moving numbers. Several well-dressed businessmen came up to congratulate the geisha and the mothers on Pontochō's excellent showing. Ichiume, looking very pretty in an expensive peach-colored kimono patterned all over in tiny dots made by the painstaking hand-tied *shibori* technique, was collecting compliments for Ichisono and Mameyuki, who were exhausted and resting in their dressing room.

Dressing rooms in Japanese theaters are like public thoroughfares. Friends, relatives, and admirers are expected to troop through this area all during the time the long recitals are in progress. The dancers are supposed to give a small gift to people who have come expressly to see their performance. Some of the other Pontochō geisha were in the dressing room with Mameyuki and Ichisono, passing out wrapped wooden boxes of

Kyoto sugar candies to visitors. The sweets, made up in the shape of butterflies and grasses to recall the theme of their dance, had been ordered from a confectioner near Pontochō.

These custom-made candies were the least of Mameyuki's and Ichisono's expenses. On the train back to Kyoto, I asked okāsan how much she figured they had spent altogether. "I know it was over 500,000 yen," she said. That was on the order of $1,500. What had cost so much?

Everything connected with a performance like this is expensive, starting from the rental of the Kabuki-za theater for an afternoon and evening. This fee was divided up and shared by all the performers. Further, each dancer provided for musicians to accompany her piece. Ichisono and Mameyuki paid the plane fare, hotel, performance fee, and tip for six gidayū shamisen players and singers to come from Kyoto to Tokyo for a single day. Their costumes, rented from the Kobayashi kimono shop in Kyoto, were yet another expense, at several hundred dollars apiece. The boxes of sugar butterflies, worth over $150, thus were mere frosting on the total amount. How, then, can geisha ever afford to perform?

They are able to do so because of a system that amounts to subsidy by the comfortably well-off customers who patronize the teahouses. Part of becoming an *intime* guest means being willing to buy up batches of tickets to a geisha's performances. A ticket will officially cost around 4,000 yen (about $12 in 1975). A customer, deciding he could manage to buy twenty, will obtain them from the geisha at a higher price. He may of course then resell the tickets at their normal rate to his friends or to people at work, but any customer who can afford to know the geisha areas so well would be more likely to give the tickets away. Such a gesture will advertise his magnanimous nature and his debonair patronage of the arts.

Style is essential to grand performances like these. They are lavish from start to finish, and, once committed to the endeavor, a geisha will see little point in cutting corners. One of the reasons it is iki for a geisha to dance in this fashion is precisely that it is so impractical. Though she may make a name for herself in geisha circles and win the admiration of a tiny group of knowledgeable customers, she will earn no more money because of her efforts. On the contrary, she may well find herself fallen into debt for her pains. A geisha does not dance for utilitarian reasons.

SOME PREFER GEISHA

If geisha are the most iki of women, they also appreciate customers who are iki. The clientele of the teahouses is now primarily limited to older and wealthier men, businessmen of one stripe or another who nevertheless vary greatly in their tastes. Some of these patrons treat geisha as mere purveyors of an expensive atmosphere that enhances the image the men cultivate. Privately, geisha tend to think of such customers as cold fish.

The atmosphere of a teahouse should be different from that of a bar. It is not overly cynical to say that bar hostesses are hardly more than human furniture. The management chooses them according to how well they fit in with the mood the bar is trying to create. Geisha will not stand to be treated in such an impersonal manner. They assume a customer has engaged them because he prefers their company. For geisha, an iki customer is one who is versed in the arts they practice, who is witty and charming, and who entertains them as much as they do him.

Paradoxical as it may seem in a situation where one side pays for the company of the other, the actual behavior of guests and geisha is anything but one-sided. This is one reason why many geisha are iki and bar hostesses seldom are. Nobody asks the furniture if it cares to be sat upon, and hostesses have little say in whose table they are directed to. Once a geisha has paid off her initial debts and become independent, she can choose which banquets to attend and which customers to associate with. A customer who is iki is attracted to this very independence.

The qualities of iki, oddly enough, are confined within a very small enclave. In Japan today, one hardly ever hears the word. International youth culture has its Japanese manifestation, and the fashions of cuteness and prettiness, so antithetical to iki, predominate. Teenagers slather themselves with suntan oil and lie on Japan's crowded beaches to tan; geisha carry parasols and daub their faces with unguents of nightingale droppings to whiten their skin. That the geisha continue to cultivate the aesthetic of iki makes them appear ever more recherché to young Japanese, whose senses have never ventured beyond the bland and the sweet. Iki, like caviar, is an acquired taste.

SIXTEEN

KIMONO

When the colors of a robe do not match the
seasons, the flowers of Spring and the Autumn
tints, then the whole effort is futile as the dew.

Tale of Genji, *chap. 2 (eleventh century)*

A month after I returned to the United States, I was invited to
appear on the "To Tell the Truth" television show because of my
odd distinction of being the only non-Japanese ever to have
become a geisha. The object for the panelists would be to guess
the identity of the real "geisha anthropologist," so I had dressed
myself and the two women pretending to be me in cotton
kimono. As we walked through the program's format during
rehearsal, each of us was to announce, "My name is Liza Crihfield," then step ten paces to our seats facing the panel at stage
left. The director shook her head in dismay before we even took
our places. "Stop," she called. "You've just given it away."

After my year-long training as a geisha, the technique of walking gracefully in a kimono had become second nature. The two
poseurs, though they had diligently studied my research proposal
in order to anticipate questions from the panel, could not, in an
afternoon, master the art of walking. It was quite obvious who
was who before we even opened our mouths.

Repeatedly I showed them the technique of sliding one foot,
pigeon-toed, in front of the other with knees slightly bent. I tried
to convey how the shoulders should have a barely perceptible
slope, how the arms should be carried gracefully, close to the

body. We tried to minimize the contrast. They made great efforts to mimic an authentic movement, while I attempted to recreate the clumsiness of my own first experience in wearing kimono. Even so, on the show the next day none of the panelists except Bill Cullen was fooled a bit. I am convinced that our body language had "told the truth."

Learning to wear kimono properly was one of the most difficult aspects of my geisha training. But it was essential so that I could fit without awkwardness into a group of geisha. No one gives geisha formal lessons in how to wear kimono. Most of them have learned how to move gracefully in kimono by virtue of their practice of Japanese dance. Awkward gestures are noticed immediately by the watchful mothers, who seldom fail to utter a reproof to a fidgety maiko.

When I lived in Pontochō, the sardonic old auntie who worked at the Mitsuba invariably had some critical remark when I checked in for okāsan's approval of my outfit before going off to a teahouse engagement. I usually managed to put together a feasible color combination of kimono, obi, and *obi-age* (the sheer, scarf-like sash that is tied so as to be barely visible above the obi), but it was many months before I could proceed on my way to a party without something having to be untied and retied properly. Only when I reached the point where I could put on the entire outfit in less than twenty minutes by myself did I finally win the grudging respect of the old auntie who tended the inn.

THE LANGUAGE OF KIMONO

Wearing kimono is one of the things that distinguishes geisha from other women in Japan. Geisha wear their kimono with a flair just not seen in middle-class ladies who, once or twice a year, pull out their traditional dress to attend a wedding, a graduation, or perhaps a retirement ceremony. They are uncomfortable in the unaccustomed garment, and it shows.

To the untutored eye, the kimono a geisha chooses are much the same as those any other Japanese woman might wear. The resplendent trailing black robe with deep reverse décolletage is the geisha's official outfit, but she actually wears it infrequently. Her usual garment is an ankle-length, medium-sleeve silk kimono in slightly more subdued colors than those other women wear. The subtle differences in sleeve openings, in color, or in the manner of tying the obi that set a geisha apart are not immediately obvious, even to many Japanese. But together with her natural way of wearing the outfit, such cues are visible to an observer who is sensitive to the language of kimono. A connoisseur will know the wide vocabulary of elements that varies according to the region, class, age, and profession of the wearer. He or she will be able to recognize a geisha easily.

The elements of the kimono costume in fact constitute a social code. This was revealed to me when I inadvertently mixed up some of them early in my geisha career, before I had acquired an appropriate wardrobe from the taller geisha in the neighborhood. In the beginning, the only kimono I owned was one that Yuriko, my well-to-do middle-aged friend in Tokyo, had given me. It was a lovely burnt orange color with a pattern of weeping willow branches in brown shot with gold. She had worn it a few times many years ago, before she had married. Now the colors were inappropriate to her age, and besides, she told me, she never wore kimono any more. She doubted she could even tie the obi by herself.

When okāsan first asked me to help her out at a party at the Mitsuba so I could see the geisha's side of the affair, I gladly agreed and planned to wear my only kimono. As she helped me put it on, she remarked that, lovely as it was, it would be entirely unsuitable in the future. It was the sort of thing a stylish bourgeois young lady might wear, not a geisha. It would have to do for that evening, though. She loaned me a tea-green obi with a pale cream orchid dyed into the back and gave me an old obi-age sash that she had worn as an apprentice many years ago.

The obi–age was of sheer white silk with a pattern of scattered fans done in a dapple-effect tie-dying technique called *kanoko*. Okāsan slipped it over the pad that held the back loop of the obi secure, and as she tied it in the front she said, "Here is a trick for keeping the front knot in place. All the geisha tie their obi-age this way." She made a loose slipknot in one end, making sure the red fan pattern showed at the front of the knot, then drew the other end through. The effect was of a simply knotted sash, but without the bulk of both ends tied together. She smoothed and tucked this light sash down behind the top of the obi, so that only a glimpse of the red and white was visible. At the time, I was reminded of letting a bit of lace show at the neckline of a blouse. Since the obi-age is technically considered part of the "kimono underwear," my thought was more apt than I first realized.

Still wearing this outfit, I went out after the party. Later that evening I met a pair of college teachers at a nearby bar. We struck up a conversation, and I told them a bit about the circumstances of my being in Japan. The bartender, half listening in, finally exclaimed, "Aha, now I realize what was bothering me about you. You said you were a student, and I could tell that you're an unmarried young lady from a proper family. Your kimono is perfectly appropriate. But I think it's your sash, something about the way it's tied, that struck me as odd for a young lady – something too much like a geisha about it." As I had not yet said anything about the precise subject of my study, I was astounded at the acuity of the man's eye.

Incongruent as it was, my outfit that evening expressed my odd position rather well. Not exactly an *ojōsan*, a demure young lady not yet a geisha, I was attired in disparate elements of each style, so I presented an odd aspect to someone with a perspicacious eye for dress. The bartender had received all the messages my outfit conveyed but was puzzled at the totality, as well he might have been.

KIMONO WEARERS

Mono means "thing," and with *ki-* from *kiru*, "to wear," kimono originally meant simply "a garment." Not all things to wear are kimono however. Today, the relevant distinction is between *yōfuku*, "Western apparel," and *wafuku*, "native apparel": kimono. Western clothes, following all the latest fashion trends, are what most Japanese women wear most of the time. Some women don't even own a kimono, and many, like my friend

Yuriko in Tokyo, have forgotten how to wear those they have tucked away in the Japanese equivalent of cedar chests. Few if any social occasions in Japan now would exclude a woman because she was not dressed in kimono.

Most women own a black kimono dyed with the family crest that they will pull out of a drawer for a few highly formal occasions. This garment was probably the main item in their wedding trousseaux. Families are encouraged to buy their young daughters the gaudy, long-sleeved *furisode*-style kimono for New Year, so a woman often has one of these packed away from her girlhood as well. Such occasional use means that most Japanese women are nearly as unaccustomed to the proper manner of wearing kimono as a foreigner would be. They sigh with relief when they can finally unwind the stiff obi from around their waists and slip back into comfortable Western clothes.

As my eye became educated to the niceties of kimono, I was more and more struck by how many women who put one on fail to achieve a graceful demeanor. A good time to view masses of kimono is the New Year holiday. Young girls, who trudge to school in loafers all year, suddenly mince about in traditional zōri that match their long-sleeved kimono. Arms swinging, knees pumping up and down as they do in skirts, the girls flock on the streets like pinioned flamingos. Colorful and clumsy, they brighten the bleak January streets briefly before donning their familiar blue and white school uniforms again at the end of holidays. Women over fifty generally feel more at home than this in kimono. They probably wore the traditional dress as children and feel a pang of nostalgia when they put it on.

Middle-class women of means are now rediscovering the conspicuous display afforded by kimono. The wearing of wafuku, as opposed to the Cacharel skirts and Dior blouses of their friends, has become a fashionable hobby. A woman who would blanch at spending two hundred dollars on a dress could easily justify spending five times as much on a kimono. After all, a kimono is an investment. It won't go out of style, it can accommodate thickening midriffs without alteration, and it can be passed on to one's daughters. In the status game, it is difficult to spend more than a thousand dollars on even the most skillfully tailored Western dress. But with kimono, one can easily wear thousands of dollars on one's back without looking too obvious. The expensive yet understated possibilities of kimono are ideally suited to this aspect of fashion one-upmanship.

Yet the wearing of kimono is not without problems in modern Japan. Aside from the matter of expense, kimono inherently belong to a different style and pace of life. That life still thrives here and there, but usually under special circumstances – as are found, for example, in the geisha world. Few would call the beautiful kimono a practical garment for modern living.

Floors Versus Chairs

The kimono was once part of a cultural totality that embraced every aspect of daily life. The garment was influenced by, and in turn it influenced, canons of feminine beauty that enhanced some parts of the body (nape, ankle, and hip) and concealed others (waist, legs, and bosom). Not surprisingly, the kimono flatters a figure found most often in Japanese women: a long waist and long thigh but small bust and short calf. Cultural notions of ideal beauty seem to influence actual physical characteristics, however; as Western notions of long-legged, big-bosomed glamor have affected postwar Japan, amazingly, such physical types seem to have blossomed. The cultivation of this new type of figure does not bode well for the kimono.

The wearing of kimono was also perfectly integrated into the arrangement of living space in the traditional Japanese home. Much of the activity of daily life was conducted close to the floor, on low tables where people knelt, not sat, to accomplish tasks. To Japanese, a shod foot treading the floor inside the house would be as gauche as shoes on a Westerner's dining room table. Floors were clean enough to permit trailing garments, and the wives of wealthy men let their robes swirl about their feet as they glided down polished halls from one tatami mat room to another. The trailing hem contributed to the overall balance of the outfit, creating an effect of elegance. Again, nowadays one must look to the geisha's formal kimono to see what that style was like. Ordinary modern kimono are adjusted, by a fold at the waist, to reach only the ankle. The line, rather than flowing, is somewhat stiff and tubular.

The integration of cultural elements that formed the whole of which kimono was a part has now fragmented. The single most nefarious artifact in this respect is the chair. Chairs are antithetical to kimono, physically and aesthetically.

Women who wear kimono of course sit on chairs, but the garment is poorly adapted to this posture; it is designed for sitting on the floor. When Americans sit on the floor, this implies a greater degree of relaxation than does sitting on a chair. Not so in Japan. A chair is comfortable and relaxed compared to the straight-spine posture required to sit properly on the tatami floor. There are two different verbs meaning "to sit" in Japanese, depending on whether it is on the floor or in a chair. If in a chair then one literally "drapes one's hips" there.

When, out of determination to show the Japanese that we understand etiquette, we Westerners endure a tea ceremony or traditional banquet sitting on the floor, after thirty minutes our knees are jelly and our legs so benumbed they refuse to obey our brain's directive to stand. We are consoled that young Japanese have much the same problem. Part of the exhaustion we feel is due to the gradual slumping of our unsupported backs. Skirts ride up, pants become constricting, narrow belts bite into our waists. But the kimono that became dishevelled and kept us perched uncomfortably at the edge of a chair now offers back support with the obi, and it turns out to be almost comfortable in the posture for which it was designed.

The back view of a kneeling kimono-clad woman shows off the garment to its best advantage. The obi often has a large single design woven or painted on the back part, which forms a large, flat loop in the common style of tying known as *taiko* (drum).[1] This flat drum, not quite a square foot in area, is framed by the contrasting color of the kimono. I have often been struck by the artfulness of a seated figure, Japanese style. In a chair, the drum of the obi is not only hidden from view, it is a positive nuisance, as it prevents one from sitting back.

The fact that the back view of a kimono-clad figure is such an aesthetic focus has to do, I think, with the way a traditional

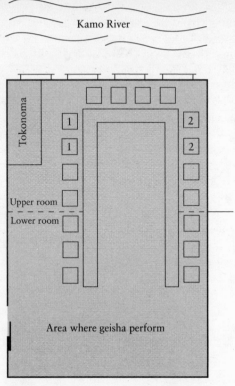

1 – Seats of highest prestige (guests)
2 – Hosts

*Floor plan of a typical banquet room in Pontochō.
The space enclosed by the three sides of the tables serves as a
no-man's-land where geisha can move about freely.*

Japanese room is arranged and how a woman in public (such as
a geisha) moves and is viewed on a social occasion. At a banquet,
low, narrow tables are laid end to end, forming a continuous row
that parallels three sides of the room. People sit on individual flat
square cushions along the outer edge of this U-shaped arrangement. In effect, everyone sits next to someone, but nobody sits
across from anyone else.

The seating positions are hierarchical: the places of highest status are in front of the alcove, and the lowest are those closest to the entrance. People usually have a keen sense of where they stand vis-à-vis one another's status in Japan, so the problem of where they sit is solved with a minimum of polite protestation. When everyone has taken a seat, the banquet can begin. After it has started, however, people leave their original places to wander across the center of the room, squatting temporarily in front of different personages to make a toast or have a short conversation. This center space is a no-man's-land, ringed as it is by the prescribed statuses of the proper seats on the other side of the tables. Here more relaxed conviviality can occur.

When geisha attend upon a banquet, they often move into the center free space, kneeling for a few minutes across from one guest after another. As they do so, their backs are turned toward an entire row of tables on the other side of the room. The first time I was a guest at a traditional banquet, I noticed the beauty of the backs of the geisha as they talked with other guests. Upon reflection, it hardly seems accidental that the view from that particular vantage point was so striking.

HISTORICAL LAYERS

The kimono has changed very little in its basic form since the Tang Chinese prototype was adopted by the court ladies of Nara period Japan, twelve hundred years ago. The number of robes worn simultaneously has varied, from the layered *jūni hitoe*, "twelve unlined robes" of the Heian period (794–1185), to the usual two layers, that is, the under-robe (*nagajuban*) and kimono of today. Materials have ranged from hemp or cotton for peasants (for whom kimono of any kind were a luxury) to the most gorgeous, costly silks for court ladies, wives of samurai, and eventually merchants' wives and expensive prostitutes.

The kimono has always been fastened by a sash of some kind. For eleventh-century Heian ladies, with their layer upon layer of robes, sashes were hardly more than narrow cords. Aesthetic ambition in dress was directed entirely to the combination of

*Heian Kimono. Twelve flowing
layers of unlined robes tied with
a narrow cord were the
fashion.*

colors at the sleeve openings and the breast, where the garments overlapped.

The obi remained fairly simple even when the courtly style of layered robes had disappeared. When the samurai took control of the country in the thirteenth century, they scorned the imperial capital of Kyoto as decadent. Twelve layers of flowing robes were regarded as effete, and the ladies of the warrior class wore a single, or at most two or three, robes secured by a relatively unobtrusive sash at hip level.

During the Edo period, Japan's two and a half centuries of internal peace beginning in 1600, the shape of the kimono changed hardly at all, but the obi appeared in a variety of widths, tied in different ways, reflecting the social position of its wearer, as well as fashion trends. Perhaps the most striking example was

Edo kimono. In the early seventeenth century a narrow sash was worn low, belting only two or three layers of kimono.

A modern kimono and obi ensemble, emphasizing a fairly stiff, tubular line.

the front-tied obi characteristic of high-ranking yūjo. Contemporary pictures show that a fairly pliant weave was used for the sash until around 1800, when heavier, stiff, tapestry-weave cloth became popular. From this time on, the obi became more highly elaborated and eventually came to demand as much attention as the gown itself. The modern kimono/obi combination is heiress to this trend – so much so that it sometimes seems the kimono is merely a backdrop for the obi.

The obi worn today is wide, encasing practically the entire midriff in a carapace of stiffly woven cloth. A woman does not have the option of choosing a narrower style of obi without appearing to be wearing a costume from a different era. She has but a small degree of leeway in how high or low she wraps the obi about her body. A few inches either way can make a great difference in the total look. There is a symbolic correlation between the primness of the wearer and the level at which she ties her obi. A proper wife will tie hers just below her breasts; and young girls, supposedly virginal and innocent, are to wear their obis highest of all, giving no clue that they even have breasts under the wide, heavy sash.

The languid beauties in Utamaro's woodblock prints with their soft, low sashes differ markedly from modern kimono-wearing women. If the more graceful loose kimono line is to be seen anywhere today, it is on the geisha, who have no stake in looking prim. Their obis are tied relatively low, giving a strikingly more voluptuous tone to the outfit. Geisha also let a wider band of the white collar show in front and expose more of their napes by pulling the layers of collar down further in the back.

KIMONO SCHOOLS

Geisha may be the only definable group of women in Japan today who, as a matter of course, wear kimono every day. New members of the profession obtain help in getting dressed from their ex-geisha mothers and their colleague sisters. They soon learn the proper way to move by example and practice. A middle-class woman who takes up kimono as a hobby does not have this surrounding environment to learn from, so instead she may actually take lessons from one of the recently established kimono schools. These institutions capitalize on the fact that many women with the means and desire to cultivate a kimono image do not quite have the required knowledge or confidence. They give classes that range from basic kimono wearing to advanced techniques of tying the obi in facsimiles of daffodils or folded cranes.

The kimono schools try to convince the public that they alone hold the secret to kimono success, by having appropriated one particular mode of wearing the garment and elevating it to an ideal. The text of one school calls for an elderly lady to wear her kimono "with dignity"; a middle-aged woman, or "missus," to wear it "composedly"; and a young girl to wear hers "neatly and sprucely." All this originates from bourgeois notions of how the upper crust once dressed – and, in particular, from the somewhat stiff samurai class tradition, where propriety was the sole aim of women's dress and demeanor. That the kimono has been and can be very sexy and alluring seems to be systematically ignored by the schools.

A certain amount of judicious padding will help most women achieve a better kimono line, to be sure, but the numerous figure-fillers advocated by the kimono schools mold a woman's figure into an absolute cylinder. A towel around the waist, a V-shaped bust pad that adds substance to the upper chest, a bust suppressor to flatten the breasts, and a back pad to fill in the curve of the lower spine are items recommended as kimono foundation garments. Various sorts of clips and elastic velcro bands are sold to keep the collars in place and the front overlap neat. Such gadgetry is a substitute for the ease that comes with familiarity in wearing kimono. Geisha somehow manage to stay put together without all these aids.

When I first began to wear kimono, I used towels and handkerchiefs here and there as padding devices, as well as alligator clips to keep my underkimono in place. As I became more accustomed to wearing kimono every day, and as my entire way of moving became more attuned to its constraints, I found I could do without all the clips and padding and still maintain a neat appearance. A novice kimono wearer will usually tie the obi too tight, cutting off breath and appetite, yet will still somehow come apart after several hours. A geisha, or other experienced woman, can tie the obi so that it is well secured but not constricting. One of my plump geisha friends, for instance, said she always wore kimono when she was invited out to dinner so she could eat more.

Learning a Foreign Clothing

We are revealed by clothes more than we are clothed by them. Only a sincere attempt to wear foreign dress makes us realize the extent to which we are not just naked without familiar clothing: we are stripped of part of ourselves. A garment as demanding as the kimono, for example, requires a whole new personality, and, like learning a foreign language, it takes a while before we are no longer self-conscious.

"You look like a rabbit, hopping along like that," the sarcastic auntie at the Mitsuba would jibe during my early days of attending parties as one of the geisha. I would then forget the errand I had been sent on while I concentrated on my manner of walking. Eventually the proper movements became natural, but in absorbing them I discovered that I had developed another self in kimono. By no accident are the relatively small gestures of Japanese body language gauged to the kimono, but I was surprised to find that after a while, I actually felt awkward speaking English when dressed as a geisha. American English body language simply does not feel right in kimono.

Much presence of mind is required to switch back and forth easily between Western and Japanese dress. Few geisha can do it. On the whole, they tend to look awkward in dresses and skirts. The stunning and sophisticated older geisha I met at a banquet one evening seemed dowdy on the street the next day in her two-piece navy blue knit. When they wear Western clothes, geisha scrape their feet along as they are used to doing in their zōri. Their manner of walking with turned-in feet, which makes a kimono rustle delicately, looks simply pigeon-toed in shoes and a dress. They seem to be wearing invisible kimono, gesturing as if long sleeves were quietly constraining their arms.

Almost every geisha I know has a weakness for kimono and a passion for collecting them. This is above and beyond the necessity of acquiring the basic number for each season that is considered a geisha's working wardrobe. Kimono are the single greatest expense in a geisha's budget. When a young woman begins her geisha career she will have had to purchase at least ten of them, along with obi, to see her through the changes of season in proper attire. About ten thousand dollars is needed to purchase a minimum wardrobe. A young geisha is thus likely to start her career in debt for the loan to buy kimono.[2]

An old proverb says that Osaka people are *kuidōraku* – prodigal in their expenditures on the delights of eating – whereas Kyoto people would eat plain rice in order to lavish their money on clothes (*kidōraku*). The Kyoto geisha exemplify their city's stereotype perfectly. I know from my own experience, too, that it is difficult to be satisfied with a bare minimum number of kimono. Once wearing kimono becomes a habit, the desire to have a chestful of kimono and obi becomes an addiction. In Kyoto, where the affectionate local dialect term for kimono is *obebe*, women talk about the enviable state of being *obebe mochi*, having lots of kimono. Every geisha wants to be obebe mochi, and she will spend thousands of dollars a year to add to her kimono collection.

Geisha will appear before guests only in silk kimono and, further, only in certain kinds of silk kimono. Although kimono today can be thought of first of all as native dress, as counterposed to Western dress, within the realm of Japanese clothing a number of important distinctions define which kimono can be worn on what sort of occasion.

A KIMONO GRAMMAR

Formality

The most basic distinction in traditional Japanese clothing is that between *fudangi*, everyday wear, and *haregi*, formal wear. Formal kimono are those with family crests, and the most common type is *hōmongi*, literally, dress suitable for visiting.[3] Fudangi and haregi create a dichotomy of informal versus formal, and because a geisha is formally presenting herself to guests when she works, she most often wears hōmongi or other kimono types of approximately the same level. Hōmongi are always silk, although not all silk kimono are hōmongi. Geisha never wear fudangi (wool, cotton, or certain weaves of silk like pongee) when they entertain.

Like hierarchy, formality can be graduated into ever finer degrees. Because clothing is one of the prime ways by which people in any culture demonstrate the differences between ordinary and extraordinary occasions, many levels exist within the basic dichotomy of formal wear/informal wear in kimono.

301

Woven Versus Dyed

The weave of cloth and type of pattern both help establish the place of a particular garment along the scale of formality. Even among silks, an *ori*, or "woven" kimono, in which the thread was dyed before weaving, differs from a *some*, or "dyed" kimono where the silk was colored after being woven into cloth. With a few exceptions, the woven kimono are usually classed as ordinary wear and the dyed silks are considered dressier.

Among dyed kimono, crests mark the most formal. Dyed silks without crests are arranged below hōmongi, according to the type and placement of the dyed design. The *tsukesage*, for example, is a useful garment appropriate for all but truly formal occasions. Its pattern comes on the bolt, with a definite front and back side that are divided at the shoulder, and its motifs are concentrated on the upper torso and the hem. A geisha will own many kimono of this type. The parties she attends vary in their level of formality, so her wardrobe must cover the range. A party by definition excludes fudangi, but a crested kimono would also be out of place in a small, relaxed gathering.

Just below the tsukesage is the *komon* kimono, with an allover pattern of some small design. This type of kimono can, to some extent, be dressed up or down depending on the obi worn with it. A geisha might wear a komon-pattern kimono to a small party of familiar customers.

There are many other varieties of kimono, but these, along with the solid color *iromuji* kimono, are the most popular today. A five-crested kimono is the most formal anyone can wear, as, for example, at a wedding. The geisha's version of this most formal level of clothing is her desho, literally, her "going out wear," a trailing black kimono marked by five crests, with a pattern dyed and embroidered at the hem.

Age

Formality is just one dimension defining the appropriateness of a particular garment. Age is another. Bright colors are seen in great profusion on young women's kimono, but they are supposed to become more subdued as a woman ages. The placement of the design on the hem of a formal kimono also changes according to the age of the wearer. The higher up it extends, the more appropriate to youth. But, though color and design are dimensions eminently capable of gradation along the scale of age, they are not the primary categories of relevance. The most basic division centers on the type of sleeve: the place where the difference between girlhood and womanhood is signified.

Sleeves

A furisode, or "swinging sleeve," is worn by a nonadult female and is considered the most formal type of kimono for a young girl. This is what a bride wears at her wedding. When the arms are held at one's side, the sleeves of the furisode reach to the ankle.[4] The maiko's kimono is of this type. Once a woman becomes an adult, most commonly signified by her marriage, she puts away her swinging sleeves and changes to a type of kimono called *tomesode*, the sleeves of which reach just below the hip. The name refers to the sleeves (*sode*) of the one who has to stay here (*tomeru*), that is, who marries into (this) house.

In the past, most women appeared in the shorter sleeved tomesode from their late teens on merely because a single woman in her twenties was a social anomaly. A twenty-two-year-old virgin geisha would traditionally have been just as odd. Nowadays, when it is no longer unusual for twenty-five-year-olds to be maidens, social adulthood involves many other things besides sex. Somewhere around age twenty-three, a young lady will probably put away her long sleeves, and a maiko, virgin or not, will also change to tomesode.

Even if they are unmarried, women in their twenties still in furisode look a little silly. This is true of maiko as well, because they often do not become full geisha until they are twenty-one or twenty-two, yet they are still traipsing about in the "little girl" paraphernalia of the apprentice.

In the past, an apprentice geisha did not graduate to a tomesode until she had gone through her sexual initiation and her patron had paid for an entire new adult-style wardrobe.[5] Adulthood in the geisha world was traditionally begun when a woman became sexually active – an event that occurred and was celebrated around the same age (seventeen to nineteen) when other women would marry. Because of their connection with a woman's sexual status, the symbolic overtones of sleeves are very evocative. Long, swinging sleeves connote innocence and purity and are appropriate to little girls and maidens. It is not seemly for a woman who is no longer chaste to wear furisode.

In the modern geisha world, the apprentice's "deflowering ceremony," the mizu-age, is no longer practiced as such. Young geisha seldom obtain a patron until they are in their mid- to late twenties, by which time they are usually not particularly virginal even if they are virgins. That is why they will long since have left their maiko kimono and hairstyles behind. For geisha, as well as for society at large, a discrepancy often exists between a woman's socially defined adulthood and her kimono.

Season

The season is yet another index of appropriateness for kimono. Like a traditional haiku poem, a kimono should have a discernible seasonal motif. Seasonality is expressed broadly in three distinct types of the garment, as well as in the colors and design.

From September through April, women should wear kimono of the lined type called *awase*. Commonly, this kimono will be a weighted silk crepe de chine garment with a lining of lighter crepe or silk mousseline. Red lining was popular twenty to thirty years ago, but now cream, white, pastels, or *bokashi* (one color fading into another) are more fashionable.

Awase kimono are worn eight months out of the year, so a woman's wardrobe will have more of these than the unlined hitoe kimono, which is worn only in May and possibly June, or the light silk leno-weave ro kimono for June through August. A good summer ro kimono might cost more than an ordinary awase, but a very good awase kimono will be the most expensive kind of kimono there is.

Unlined hitoe kimono are not much in demand today. Women usually do not have a kimono wardrobe large enough to justify

Poster for the Kamogawa Dances, showing young geisha in full formal attire. The style of these kimono is that of two hundred years ago. Ichiume is at far left.

buying a garment that can be properly worn for only two months of the year. Nobody would raise an eyebrow if a woman wore an awase kimono in May, but hitoe would be out of place for ten of the twelve months. Although relatively inexpensive because unlined, such a kimono remains a luxury because it has such a short season.

A geisha's kimono wardrobe takes even more account of the seasons than does that of an ordinary woman. Her formal, long black robe (*kuro mon-tsuki*) at New Year is succeeded by the same type of robe in a color (*iro mon-tsuki*) for the rest of January. During February and March she should wear two layers of kimono (*nimae gasane*). In April a formal occasion demands a single lined robe with padded hem and in May one without padding. June brings out the unlined hitoe, July light silk crepe, and August leno-weave striped silk; from September, one returns to lined awase.

Japanese are fond of saying how much the natural change of seasons has affected the development of Japanese aesthetic sensibilities. It is also true that cultural categories of nature (for example, the seasons) have been turned back upon those same natural phenomena. No matter how hot the weather may get in May, one cannot appear in the summer ro kimono, the light, open weave designed to express coolness. The physical fact of summery weather, in other words, is not as important as the cultural fact that summer does not begin until June.

On June first, in every house in Pontochō where geisha live, the same activity takes place. Kimono undergarments are spread out on the tatami mats, and the mother of the house snips the threads that attach the white silk grosgrain collar to the under-robe. The wide collar is the only part of this robe that shows, but it is very conspicuous. The geisha can use benzine to dab at the makeup stains that inevitably soil it, but after a point it will have to be taken off and a clean one sewn on. Women feel they are sloughing off the last remnants of winter when, dirty or not, the old collars come off on June first, and a silk collar of the open-weave striped ro is attached.

Flowers, birds, and insects are common design motifs for kimono. Unlike more abstract patterns, or representations of such auspicious objects as fans, the natural objects usually have a seasonal significance. Some are expressly associated with a particular month – pine for January, plum for February, iris for May – but most are more broadly appropriate for a season: cherry blossoms in the spring, little trout for summer, or maple leaves in the fall.[6]

When a woman has only a few kimono, she may purposely avoid buying those with too obvious a seasonal design because she wants something she can wear at almost any time of year. But the fact that seasonal designs limit the times a particular garment can be worn merely increases its cachet when it is brought out. Geisha wear kimono through every month of the year, so they are in a perfect position to season their wardrobes with spring plums, summer plovers, and autumnal deer.

Colors

Colors can also have seasonal flavors. Traditional color combinations, for the most part named after flowering plants, are specific to each month. For example, January's colors are pale green layered on deep purple. The combination is called pine. October's are rose backed with slate blue, called bush clover. These are preeminently cultural categories, for although the names of the combinations – pine, peach, cicada wing, artemisia, and so on – reflect a connection to the natural world, the colors themselves have little to do with the name. May's combination, called mandarin orange flower (the actual blossom of which is white), consists of purple and a color known as deadleaf yellow.[7]

An extensive knowledge of these traditional seasonal layers of color is, admittedly, rare in modern Japan. But the artists who dye or hand-paint the finest silk kimono are aware of the traditions, and connoisseurs still appreciate these expressions of the gradual and subtle change of the seasons.

A geisha's kimono constitute a large part of her life as art. It is not only her dancing or singing, or any other specific sort of gei she has, but the presentation of her self in an aesthetic fashion that makes her kimono such an important part of her profession. The amount of money geisha spend on clothes makes many people gasp, yet expense as such does not mean one is a clothes horse. American high fashion encourages a woman to display herself in a paroxysm of individuality; the eternal quest to find exactly the right pieces of clothing to create the ever-elusive individual image. The purpose is to make oneself stand out, within an acceptable range of what is "in," of course, and one must always keep pace with the changing definition thereof.

The kimono aesthetic is different. The point is not to stand out, but to harmonize with one's surroundings, both natural and social, mindful of the season and the event. The criteria defining the appropriateness of kimono are highly ramified, yet while some of the rules are quite strict (wool kimono are not worn to a party, married women do not wear swinging sleeves, ro is not worn in the fall), a range of choices exists in all of these dimensions: formality, age, and season.

Within the framework of the times of year, a woman's age, and the occasion, personal taste enters in to combine these elements into an expression of an individual woman in a particular setting. Of course, a calibration so fine demands a keen aesthetic sensibility, as well as knowledge of the domain of kimono, and it is not something that can be observed every day. Bad taste in kimono is as common as bad taste in anything else. But when all these things do come together, and one meets a woman whose carefully chosen outfit is precisely right in every detail, the sense of harmony of time, place, and person can be breathtaking.

SEVENTEEN

EXOTICS AND RETROSPECTIVES

KAI YO KEN BI RYŌ NYŌ JŌ BUTSU

All beheld from afar the dragon maiden,
now become a buddha.

The Lotus Sutra

THE TEMPLE OF GREAT VIRTUE

AN ALMOST PALPABLE stillness descends upon Kyoto in
the summer. Daytime life slows down under the continuous
drone of cicadas, a sound that "penetrates the rock," in the
image of a well-known haiku.[1] The constant "mi mii miim" is the
auditory equivalent of the oppressive humid heat. Mornings are
pleasant, though, and except for the geisha, who sleep late as
usual, people often get up early to take advantage of the cool. In
the Zen temples, acolytes do their first meditation at 4:00 A.M.,
another at 6:00, and another at 9:00. They break during midday
because of the heat.

Walking into the garden of the Mitsuba early one July morning, I was startled by the sudden whirring of doves' wings from a
bush by the gate. In that instant, the familiar sound brought a
sharp memory of the first time I had lived for a summer in Kyoto.
I was nineteen, in the midst of an austere Wanderjahr, looking for
ultimate meanings and a cure for adolescent morbidity. I had
joined a group of young Japanese and foreigners who "sat," that
is, followed the Zen prescription for meditation, at Kōtō-in, one

of the small temples within the large compound of Daitokuji, the Temple of Great Virtue.

I remembered the thick whitewashed walls of the meditation hall, and early morning dew on the leaves of a shaggy banana plant in its garden. If I were the first to arrive, I might surprise a dove or two when I opened the gate, or disturb a somnolent lizard perched on the edge of the wooden door. At the time I knew nothing of the Kyoto of Pontochō or Gion, or of the neon night life that glowed in narrow alleys at the center of the city.

I had lived next to the Kamo River in 1970, too, but it was a different river in its northern reaches, tranquil and dark at night. Now, six years later, I had little occasion to take the streetcar up to the northern edge of the city, to walk along wide stone pathways past the imposing buildings contained in the Daitokuji compound. If my life had been simplified to bare essentials then, now it was ensnared in countless details: lessons, banquets, obligations to this person and that. I was as immersed in worldly affairs as I had been aloof from them before.

One July afternoon, as a geisha caught in a traffic jam downtown, I was looking across the river at Pontochō, thinking what a nice view it is from that vantage point – the row of teahouses on the opposite bank seen through waving branches of willow – when two Buddhist priests came striding past the line of stopped cars. They wore stiff black gauze robes, straw sandals, and great dome-like hats of closely woven reeds, like baskets, that covered their faces but for a glimpse of set jaws. They were Zen monks on their begging rounds (*takuhatsu*), still part of the Zen regimen for monks. Something about one of them caught my attention. I rolled down the car window, craning to see better. When they took off their hats I was almost certain, and I called out, "Chris!" The first monk wheeled around, startled. He was one of my old confreres from Daitokuji.

Chris had arrived in Japan six years before, not knowing a word of Japanese but determined to devote himself to Zen. About twelve foreigners I knew in Kyoto had had the same idea. Few of us lasted more than a year. I left the temple after four months to go to a Japanese university, and many others left to continue their treks in Nepal and India. I had not realized that

Chris was still in Kyoto until the moment I sensed something familiar about one of the shaven monks. After four years of doggedly proving his sincerity, he had been accepted into the order, which fewer than half a dozen foreigners have ever been able to do.

Puzzled, the pair of bonzes came over to the taxi. My hair was done in a geisha-like manner, but Chris recognized me immediately. It would hardly have been proper to begin chatting on the street, so as the line of cars started to creep forward, I scribbled my phone number on a calling card. "Here, call me sometime when you can get to a phone. I'll be in Kyoto for another month." He put my card somewhere within the many folds of his voluminous robes and ran his hand over his stubbly bald head. Then he raised his hands, palms together, in the Buddhist greeting, and as the cab crossed the bridge I saw the two monks tie on their hats again. No one would ever have guessed that one of them was not Japanese.

Early the following week I was awakened at about six in the morning by the deep voice of a Zen monk chanting a drawn-out mantra as he walked down the street outside my window. I jumped up and folded my bed mat, stuffing it in the closet, expecting my doorbell to ring any moment. It didn't. Later that morning several more priests came down our street, Chris not among them. I asked okāsan about them and she said that at this time of year the monks from all the Zen temples came out on rounds. They had set routes, though, and only "begged" from houses of parishioners. Her family belonged to a different sect of Buddhism, so none of these monks stopped at the Mitsuba. Every time I heard an approaching monk that day I went to my window, only to catch a back view of a mountainous hat disappearing around the corner. Finally, one afternoon at about one o'clock my doorbell did ring, and I went down to greet this unorthodox Zen monk.

"I had no idea you were still here," I told him. Chris settled himself on the tatami, resting one foot on the opposite thigh in the semi-lotus posture that, as he assumed it, seemed as natural as crossing his legs. He was relaxed and cheerful. "You look fine," I said. "Your austerities seem to agree with you." "And yours with you," he laughed, glancing at my shamisen and a kimono hanging out to air. We both felt a trifle self-conscious in these personae we had adopted: a Zen monk and a geisha, neither of them Japanese. Six years ago we had once spent an afternoon in a music coffeeshop that played nothing but Bob Dylan records. "It's disappeared by now, I suppose," he said. "I don't get much chance to listen to music these days, anyway."

Soon his companion came past the window, intoning his resonant call, and Chris had to leave. "Listen," he said, "there's a *sōmen* party at the temple on the fifteenth. We make big vats of it and serve anybody who shows up." Sōmen is Japanese vermicelli, eaten cold in the summer. The monks all make lanterns," he continued, "and give them away. Come. And bring some of your geisha friends." Outside, he tied his hat under his chin. "Goodbye, Kikuko, see you on the fifteenth." Taking a deep breath, he sounded the mantra that heralds the begging monk and strode off down the street.

I told okāsan about Chris and his invitation to eat noodles. "I've heard of that custom," she said. "As you know, Kyoto has O-bon by the old calendar [mid-August], except for that one temple, which celebrates it on the new calendar date [mid-July]."[2] Nobody had booked the Mitsuba for the fifteenth of July, so okāsan decided to come with me.

LANTERNS

Bon is the most important Buddhist holiday in Japan. Feast of Lanterns, Festival of the Dead, Buddhist All Souls Day – these are various names for it. On the thirteenth of July (or August, depending on which calendar is followed) the souls of ancestors are said to visit their descendants to be feted with offerings of food and flowers on the family Buddhist altars. Then, on the fifteenth or sixteenth, they are politely shown the way back home to the netherworld.

One way the ancestral souls are escorted back is by *okuribi*, fires or lanterns lit to illuminate their path. In Kyoto on the evening of August 16, bonfires are lit on different mountainsides, arranged in the shape of auspicious characters, a boat, and the traditional square *torii* arch. The centerpiece is the character DAI, meaning BIG, which is laid out on the eastern mountain that takes its name from that fact: Daimonji. It is an awesome sight to see a whole mountaintop blaze forth with the grand character DAI. The entire city of Kyoto, full of tourists from all over Japan, turns out to view this most spectacular version of okuribi.

In other places, people follow the custom of lighting candles in paper lanterns and floating them down the river in the evening. The visiting spirits are supposed to follow the bobbing, flickering stream of lights away from the towns and villages of human habitation, back to the spirit world. Sometimes the food offerings from the altar are wrapped in a lotus leaf and placed on the raft, too, as a spiritual lunch-box to make sure no hungry souls linger in the world of the living.

Sōmen is primarily a summer dish. Thread-like white noodles served in a bowl of ice water are plucked out and lightly dipped into individual cups of thin sauce. Somen is associated with Bon because it is seasonally appropriate, but it is ceremonially appropriate as well. The *so* of sōmen means "simple, unadulterated," and, in Chinese cooking, denotes vegetarian or Buddhist dishes. *Men* means "noodles."

Because the ancestral spirits are good Buddhists (everybody is thought to become a buddha after death) they are never offered meat. Rather, sōmen, eggplants and cucumbers, and such fruits as peaches, pears, and persimmons are placed on the altar as offerings to the visiting souls. In some areas of Japan, toothpicks are stuck into the small eggplants and cucumbers to make crude representations of horses or oxen. The idea is that these animals can help carry the souls on their long journey to and from the netherworld.

Chris had said to come to the temple early, around five o'clock, before all the lanterns were claimed. The monks had spent several days making them, each according to his own whim, and it was a motley display indeed. Most of the lanterns were squarish, made of little more than rice paper pasted on a balsa wood frame, but some were hexagonal, or took the shape of boats, including one balanced on beer-can pontoons. The lanterns were displayed in the meditation hall, where strips of matting had been laid on the stone floor for visitors to walk on. When okāsan and I arrived, a number of people were already milling about, viewing the lanterns and choosing the ones they would take home. We went in and put scraps of paper with our names on two rather plain ones; the more interesting lanterns had already been claimed.

I caught a glimpse of Chris' friend, the young monk who had been with him the day we met, and went to say hello. Just then Chris himself came hurrying along the outside corridor. I introduced my okāsan to the two men, and she urged them to stop at the Mitsuba the next time they were on their begging rounds. "Sometimes you probably have to use the bathroom when you're out," she said. "Of course a monk can hardly go against the side of a wall someplace, so please feel free to use our facilities." They thanked her. Chris was on the cooking detail, so he had to go back to the kitchen. His friend showed us to the monks' dining hall, where the sōmen was being served.

Whole families were there: men in shirtsleeves, women in summer dresses, little boys in shorts, and little girls in bright yukata. It was a gay and informal gathering with no hint of the austerity usually associated with a Zen temple. People were gathered into a group large enough to fill the hall, seated, and served. When they were finished, another group was ushered in. There was no reverent solemnity here – the monks were fast and efficient in serving, the visitors fast and efficient in slurping down the sōmen.

The temple, with its deep, overhanging eaves and stone floors, was cool inside, and the late afternoon light made the enclosed garden glow with fresh green. The moss and stones had been sprinkled with water in preparation for the visitors. We finished just at dusk. Okāsan and I picked up our lanterns and left the temple, hailing a cab on Kita-Ōji Boulevard.

"What about floating our lanterns on the Kamo River?" I asked. I had read about the custom but never seen it. "Nobody does it on the Kamo," she said. "Well, I'll try to make some rafts out of something when we get back," I said, thinking of some flat pieces of wood I had seen in the shed. Okāsan gave me her lantern to see what I could do with the scraps.

With thumbtacks and string I anchored the fragile paper boxes to chunks of wood, then I secured the candles with nails so they wouldn't tip and brought the floatable lanterns next door to the Mitsuba. Okāsan was game for the experiment, so we went around back, down to the riverbank, crowded with people strolling or sitting on the stone embankment. Okāsan cupped her hand over several matches to light the candles against the breeze off the river.

I set the lanterns in the river at the water's edge, but they just bobbed there, nosing back into the bank. "Ah, it's not going to work," said okāsan. Hitching up my skirt, I fished the rafts out and waded toward the middle of the river, where the current was faster. This time they took off, riding atop the ripples down the stream. People on the bank applauded. It seemed as if the two lanterns were racing each other, first one bobbing ahead, then the other. Soon one took the lead and kept it.

Okāsan and I walked down the bank, keeping pace with the boats. Just above the Sanjō Bridge there is an artificial step in the river, where the water drops suddenly about four feet. That would be the end of our lanterns, I realized, as they calmly wafted along toward this small Niagara. This was the reason, of course, why nobody sent the spirits home with platoons of lights down the Kamo River. The first lantern went rolling over into the fall, but to our surprise it popped out at the bottom, its candle doused but right side up and floating steadily on. The second lantern sailed right over the drop. Still lighted, it followed the first down the long stretch of smooth water before the next step above the Shijo Bridge.

The crowd on the bank had gotten involved in this small drama, and a cheer went up when the lanterns were seen to have survived. Okāsan herself was skipping along like a young girl. We were walking faster now, the teahouses of Pontochō at our backs. I stumbled on a rough stone in the dark, breaking the strap of my wooden clog. Okāsan called up to one of the verandas where people were partying. "Oi, Fukumoto-san. Kikuko broke her *geta*, can you toss down a pair?" "Right away," floated down the response. "Do you see somebody's sailing lanterns out there?"

"Those are ours," okāsan shouted back. A maid appeared at the back with a pair of garden clogs. "They're dirty," she apologized, "but it's all I could find at the moment." I thanked her and we hurried on, having fallen behind the swift lanterns.

People were standing along the Shijō Bridge, pointing at the one lighted candle making its way down the river – they couldn't see the unlit lantern in the dark. The step at Shijō was higher than the previous one, yet okāsan and I stood there, hoping that somehow the lanterns would survive here too. They were dashed to pieces. Not a splinter emerged at the lower level. Yet, there was something satisfying about the finality with which they were swallowed up into the dark water.

A week or so later I heard the monks go down our street at dawn again. This time I pulled the light blanket over my head and went back to sleep. Five minutes later my phone rang. "Kikuko, friends of yours here," said the auntie, in none too good humor, and then she hung up. I whipped on an old kimono I used for a bathrobe and hurried out. Chris and his friend were sitting on the step at the entryway as if a 5:00 A.M. visit were nothing out of the ordinary. "Good morning, we came to use the bathroom," he said. Okāsan was asleep in the inner recesses of her apartments, so it was the auntie who had been wakened to open the gate for them. "Would you be so kind as to make some tea for the priests, auntie?" I asked her, having never dared request a favor from her before. She repeated my words under her breath, but glancing at the young men in their Buddhist robes, she went to the kitchen to make tea.

They drank their tea quickly and stood up to leave, bowing with brisk dignity I walked them out to the gate. That was the last I saw of Chris. Two weeks later I returned to the United States to write my dissertation. Precisely two years after this, once again in mid-July when I was back in Pontochō for a visit, I went to the Temple of Great Virtue to see whether Chris were still there. A monk tending the vegetable garden at the edge of the compound told me he had gone away – to Kyushu, he thought, but he wasn't sure.

CROSS-CURRENTS

A great deal of water had flowed beneath the bridges of Pontochō in the two years I had been away. I burned a stick of incense in memory of Ichiume, my young older sister, and met a new maiko-to-be who was being groomed for her autumn debut as Ichimomo. For the first time, my okāsan was to sponsor a geisha from her own house – actually the second time, if Ichigiku the American geisha can be counted as the first. Okāsan was busily preparing the future Ichimomo's maiko wardrobe.

During my visit I was pressed into geisha duty for several parties. Borrowing a summer kimono from okāsan, I was glad to oblige. My legs were a bit out of practice for sitting properly, though, and once when I slipped out of the room to stretch them I met Ichimomo in the hall doing exactly the same thing. If anything, she was less accustomed to sitting on her feet than I was. She spoke to me in Kyoto dialect, but it did not yet slip easily off her tongue. A distant relative of my okāsan's brother's former wife, she had grown up in Nagoya. The first part of her training involved teaching her to speak in the soft, undulating tones of Kyoto.

This seventeen-year-old was chafing under the supervision of the mothers and the other geisha. "Anything I say, they tell me I'm being fresh," she complained to me. I could easily imagine them doing just that. Ichimomo had no real intention of becoming a geisha. She had agreed to be a maiko for two years, then she was going to quit to marry her boyfriend. She made no secret of the fact that she was attracted to family life, not to the mizu shōbai. But she had been persuaded that it would be interesting to play maiko for a few years. Okāsan was convinced she would change her mind and want to stay on longer, but as I listened to Ichimomo, I felt doubtful.

My okāsan has spent her entire life in the mizu shōbai. She has been buffeted by the uncertain currents of the geisha business, but she has always managed to emerge on top of things. Her success arises from the energy she plunges into her projects and protégés, like Ichimomo and me. She does not stop to brood over the enterprises that sink. I knew she would be disappointed when the

*Liza Dalby's okāsan in 1976 during a visit
to the Daitokuji Temple.*

inevitable break with Ichimomo occurred, but then, I knew too
that she would go on and try again. I liked to think that because
she had enjoyed having her American "daughter" in her house
she now pursued a more permanent arrangement of the same
sort.

One of the last things we did together during my visit was to
drive out to the hospital where Ichiume's okāsan languished.
Tsunehiko drove us there in the new Toyota. The Hatsuyuki teahouse was now just an empty lot with some charred beams in a
pile, its mistress a frail old woman sitting on a hospital bed with

her legs tucked under her. She was very thin and pale and seemed to have drawn all her grief into herself, where it was slowly consuming her. We stepped into her room and tears came to my eyes. Other geisha had come to visit that day, along with some relatives. Gradually the sound of weeping spilled out into the hall.

We stayed for about an hour. Then okāsan glanced over to Tsunehiko, who had been sitting glumly in the corner. I bowed in farewell to Ichiume's mother, and she bent over in a low bow from her bed. On the way back to Pontochō, okāsan said that the sick woman's son had just eloped with one of the maiko. If her heart could possibly be torn any further, this would do so. The news was being kept from her.

My okāsan and the other mothers held full knowledge of the tragedy at Hatsuyuki. They knew of other such things, too – of the proprietress who hanged herself, of the love triangles and the intrigues, of the emotions that seem to run stronger in the geisha world, where romance is trade. Everyone's life is rocked, from time to time, by the waves of fortune, but the geisha live in rougher waters than most. I think of my okāsan as I do the buoyant lanterns we sent floating down the Kamo River in the middle of July.

NOTES

PREFACE

1. Among women aged twenty-five to fifty-five (a high percentage of whom are married) the rate of participation in the labor force is around 25 percent. See Alice Cook and Hiroko Hayashi, *Working Women in Japan*, esp. p. 102, Table 3, "Women Employees by Age."

2. This is considered the upper limit for women hired as clerks or secretaries in many companies. Called "office flowers," they are expected to retire gracefully when they marry or age much beyond thirty. Although this is still common practice, there have been several court cases since 1966 in which women challenged their companies on the issue of forced early retirement, and won. See ibid., pp. 45–63.

3. To select two recent examples: Germaine Greer uses the neologism "geishadom" to refer to women in a state of slavery to male whim ("Being Shrewd About the Shrew," *The Dial* [Public Broadcasting Communications, Inc.], January 1981); Susan Brownmiller's eulogy of John Lennon speaks of Yoko Ono as "hardly cut out for the geisha role" – meaning that she is not meek, subservient, and passive ("Yoko and John," *Rolling Stone*, January 22, 1981).

4. These geisha communities, or *hanamachi*, were as follows. In Tokyo: Akasaka, Asakusa, Mukōjima, Oimachi, Shimbashi, and Yoshichō. In Kyoto: Gion, Higashi Shinchi, Kamishichiken, and Pontochō. Other areas were Atami, Hakata, Nagoya, and Tamazukuri. Within these hanamachi, many of the names of people and establishments are fictitious.

5. A translation of this questionnaire with tabulated responses is in my Ph.D. dissertation, "The Institution of the Geisha in Modern Japanese Society."

6. Minarai in this case comes very close to the idea of participant observation, but with the crucial difference that it is actually a part of geisha society. I can think of no society (except, perhaps, American universities) where participant observation is a native category.

CHAPTER 1

1. "Double registration" (*nimae kansatsu*) dates from the days when prostitution was legal in Japan. Prostitutes had to be licensed as such, and geisha were licensed as geisha. A woman could not hold both licenses, so double registration became the derogatory description for a geisha who slept around.
2. A geisha cannot be married, but the "mother" of a teahouse can be.

CHAPTER 3

1. The *kaimyō* is the Buddhist name given to the spirit of the dead, engraved upon the tombstone. For an excellent discussion of kaimyō, see Lafcadio Hearn, *Exotics and Retrospectives:* "Exotics IV: The Literature of the Dead," pp. 130–153.
2. The character *ichi* as such means market or city, but these meanings are not automatically called into play when the character appears in a name.
3. The custom of inheriting the first character from the name of a main house or shop when setting up a branch is common in Japan. As with people's names, the shared written character expresses the continuity and connection of the establishments.
4. See Harumi Befu, "Ritual Kinship in Japan," *Sociologus*, 14 (1964), 150–169, for an analytical description of Japanese ritual kinship.
5. As with the use of the sansan-kudo ritual, I think it is not that geisha have copied the rites and language of the marriage ceremony, but rather that both marriage and ritual sisterhood express the same underlying concept of creating kin out of nonrelatives.
6. The term en used in words referring to relatives (*enrui, enja*) can have the broader meaning of "kin," but usually it refers specifically to affinals, as in *enka*, a "family (house) related by marriage."
7. In Kyoto the teahouse (*ochaya*) can also function as a geisha house (*okiya*), whereas in the Tokyo area these are always separate establishments.
8. This, too, has a parallel in the wedding ceremony. A bride exchanges cups with her husband's parents to show that she, as a dutiful daughter-in-law, accepts the rules and customs of their house.

9. According to one geisha I spoke with, there can be two versions of this ceremony. If a woman leaves the geisha world with no expectation of returning (if she marries, e.g.) she distributes the "red rice." If she wants to leave open the possibility of return in case her new venture falls through, she gives plain boiled white rice.

10. As an announcement of her changed status, she passes out triangular paper notices with the characters *hiki* and *iwai* printed in the middle. Written in brush to the side, and smaller, is the phrase: [her geisha name] *kai kai* (has reverted to) [her original name].

11. When the teahouse mother calls geisha for parties, a particular house will favor its own trainees. Geisha, in turn, honor their commitments to that house first, should a conflict of any kind arise. Chapter 6 discusses some of the ceremonial obligations entailed by this relation to a minarai-jaya.

12. This practice is reminiscent of the role of the *uchi deshi*, the "house pupil," in many of the traditional arts. A favored pupil is allowed to live in the master's house, performing all manner of menial chores for the privilege of being able, by sheer proximity, to absorb something of the essence of the master's art.

CHAPTER 4

1. *Yōnaki*, "crying out in the night," means orgasm. The yūjo coolly referred to it as *naki o ireru*, "sticking in some cries," as part of their technique of fakery. Nakano Eizō, *Yūjo no seikatsu*, p. 127.

2. The woman who is usually credited with being the first female geisha was Kasen, of the house Ogiya in Yoshiwara. She was originally a yūjo who paid off all her debts and then went into business for herself as an entertainer, or geisha, around 1761.

3. Cited in Keisuke Watarai, *Miyako no hanamachi*, p. 147.

4. The best known of the Meiji oligarchs who married a geisha was Katsura Kōgorō (1833–1877), later known as Kidō Takayoshi, of Chōshū; he married Ikumatsu of Gion. Itō Hirobumi, Sakamoto Ryōma, Yamagata Aritomo, and even Saigō Takamori all had geisha mistresses.

5. "Nonexistent things: square eggs and a yūjo's sincerity," says a proverb.

6. See J. E. DeBecker, *The Nightless City*, esp. page 82, for a detailed discussion of how the sumptuary laws were applied to geisha and courtesans.

7. The one Tokyo group that did not participate at that time was Yoshiwara, the old licensed prostitute quarter of the city.

8. Tora no maki means handbook, or tradebook. Many schools of arts or crafts had such books, graduated into different levels for apprentices. The supposedly highest and most esoteric was the tora (tiger) volume. There were actually no such primers for geisha; this title is a semi-facetious reference to that custom.

CHAPTER 5

1. The Gion geishas' style of dance is called kyō-mai (dance of the capital, that is, Kyoto) and it comes from the Kansai regional *jiuta* musical tradition, which is on the whole more sedate than some of the livelier musical styles developed in Edo. Gion has but one dance teacher, the renowned Inoue Yachiyo, now an old woman and a cultural institution in her own right since she was awarded the prestigious Living National Treasure award in 1955.

2. In the years 1930–1934, the number of jokyū jumped from about 50,000 women to over twice that. They outnumbered geisha, whose population had fallen from a high of over 80,000 in the country as a whole in 1929 to around 72,000 in 1934. *Naimushō Keisatsu Torishimari Tōkei* [Department of the Interior, Police Regulation Statistics] (Tokyo, 1934), no. 11, p. 98.

3. Cited in Miyake Koken, ed., *Geigi tokuhon*, pp. 73–74.

4. This book was compiled by Miyake Koken and published under the auspices of the "newspaper for the national association of chefs" in 1935. It is the most comprehensive collection of its kind, but by no means the first. Numerous books about geisha appeared in the late 1920s and early 1930s. Some of them, e.g., Hayashida Kametarō's *Geisha no kenkyū* [Geisha studies], were literary and idiosyncratic essays that used the idea of geisha more as vehicle than as subject. The *Geigi tokuhon*, however, was written in a simple, readable style that even geisha with only a grade school education could read.

5. Miyake Koken, *Geigi tokuhon*, pp. 35–37.

6. Ibid., pp. 43–45.

7. Ibid., pp. 101–110.

8. Ibid., p. 221.

9. See esp. Kaffū's 1918 novel *Ude kurabe*, translated by Kurt Meissner as *Geisha in Rivalry* (Tokyo: Charles E. Tuttle, 1963).

10. Miyake Koken, *Geigi tokuhon*, pp. 293–297.

11. Although all are equally *okyakusama*, honored guests, to the geisha, one man is usually host of the party in the teahouse for someone else, who is *his* guest. This person who is being treated will be seated in the *kamiza*, the seat of highest prestige in front of the

tokonoma, and the host (who is paying for everything) is seated below him.

12. See Thomas R. H. Havens, *Valley of Darkness*, pp. 15–32.

13. *Shukuzu* was Shūsei's last major novel. It began serial publication in the *Miyako shimbun* in June 1941, but because of the censorship of the wartime government it was never completed. Publication was suspended in mid-September 1941 after eighty installments. This section was translated by William F. Sibley (unpublished), and the text can be found in the *Tokuda Shūsei zenshū*.

14. See Kishii Yoshie, *Onna geisha no jidai*, p. 133.

CHAPTER 6

1. The weighty glutinous masses, called *kagami mochi* (literally, mirror [round] rice cakes), have heavy import. Rice is synonymous with sustenance, and because mochi are concentrated rice, they are considered particularly fitting as objects for ceremonial offering. The traditional New Year decoration (an offering to the deity of the new year) consists of these rice cakes, citrons, *konbu* (kelp), fern fronds, and other items to evoke longevity and prosperity. The custom of offering rice cakes to one's mentors in the geisha world thus partakes of the meanings already attached to mochi in Japanese society in general.

2. Bowing is a complicated art. One's bow can be infinitely adjusted to take account of the person, the occasion, and so on. Bows range from a slight inclination of the head and shoulders toward an acquaintance on the street to kneeling on the floor with palms flat, one's nose a few inches above the ground. The longer the position is held, the more respectful the bow.

3. Not wearing underpants is thought to be risqué in modern Japan, just as it is in American culture. (Witness the advertisement for designer jeans: "You know what comes between me and my Calvin Kleins? Nothing.") Perhaps it is not so surprising that panties have, at various times, been taken up as a symbol of liberated womanhood, but it is interesting that both wearing them and not wearing them have been advocated for the emancipated woman. In the 1960s, Germaine Greer called for women to throw away their panties and taste their own menstrual blood; but in the 1930s, the equally daring feminist Tsukamoto Hamako spoke out for Japanese women to wear underpants to free themselves from the worry of exposure should their kimono go awry.

Tsukamoto's efforts were somewhat trivialized when they were dubbed the Wear Panties Movement, but the initial impetus for her speeches was serious enough. In 1932 a large department store called Shirokiya in Asakusa caught fire, and several scores of women customers died in the flames despite the fact that firemen arrived in plenty of time with safety nets. The women apparently were afraid of exposing themselves by jumping and landing in ungraceful postures. Tsukamoto seized on this incident to exhort women not only to wear panties, but to overcome their timidity in general.

4. Drinking is such a large part of a geisha's job that it can be considered an occupational hazard. Even women who definitely should not drink because of their health must still pretend to do so. Geisha help each other disguise the fact of not drinking, and some of their ruses are quite ingenious. A symbolic sip in front of the customer satisfies the social necessity to take the cup, and he need not notice that most of the sake is dumped into the bowl of rinse water provided on the table. An older geisha can more easily get away with not drinking for medical reasons. She may sometimes call a younger woman to down her cup by proxy.

5. The etymology of mizu-age, like so many terms used in the karyūkai, involves a series of associated meanings which are often originally euphemistic. *Mizu*, water, and *age* (from *ageru*, to raise) originally meant the unloading of goods from transport barges. Mizu-age thus came to mean "commercial income" in general, especially when applied to places in the entertainment world – the mizu shōbai, or water business. In the licensed quarters (prostitution is an example par excellence of the mizu shōbai), the fees paid to the women were written down in a register called the *mizu-age chō*, the income account. Because the prostitutes' income was based on sex, mizu-age and sex became closely related terms.

   A lascivious image also comes to mind when one says "raising water" in the context of sex. In fact, most people whom I asked about the meaning of the term thought it meant the sexual equivalent of priming the pump.

6. Japanese rice-flour, sweet-bean, and pure sugar cakes are never taken after a meal as dessert. These confections are of a sweetness to make one's teeth ache. They are customarily eaten in the afternoon, balancing the unsugared green tea that accompanies them.

7. The five- or six-inch-high wooden clogs (*okobo*) that a maiko wears are, along with her dangling *darai* obi, one of the most distinctive elements of her outfit. Because her coiffure adds another couple of

inches to her height, a well-fed young maiko in her tall clogs can tower over an elderly customer.

CHAPTER 7

1. Once in a while, following the adjustment of the day of the spring equinox, it falls on February 5 instead.
2. A day called Setsubun occurs before the first day of each of the four seasons, but the Setsubun before spring is the only one widely celebrated now.
3. Buildings, sculpture, paintings, and other pieces of art can be designated as Important Cultural Properties in Japan and can receive government aid for their preservation and upkeep. Artists in various fields can be honored with a similar designation as Living National Treasures and can also receive a government stipend.
4. The rules of adoption, inheritance, and establishing branch houses in the Kyoto geisha quarters are not as clear as they once were. Inheritance of an establishment can take two basic forms. In the more limited version, what is passed on is the right to manage the place as the okamisan, using the same *yago*, or shop insignia. In the full form, actual ownership of the property, the family name, and even ancestral obligations are passed on, and the heiress becomes, in effect, a family member.

   Before the Second World War, only in the latter case was the heiress said to hold the position of *musume-bun*, the "daughter role." At present, both types of heiress are called musume-bun, and only those familiar with the particular case know exactly what was inherited. In the case of Michiko's mother's house, the nakai took over only the management at first; but years later, Michiko sold the house to her.

CHAPTER 8

1. Although the party from the geisha's perspective is called a zashiki, the customers would never refer to it as such. From their position it is called an *enkai*, a feast, dinner party, banquet.
2. Most of the Pontochō teahouses are not equipped to handle large formal banquets on the premises; the parties at the teahouses are small gatherings, often taking place after the main formal banquets. Still, the engagement of Pontochō geisha for a large party somewhere outside the hanamachi is always made through the auspices of one of the teahouses.
3. Americans who tune into the 11.00 P.M. adult television programs

in Japan are amazed at the nudity (bare breasts, but panties) allowed, and they come away with the impression that Japan must be a voyeur's paradise; if that's what's allowed on television, they surmise, then the other communications media must be even freer. Not true. For example, most modern editions of the old *shunga*, erotic woodblock prints, are prudishly trimmed to show ecstatic faces over gray blanks; movies are fuzzed over wherever improper parts are exposed; and a film like Ōshima's spectacular *In the Realm of the Senses* (Ai no corrida) has never been shown uncut, as it were, in his own country.

4. The real name of this teahouse is Mantei. "Ichiriki" comes from a fey reading of the first character, *man* (ten thousand), which appears as its shop crest. Broken up, it looks like the single-horizontal-stroke character for "one," *ichi*, with the character for "strength," *riki*, underneath.

5. Dodoitsu are short: three lines of seven syllables each, ending with one line of five syllables. The subject is usually male/female relations, unadorned with polite language. Dodoitsubō Senka (1796–1852) was the musician and comedian who unified the style into what became known, after him, as dodoitsu.

6. The most common Japanese word for "funny" is *okashii*, which has exactly the same ambivalent usage as the English word: funny, ha-ha, and funny, strange.

7. A Japanese friend told me the following story as an example of typical Japanese humor: A sudden cry of "Fire!" caused panic in a public bathhouse. The naked bathers, with no time to grab their clothes, rushed out into the street clutching only their washcloths. Rather than using them to cover the obvious places, they held the cloths over their faces.

Another story is from a collection of classic comic pieces: A master decided to reward a loyal servant with a day off. "Tell me what you'd like to do most," he told him, "it's on me." "Well," the servant replied, "my second favorite is sake."

8. The generic term for apprentice geisha (maiko in Kyoto, *han'gyoku* in Tokyo) is *oshakusan*, "those who do oshaku." Oshaku is the first thing an apprentice geisha learns, and even if she has no other gei to present, she can at least pour sake.

9. On this point, see Doi Takeo's reminiscences of being offered food and drink during his early days in America in chap. 1 of *The Anatomy of Dependence*. Doi felt that the American practice of catering to the individual's freedom to choose was a form of

thoughtlessness. As a Japanese, he felt that true politeness was manifested when a host had the foresight and took the trouble to choose for his guest.

10. The cycle of animals repeats itself every twelve years. The year I was born, 1950, was a tiger year, so every year in multiples of twelve before that was a tiger year, too. Kazue was either forty-nine, sixty-one, or seventy-three, and only sixty-one was plausible.

CHAPTER 9

1. What are termed ochaya in Kyoto are known as *machiai* in the Tokyo area. The word is a shortened form of *machiaijaya* (rendezvous teahouse). Although the term machiai is still common in Tokyo, it was officially abolished during the Allied occupation. The technically correct word now is *ryōtei*.

2. Bazoku geisha is a well-known term for the geisha of Fukuoka, although not many people seem to know its origin. It was explained to me as having originated during the 1930s, when the Japanese army and a large population of civilians occupied Manchuria. A contingent of geisha from Fukuoka apparently made the journey to Manchuria to entertain the troops, and this experience provided them with the epithet bazoku, calling to mind a romantic (if misplaced) image of the horse-riding Mongols of the thirteenth century.

3. This practice is not uncommon in Japan. If a family has daughters but no sons to carry on the family name, arrangements will be made for a daughter to take a husband who will adopt her family's name. He is called, literally, an adopted bridegroom, *muko yoshi*.

4. This group, the National Confederation of Geisha and Geisha Houses, has a membership today drawn almost exclusively from the less prestigious hanamachi. If there is a connection between this present-day organization and the National Confederation of Geisha Houses of the first decade of the 1900s, it is in name only.

5. The most famous example is the Shimbashi geisha Okoi (1880–1948), mistress of Prime Minister Katsura Tarō during the first decade of this century. At his death she cut her hair and became a Buddhist nun. The temple she joined, Hyakurakkan-ji, is in Meguro ward in Tokyo. There I visited another ex-geisha from Shimbashi, who had known Okoi as an old woman: the eighty-four-year-old Fukuda Shōun. Shōun had entered the life of a nun gradually; she even danced one last stage performance when she was seventy-eight, before shaving her head and taking her final vows.

6. One can express hierarchy in Japanese by using special nouns, verb endings, and locutions that place oneself in a lower position than the person addressed, or vice versa. This phenomenon, called *keigo* (polite speech), provides two forms for certain words: the *kenjōgo*, or humble form, and the *sonkeigo*, or honorific form. As might be expected, a Japanese host makes great use of keigo in his speech with a guest.

7. Emigiku Kanzaki (Kikuya of Akasaka), *I, a geisha.*

CHAPTER 10

1. Namely: Fukagawa, Yanagibashi, Yūshima Tenjin, Shiba Takanawa, Nichōmachi, Ryogoku Yagenbori, Sukiyamachi, and Shiba Tenmei Mae. The first three are still hanamachi of the same name today.

2. One of these women, Hida Chiho, has left an autobiography, *Shimbashi seikatsu yonjūyonnen* [Forty-four years in Shimbashi], in which she recounts her move to Shimbashi and the types of people who patronized her establishment – mostly famous political figures, actors, and business magnates.

3. These figures, for previous years, are listed in the *Fūzoku kankei Eigyō* [Statistics from the Metropolitan Police Bureau], 1967.

4. Han'gyoku and *oshaku* were the common terms for apprentice geisha in the area around Tokyo. *Gyoku* refers to a flowery term for geishas' wages: *gyokudai*, or jewel money. The apprentices received only half (*han*) the wages of a full geisha, thus han'gyoku.

5. From my questionnaire I learned that 68 percent of my sample of Tokyo geisha live in their own apartments, compared with only 15 percent of the Kyoto group. The Kyoto sample included maiko, who never live on their own; but excluding them, the Kyoto figure is still only 18 percent.

6. When asked where they had lived when they started their geisha careers, almost half of the Tokyo respondents said in an okiya. Only 8 percent had lived on their own. Most of the remaining 40 percent had lived with their parents.

CHAPTER 11

1. Merchants and artisans were the primary inhabitants of the downtown, or *shitamachi*, part of the city. The cultural style they developed, which is still characteristic of the shitamachi manner, is one of confident sophistication, just bordering on the brash; of a studied casualness of dress with a faint undertone of the erotic; and of frank

enjoyment of the pleasures of life. The shitamachi style contrasts, first, with the rustic crudeness of the farmer and, second, with the stiff and proper demeanor of the samurai.

2. To turn one's collar (*erikae o suru*) is a synonym for attaining full geisha status. When a new geisha is presented to the hanamachi community, she turns back part of the white collar of her underkimono to reveal a small triangle of the red chemise beneath. She wears her kimono thus for the ceremonies in which she is formally introduced to customers and peers.

3. Mukōjima is an old hanamachi located on the bank of the Sumida River, opposite the main part of Tokyo. In the heyday of the Yoshiwara licensed quarter, guests would take a ferry across the river to Mukōjima to continue their revelry with the geisha there. These small, canopied ferryboats (called *yakatabune*) were very popular – especially when one had a geisha from Mukōjima along to share the temporary floating world.

4. The gesture of holding the kimono hem in the left hand (*hidarizuma*) is another sartorial image associated exclusively with geisha.

5. Decorated envelopes, called *go-shūgibukuro*, are another way of veiling the appearance of cash in the karyūkai.

6. For comparison, in 1975 a college graduate's starting salary was about 70,000 yen (about $210) a month, and an executive in a large steel company could expect a monthly salary of about 300,000 yen ($900). The geisha's wages are also high compared to the salary scale of most working women.

CHAPTER 12

1. Of the respondents from Kyoto, 95 percent of those whose mothers had been geisha said their parent(s) approved their choice of occupation. Of the Tokyo second-generation geisha, 78 percent claimed approval.

CHAPTER 13

1. Atami's kenban is the office of its Association of Geisha and Geisha Houses. This association owns the building that serves as the geisha school (*geigi gakkō*) and kenban, and it employs retired geisha or operators of okiya to administer its several offices. The department of performances, or engeibu, is always run by an active geisha who is an experienced dancer or musician.

2. *Karayuki* means "those who traveled to China," but the word refers specifically to Japanese prostitutes who went abroad, not

only to China, but to India and Southeast Asia, from about 1880 until the 1920s. By far the greatest number of these women were from Kyushu, from the Shimabara peninsula and the Amakusa Islands. (See Tomoko Yamazaki, *Sandakan hachiban shōkan: Teihen joseishi joshō* [Sandakan number eight brothel: introduction to the history of women in the lowest social stratum].) Some excerpts from this book, translated into English by Tomoko Moore and Steffan Richards, appeared in the *Bulletin of Concerned Asian Scholars*, October–December 1975.

3. For a dance recital, participants must rent the stage and pay for their costumes, the musicians' fees, and a "tip" for their teacher. All of this easily adds up to hundreds of dollars.

4. A geisha's wages are still known by any number of flowery terms, the most common of which is actually "flower money" (*hanadai*). Hanadai is counted in units called sticks (from the original method of calculating a geisha's wage according to the time it takes a stick of incense to burn down). In Atami, the first party, from 6:00 to 7:30, is worth three sticks. One stick equals 1,220 yen (about $4 in 1975). The unofficial record in Atami was held by a hard-working geisha who amassed two hundred "sticks" (about $800) a month. A geisha also receives 800 yen from the inn as "carfare" every night she appears.

CHAPTER 14

1. The narrative (*katarimono*) style of music called gidayū is also very much alive, but it is mostly the preserve of professional musicians, unlike the more lyrical (*utaimono*) styles, which are practiced by numbers of enthusiastic amateurs as well. The popular kouta schools emphasize singing rather than shamisen, and no one would take lessons in kouta shamisen without knowing the songs first.

2. The shamisen player inserts soft calls of "iya" or "iyo" at the point where each phrase of the vocal line starts in order to orient the singer.

3. When Ennosuke led the Grand Kabuki on a tour of the United States in 1978, the American audience applauded the shamisen players after a brilliant instrumental transition to a new scene on stage. So dumbfounded were the normally poker-faced musicians that a few cracked bewildered smiles.

4. The geisha of Pontochō also present tea at their dance. Learning the rudiments of tea ceremony is part of the geishas' training in Kyoto, and they all dutifully attend lessons from teachers of the Urasenke

School of Tea. Gengen Sōshitsu, the great-great-grandfather of the present head of Urasenke, devised a special shortened version of the ritual in 1877, called the *ryūreishiki*. In this ceremony, the participants sit on chairs and the tea is prepared at a table rather than on the tatami mat floor. This is the version the geisha learn first and use at their dances, although many of them go on to study the more formal and orthodox versions as well.

Most people think of the tea ceremony, or the Way of Tea, as an austere, meditative, Zen-infused ritual developed by the samurai. This is all true, but there is another side to Tea as well. Some of the utensils are fine porcelain rather than earthenware, richly decorated in opulent floral designs and bright colors. Tea served in such bowls by beautifully dressed young women in an ochaya naturally has a different "flavor" than does the hermit's bowl prepared quietly in a tearoom (*ochashitsu*).

5. The twenty-eighth year of this program of music and dance, which featured all the hanamachi of Kyoto, was 1976, when I saw it. Until 1975, participants came from the *rokkagai*, the "six geisha communities," but in 1976 the number of communities had been reduced to five: Shimabara had no geisha to perform. These programs are exhibitions for connoisseurs more than for tourists. The audience consists largely of other geisha, dancers, and musicians.

6. Some of the larger and more businesslike geisha communities, onsen towns like Atami, e.g., do advertise for recruits in newspapers and magazines.

CHAPTER 15

1. There are many examples of this particular concatenation of linguistic images. The word *nureta* (wet) often occurred in classical poetry describing sleeves wet with tears because of a lover's absence or fickleness. This usage established a connection between "wet" and "emotional." Even the Japanese loan words from English, *uetto* (wet) and *dorai* (dry), have the specific meanings of "emotional" versus "rational, calculating."

In the geisha world, it is no accident that the willow, or *ryū* of karyūkai, is a tree associated with flowing streams; that the term for sexual initiation is mizu-age; and that a geisha who sleeps around is a *mizuten*. Mizu, "water," has a homonym in *mizu*, "unseen" or "unseeing," and the original version of mizuten probably meant "indiscriminately tumbling." Given these associations, substituting the homonymous character "water" is not strange at all. A coquettish glance between members of the opposite sex is a *nagashi-me*, a "flowing eye," and a woman of a *mizushō*, a "water temperament," has a wanton nature.

2. That the etymology of this term is somewhat muddy only strengthens its appropriateness. Water symbolism is very evocative. In this case it calls to mind women and sex as part of its penumbra of meaning, but also other characteristics of water that have symbolic associations in the businesses so named. Such trades are dependent on the whim of customers; people often float from one position to another; the hours are fluid; they deal with liquor; and so on.

3. When the geisha of Fukagawa (or Tatsumi, as their quarter of the city was sometimes called) began wearing haori, the practice was iki because it was original. By the 1930s, when women wearing haori had become a common sight, the geisha stopped doing so. Even now, when a haori is the accepted "coat" while wearing kimono, geisha rarely don one.

4. Cited in Shinohara Haru, *Kikugasane*, pp. 124–126.

5. Like geisha, hakoya were registered at the kenban, and their fee came out of the geishas' wages. Some geisha houses had a live-in servant (usually a woman) called an *uchibako* who served the same purpose. Neither of these occupations is pursued in modern Japan.

6. The Onoue house, or school, of classical dance comes directly from Kabuki. The founder was Onoue Kikugorō VI (d. 1949), probably the most famous and popular Kabuki actor of modern times. Although the famous Rokudaime ("the Sixth," as he is affectionately referred to by aficionados) was both a choreographer/teacher and an actor, he split the two aspects of the art: he had his son Baikō take the leadership of the Kabuki line, and his son Kinjirō became the master of the school of dance, under the new name Kikunojō.

CHAPTER 16

1. This particular way of tying the obi, considered the basic adult style today, was originated by the geisha of Fukagawa in Tokyo. In November 1818, when the Taikobashi (drum bridge) at the Kamedo Tenjin Shrine was rebuilt, these geisha fashioned a way of tying their obis that was meant to call to mind the name of the bridge. The style caught on, and by now it has largely supplanted all other ways of tying the obi among adult women.

2. Sometimes a geisha house will make the loan to a new member, but the terms of repayment and the rate of interest are regulated by the geisha registry office. The new geisha usually needs a guarantor

from the outside when she enters such an agreement so that the house will have some security for the loan. It is also becoming more common for a new geisha to arrange a loan from a bank, or some sort of pay-by-installment agreement with a kimono shop.

3. Different types of haregi are: a black kimono with five crests (most formal), a colored garment with five crests, and hōmongi, which customarily have one crest at the top center of the back seam but may have three, on the back and on either side of the collar in front. The pattern will be dyed, painted, embroidered, or a combination of these, on the shoulder, sleeve, and hem only. The development of the hōmongi style as proper semiformal to formal attire for women is relatively recent. It was first seen in the Meiji period but only came into common use during the Shōwa era.

4. Today the *chū-furisode*, or "mid-swinging sleeve", version has become popular. It is almost as formal as the true furisode, but the sleeves reach only to the knee when the arms are held relaxed at the sides.

5. Given the expense this would entail today, I was told that it is no longer the way things usually happen. Rather, a maiko who turns twenty-one is sponsored by her house (or, in one case I know of, by her parents) in obtaining a new wardrobe of tomesode kimono. Her elaborately embroidered furisode are usually the property of the geisha house she belongs to, and they are carefully packed away for a future maiko to use.

6. The sheer number of seasonal designs for spring and fall greatly outnumber those for summer and winter. Patterns representing flowing water are often seen on summer clothing, but the water motif is not limited to summer. A stylized design of a snowflake is also popular, but it is not limited to winter. The winter season, however, includes the New Year, which calls for cranes, rising suns, and the auspicious *shōchikubai* (pine, bamboo, plum) combination.

7. This layering of colors (*irome kasane*) was developed in intricate detail during the Heian period (794–1185) but has continued with variations and simplification until recent times. The following list, given by the Ogasawara School of Etiquette, is representative:

	Name	*Obverse*	*Reverse*
JANUARY	pine	sprout green	deep purple
FEBRUARY	redblossom plum	crimson	purple
MARCH	peach	peach	khaki
APRIL	cherry	white	burgundy

	Name	*Obverse*	*Reverse*
MAY	orange flower	deadleaf yellow	purple
JUNE	artemisia	sprout green	yellow
JULY	lily	red	deadleaf yellow
AUGUST	cicada wing	cedar bark	sky blue
SEPTEMBER	aster	lavender	burgundy
OCTOBER	bush clover	rose	slate blue
NOVEMBER	maple	vermilion	gray-green
DECEMBER	chrysanthemum	lavender	deep blue

CHAPTER 17

1. *Shizukesa ya*   The quiet.
   Iwa ni shimi-iru   Penetrating the rock,
   Semi no koe   Voices of locusts.

Matsuo Bashō

2. Bon occurred in the seventh month by the lunar calendar, but that time of year now, in the Gregorian calendar, is August. Generally the Kantō region (eastern Japan, including Tokyo) observes Bon in the seventh month of the *new* calendar – July – whereas the Kansai area (western Japan, including Kyoto) observes it in August.

GLOSSARY

ai no te	An instrumental set piece interlude within the lyric genres of shamisen music.
awase	From the verb *awaseru*, "to put together": a kimono with a lining.
bazoku	"Horse-riding tribes," a nickname for geisha from the city of Fukuoka.
Bon	Midsummer Buddhist festival of souls.
bonchi	A basin or valley ringed by mountains.
bungo-bushi	A style of shamisen music now rarely heard.
butsudan	The household Buddhist shrine.
chatate onna	Waitresses (literally, tea-brewing women) in the early eighteenth century.
chaya	See *ochaya*.
chidori	Small bird associated with rivers: a plover. Crest of the Kyoto geisha community of Pontochō.
chōnin	Literally, town dweller. Refers to the merchant class of feudal times.
danna	A geisha's patron.
dansu geisha	In the 1920s, geisha who danced in Western ballroom styles.
darari	A style of tying the obi sash that is used only by apprentice geisha.
desho	A geisha's most formal kimono.
dodoitsu	A humorous, bawdy ditty accompanied by the shamisen.

doyō no ushi Climax of hottest summer, as calculated by the traditional calendar.

en Karma, a metaphysical connection.

en musubi "The tying together of destinies," a common metaphor for marriage.

enkai A banquet.

ennui Kin.

erikae o suru "To turn one's collar," the sartorial expression that marks the transition from maiko to geisha.

fudangi Kimono: everyday wear. The opposing category is *haregi*, formal wear.

furisode "Swinging-sleeve" kimono worn by unmarried girls.

gei Art.

geigi Alternate term for geisha.

geigi gakkō A geisha school.

geigi kumiai A geisha association. The organized body of geisha belonging to each community, or hanamachi.

geiko Kyoto term for geisha.

geimei A geisha's professional name.

geisha asobi Entertainment involving geisha.

geta Informal wooden sandals.

gidayū A narrative style of shamisen music.

giri Duty honor, obligation.

giri ninjō (The conflict between) duty and human feeling.

go-shūgi See *shūgi*.

gyokudai "Jewel money," a term for geisha wages.

hakoya Manservant who carried a geisha's shamisen box to engagements, a job now obsolete.

hakujin "White ones," a class of amateur prostitutes in Kyoto before the early twentieth century.

hanadai "Flower money," a term for geishas' wages.

hanamachi	"Flower ward," a licensed geisha community.
haori	Jacket worn over kimono.
haori geisha	Geisha of the Tokyo community of Fukagawa, renowned for their chic.
haregi	Kimono: formal wear. The opposing category is *fudangi*, everyday wear.
hauta	A style of short lyrical songs accompanied by the shamisen.
hidari-zuma	"Left-held hem," a pose characteristic of geisha.
hiki iwai	Celebration of a woman's departure from the geisha life.
hitoe	Kimono: a "single-layer," that is, unlined, garment.
hōkan	A comedian who entertained the women of pleasure and their customers in the licensed quarters of the past.
honne and *tatemae*	True intent versus facade.
iemoto	The grand master of a school of traditional art.
iki	Japanese chic.
irome kasane	"Layering of colors," an aesthetic of color combinations developed in the Heian period.
iromuji	Kimono: in solid colors without patterns.
itchū-bushi	A style of shamisen music now rarely heard.
jikata	Geisha shamisen musicians, the "seated ones," as opposed to the dancers.
jimae	Geisha independence.
jingi	A gambler's or gangster's formal self-introduction.
jokyū	Café waitress popular in the 1920s and 1930s.
jū ni hitoe	"Twelve layers of unlined robes," worn by Heian period noble ladies.

kagami mochi	Round, hard cakes of pounded glutinous rice.
kaimyō	Buddhist posthumous name.
kakae	Strict form of indenture amounting to captivity
kamiza	The seat of prestige in a formal banquet room.
kangeiko	"Lessons in the cold," a discipline thought to build character.
kanoko	Dapple-effect tie-dying pattern.
karayuki	"Those who went to China," referring to Japanese prostitutes sent to China and Southeast Asia from about 1880 to the 1920s.
karyūkai	"Flower and willow world," a conventional term for geisha society.
kenban	The geisha registry office. Each *hanamachi* has its own *kenban*.
kiseru	A long, bamboo-stemmed pipe.
kiyomoto	One of the more commonly heard styles of lyric *shamisen* music today.
komon	Kimono: of over-all patterns.
korobi geisha	"Roll-over geisha," prostitute.
koshimaki	Kimono underwear: a length of thin cloth wrapped and tucked at the waist.
koto	Thirteen-stringed rectangular harp.
koto hajime	December 13, when everyone begins rushing around to finish the old year's business before January 1.
kouta	Short lyrical songs accompanied by shamisen.
kurōto	"Professional," as opposed to *shirōto*, "amateur." *kyakusama* Honored guest.
kyōmai	Style of traditional dance originating in Kyoto.
kyū shōgatsu	New Year's day as determined by the old calendar.

machiai	Old term for places in Tokyo where geisha entertainment takes place.
machi geisha	Geisha working outside the licensed quarters.
maiko	Apprentice geisha in Kyoto.
marumage	Traditional hairstyle for adult women.
minarai	Learning by observation.
minarai-jaya	The teahouse that sponsors a new geisha's training in Kyoto.
mizu shōbai	The "water business," that is, the service or entertainment trades that are subject to fluctuations of personnel and income.
mizu-age	Sexual initiation of an apprentice geisha.
momoware	Traditional hairstyle worn by young girls, now seen only on the maiko of Kyoto.
mon	A crest or insignia.
muko yoshi	An "adopted bridegroom" who goes to live in his wife's family and takes her last name.
musume-bun	The "role of daughter" in the fictive kinship system of geisha communities.
nagajuban	Kimono: the single-layer under-robe worn with kimono today.
nagauta	The most commonly heard lyric style of shamisen music today
nakai	Maidservant.
obake	The custom of wearing disguises (similar to Halloween costumes) for the holiday of Setsubun.
obebe	Kyoto dialect term for kimono.
obi	Wide, heavy sash that completes a kimono outfit.
obi-age	Thin length of silk that shows just above the obi.
ochaya	A teahouse.
odoriko	A geisha specializing in traditional dance.
oiran	A high-ranking lady of pleasure in the licensed quarters.
ojōsan	Polite term for a young unmarried lady.

340

okamisan	Proprietress of a shop or teahouse.
okāsan	"Mother," the term used by geisha for teahouse managers.
okiya	A geisha house, an establishment where geisha are affiliated in order to be registered in their communities. Many geisha live in the okiya.
okobo	Special high clogs worn by maiko.
okuribi	Fires lighted at the Bon festival to send the visiting souls of ancestors back to the netherworld.
okusan	Polite term for a wife, literally "lady of the interior."
on	A state of indebtedness for favors received.
onēsan	Older sister.
oniisan	Older brother.
onsen	Hot springs, spa.
oseibō	Presents given at the end of the year.
oshaku	To pour a drink, usually sake, for someone.
oshiroi	White face makeup.
otoko geisha	Male geisha.
otōsan	Father.
risshun	The first day of spring according to the old calendar.
ro	Kimono: a weave of cloth containing openwork stripes, suitable for summer.
rokkagai	The "six geisha communities" of Kyoto.
ryōtei	The term now used for what were once known as *machiai*: Tokyo restaurants where geisha can be called to entertain.
sakura	Cherry blossoms.
sambasō	Auspicious dance prelude to a traditional performance.
sansan-kudo	"Thrice three, nine times," the ritual exchange of cups of sake in a wedding ceremony or the sisterhood ceremony of geisha.

sekihan	Steamed rice with red beans, a dish served on auspicious occasions.
seppun	Kissing.
shakuhachi	A thick bamboo clarinet.
shamisen	Three-stringed fretless instrument associated with geisha.
shibori	A tie-dye technique creating a dapple effect.
shihō mairi	"Paying respects in the four directions": the custom of visiting certain shrines to obtain blessings at the time of the spring new year.
shikomi	A young indentured servant: for example, a girl before she became an apprentice geisha (now obsolete).
shin hōgaku	Music of traditional style being composed today.
shinnai	Plaintive ballads accompanied by shamisen.
shirōto	"Amateur," as opposed to *kurōto*, "professional."
shitamachi	"Downtown": the area of Edo (now Tokyo) that was originally inhabited primarily by merchants.
shōchikubai	Pine, bamboo, and plum: the auspicious trio that symbolizes New Year.
shokugyō fujin	Working women.
shomben geisha	"Toilet geisha," prostitute.
shūgi	An "honorarium," or tip, to a geisha.
shūgibukuro	Special decorated envelope to hold cash meant as a tip.
shunga	"Spring pictures": erotic woodblock prints.
sonehachi	A style of shamisen music now rarely heard.
Suimeikai	Dance put on every March by the Kyoto geisha community of Pontochō.
tabi	Split-toed socks worn with Japanese sandals.

tabi geinin	Traveling entertainers, like gypsies.
taiko	A drum. Also the name of a common way of tying an obi.
taiko-mochi	A "drum bearer," or jester. See *hōkan*.
takuhatsu	The practice in certain Buddhist sects of monks begging rice – or, more commonly now, money – from parishioners.
tayū	Kyoto term for the highest-ranking ladies of pleasure in the licensed quarters.
tekirei	The "appropriate age," describing young men and women of marriageable age.
tenjin	Term used in the Kyoto licensed quarters for the rank just below tayū.
tōde	"Distant outings": term used for the engagement of a geisha outside the registered establishments of her community.
tokiwazu	A ballad style of shamisen music.
tokonoma	Alcove in a traditional room where flowers and a hanging scroll can be displayed.
tsukesage	Kimono: garment with a design on shoulder and hem.
tsuyu	The rainy season in May–June.
uchi geisha	"House geisha," women who entertain at one establishment as employees rather than making the rounds of a number of teahouses.
uchibako	A womanservant who carried a geisha's shamisen box to engagements; now obsolete. (See *hakoya*.)
ukiyo	The "floating world," referring to the demimonde society of feudal Japan.
ukiyo-e	"Pictures of the floating world," a genre of woodblock print.
urekko	"Popular," of geisha or other entertainers.
wafuku	Japanese "native dress," as opposed to *yōfuku*, Western dress.
yagō	A trademark, shop insignia.

yakata-bune	A small, canopied boat that once ferried passengers across rivers in Edo.
yakuza	Gangster.
Yamato nadeshiko	A "native wild pink," floral image used as a symbol of a gentle young lady.
yōfuku	"Western apparel," as opposed to *wafuku*, native apparel.
yūjo	A "woman of pleasure," prostitute.
yukata	A cotton kimono, worn for very informal occasions; bathrobe.
zashiki	A banquet room. Also the term used by geisha for their engagements.
zashiki gei	Music and dance performances by geisha for guests in the banquet rooms (as opposed to their stage performances).
zōri	Japanese sandals.

BIBLIOGRAPHY

Befu, Harumi. "Ritual Kinship in Japan: Its Variability and Resiliency." *Sociologus*, 14 (1964), 150–169.

Cook, Alice, and Hiroko Hayashi. Working Women in Japan. Ithaca: Cornell University Press, 1980.

Crihfield, Liza. "The Institution of the Geisha in Modern Japanese Society," Ph.D. dissertation, Department of Anthropology, Stanford University, 1978. Ann Arbor, Michigan: Microfilms International.

——. *Kouta: Little Songs of the Geisha World*. Tokyo: Charles A. Tuttle, 1979.

DeBecker, J. E. *The Nightless City*. Tokyo: Charles A. Tuttle, 1960.

Doi, Takeo. *The Anatomy of Dependence* [Amae no kōzō]. Translated by John Bester. Tokyo: Kōdansha, 1973.

Geishagaku nyūmon. Atami: Kinjōkan, 1969.

Havens, Thomas R. H. *Valley of Darkness: The Japanese People and World War Two*. New York: Norton, 1978.

Hayashida, Kametarō. *Geisha no kenkyū*. Tokyo: Chōbunkaku, 1929.

Hearn, Lafcadio. *Exotics and Retrospectives*. Tokyo: Charles A. Tuttle, 1971.

Hibbett, Howard. *The Floating World in Japanese Literature*. Tokyo: Charles A. Tuttle, 1959.

Hida, Chiho. *Shimbashi seikatsu yonjūyon-nen*. Tokyo: Gakufushoin, 1956.

Ida, Yoshisato. *Maiko no shiki*. Kyoto: Shinshindō, 1975.

Jackson, Laura. "Bar Hostesses." In *Women in Changing Japan*, edited by J. Lebra, J. Paulson, and E. Powers. Boulder, Colo.: Westview Press, 1976.

Kanzaki, Emigiku (Kikuya of Akasaka). *I, a Geisha*. Tokyo: Tokyo News Service, 1969.

Kishii, Yoshie. *Onna geisha no jidai*. Tokyo: Sei-A Senshō, 1974.

Kobayashi, Toyoko. *Kimono kyōhon*. Nagoya: Kobayashi Toyoko Kimono Gakuen Shuppan-bu, 1975.

Kuki, Shūzō. *Iki no kōzō*. Tokyo: Iwanami Shōten, 1930.

Kumagai, Yasujirō. *Gion to maiko*. Kyoto: Tankōsha, 1974.

Malm, William. *Japanese Music*. Tokyo: Charles A. Tuttle, 1965.

Masuda, Sayo. *Geisha kutō no han shōgai*. Tokyo: Heibonsha, 1973.

Minakami, Tsutomu. *Onna no mori de*. Tokyo: Iwanami Shoten, 1975.

Miyake, Koken, ed. *Geigi tokuhon*. Tokyo: Zenkoku Dōmei Ryoriya Shinbunsha-han, 1935.

Nagai, Kafū. *Geisha in Rivalry* [Ude kurabe]. Translated by Kurt Meissner. Tokyo: Charles A. Tuttle, 1963.

Nakano, Eizō. *Yūjo no seikatsu*. Tokyo: Yūzankaku, 1966.

Noma, Seiroku. *Japanese Costume and Textile Arts*. Heibonsha Survey of Japanese Art, vol. 16. Tokyo: Heibonsha, 1974.

Otake, Victor. "A Study of Japanese Taste with an Observation Concerning Fūryū and 'The Structure of Iki' by Kuki Shūzō." Ph.D. dissertation, Syracuse University, 1957. Ann Arbor, Michigan: Microfilms International.

Perkins, P. D. *Geisha of Pontochō*. Tokyo: Tokyo News Service, 1954.

Ryūtei, Tanehiko. *Geisha tora no maki*. Original woodblock ed., circa 1830.

Scott, A. C. *The Flower and Willow World*. London: Orion Press, 1960.

Setouchi, Harumi. *Kyō mandara*. Tokyo: Kōdansha, 1972.

Shinohara, Haru. *Kikugasane*. Tokyo: Tanshiki Insatsu, 1956.

Shively, Donald. "Sumptuary Regulations and Status in Early Tokugawa Japan." *Harvard Journal of Asian Studies,* 25 (1965).

Smith, Robert J. *Ancestor Worship in Contemporary Japan.* Stanford: Stanford University Press, 1974.

Tokuda, Shūsei. *Shukuzu in the Tokuda Shūsei zenshū.* Tokyo: Sekkasha, 1961.

Watarai, Keisuke. *Miyako no hanamachi.* Tokyo: Tairiku Shōbō, 1977.

Yamazaki, Tomoko. *Sandakan hachiban shōkan: Teihen joseishi joshō.* Tokyo: Chikuma Shōbō, 1972.

INDEX